Second is Nothing

Second is Nothing
Creating a Multi-Billion Rand Cellular Industry

Alan Knott-Craig
with Eunice Afonso

MACMILLAN

First published jointly 2009
by

Pan Macmillan South Africa
Private Bag X19
Northlands
Johannesburg
2116
www.panmacmillan.co.za

and

Rollerbird Press, a division of Troupant Publishers (Pty) Limited
PO Box 4532
Northcliff
2115
www.troupant.co.za

ISBN 978-1-77010-1-647

© Alan Knott-Craig

All rights reserved. No part of this publication may be reproduced, stored in or introduced into a retrieval system, or transmitted, in any form, or by any means (electronic, mechanical, photocopying, recording or otherwise) without the prior written permission of the publisher. Any person who does any unauthorised act in relation to this publication may be liable to criminal prosecution and civil claims for damages.

Editing by Mark McClellan
Proofreading by Andrea Nattrass
Cover design by Interactive Africa
Cover photograph by Brandon Fisher
All other photographs courtesy of Alan Knott-Craig collection
Typesetting by Manoj Sookai
Index by Christopher Merrett

Printed by Ultra Litho

Contents

Author's Note vii
Acknowledgements ix
Foreword by Wendy Luhabe xi

1. Killing me Softly 1
2. Endless Sunny Days in the Karoo 12
3. Working in the Trenches 21
4. The Rise of a Giant 33
5. Chasing the Dream 44
6. It's a Deal 58
7. Connecting the Dots 64
8. With a Little Help from my Friends 72
9. Covering the Nation 83
10. Rollercoaster Ride 92
11. The Yebo Gogo Brand 104
12. Bringing Entertainment to Millions 115
13. The Power to do Good 123
14. A Cellular Disneyworld 133

15. Stepping into Africa 141
16. Infinite Possibilities 149
17. The One that Got Away 159
18. New Millennium: New World – New Life 169
19. The Legacy 181
20. Every End is a New Beginning 188

Notes 194
References 196
Index 197

Author's Note

When Eunice and I started this book, my hope was that young people would find some hope and inspiration in the fact that very ordinary people can do extraordinary things, and that your first chance to show the world that you can be different may only occur much later in life than you might have hoped for. It was also my hope that people would see that trust and respect would bring them more success than simply outwitting one another.

As I read the text for the last time, I found it emotionally tiring. It is a sobering experience to see your life, including many private moments that you thought you would always keep secret, being laid out for all to see. It is quite stressful to see things for yourself, and ponder on those events that have clearly shaped your life, without you ever having consciously considered them as defining moments. But when laid out chronologically, defining moments they are indeed.

Many of the events seem clever, brave and even silly in retrospect, but they were none of these at the time. They were simply events that happened, ordained by another hand.

Things that seemed so important at the time, seem trivial now. Things that seemed so trivial then, seem much more important now. People who I fought with all my might and who seemed wickedly devious at the time, now seem like ordinary people. Nothing people. Hardly worth a memory.

Is it possible that I spent so much energy in clearing a path for myself and my dreams? Is it possible that I tolerated so little in anyone who even dared to stand in my way? Where did I find the arrogance to be so sure of myself?

Building something with other people's money certainly made me a lot braver than I might have been had it been my own. But since I never had any money, it has never impressed me much, and whenever I had a windfall, I would be driven to spend it so that I might relax and not dwell on having it for too long.

I was blessed with being able to work with some of the smartest, most intelligent, daring, devoted and kind people ever put on this Earth. They more than made up for the 'nothing people'.

What I have learnt is that what brings you the most happiness is good health, being loved and having someone to love, and desperately striving with every fibre of your being to make a positive difference to this world.

Second really is nothing.

Alan Knott-Craig
August 2009

Acknowledgements

This book is more than an insight into the growth of South Africa's multi-billion rand cellular industry: it reveals the extraordinary man behind its success. I would like to thank Alan for trusting me to tell his story and for his honest and forthright account of the people and events that marked his life. Alan's recollections were by turn amusing, compelling, thought-provoking, sometimes distressing, but always told with appreciation for the opportunities and experiences that propelled him to the pinnacle of success. His sense of humour, enthusiasm and candid, tell-it-like-it-is style that he infused into his anecdotes made for an unforgettable story. It has been a pleasure and a privilege to share in Alan's journey through the life and times of Vodacom and the people that made an impression on his world. Many thanks to Alan and Surina for their gracious hospitality and infinite patience with the long and arduous interviews.

There were many people who contributed to the creation of this book. Sincere thanks to Alan's colleagues, friends and family who shared their stories about Alan with unreserved wit and insight, showing him to be an uncompromising perfectionist who played the game better than anyone else, but at the same time revealing a fun-loving, loyal and true friend. For their candour and willingness to recount their memories, many thanks to: Mark Attieh, Selwyn Chatz, Leon Crouse, Americo da Silva, Francois de Villiers, Johan and Ibeth Engelbrecht, Dot Field, Joan Joffe, Shameel Joosub, Alan Thomas Knott-Craig, Janet Knott-Craig, Ivo Lazic, Wendy Luhabe, Dillie Malherbe, Dietlof Maré, Alwyn Martin, Ravi Naidoo, Andile Ngcaba, Ryan Noach, Theo Rutstein, Kevin Schmidt, Leon Shirk, Mthobi Tyamzashe, Pieter Uys, Anthea van Heerden, Rae van Zyl, Gavin Varejes and Phil Williams.

I am especially grateful to the Pan Macmillan team – Terry Morris, Andrea Nattrass, Wesley Thompson, Nina Gabriels and Mark McClellan – for their support and advice, and to Dale Cupido from Interactive Africa for the excellent cover design.

My deepest gratitude to my family for their love and affection, especially my mom, Olinda Afonso. Your memory will live in my heart forever.

Eunice Afonso
August 2009

Foreword

For centuries people have assumed that organisations owe their success to leadership that is visionary and inspiring. These two criteria, of course, are critical, but the demands of the twenty-first century have made it abundantly clear that leadership is much more than that – it requires innovation, courage and accountability. In my view, no one exemplifies innovative leadership more than Alan Knott-Craig.

Not only did Alan create a best-of-breed, new-generation company, but he also established a corporation that is by far one of the most inspiring of our democracy in the post-apartheid madness. Vodacom revolutionised the way South Africans communicate. This gave millions of people a sense of self-worth, and it left a unique legacy that gives us all hope for the future.

My relationship with Alan as the chairperson of Vodacom was characterised by trust and acceptance from day one – and we had never met before. These are by far the least-practised values in business, but they are nonetheless mandatory if we are to understand each other and collaborate to create a better future. Alan understood this better than anyone else.

Alan's gift to all the founding employees of Vodacom has been to enable us to appreciate our value, to create something of significance, and to experience a sense of pride in our achievements. As for Alan, it took a considerable leap of faith for him to be a pioneer in an industry people knew little about. It developed in him a sense of courage, a taste for risk, an ability to embrace the unknown with confidence, and a talent for delivering on his promises on an incredible scale.

Albert Einstein said that good leaders possess 'intuition to enable us to know, imagination to take us everywhere and experience as a source of wisdom'. I can confirm from my experience of working with Alan for six years that he has all three of these qualities in abundance. This has been Alan's contribution to South Africa: he has used these qualities so effectively that he deserves to be called the Godfather of South Africa's Cellular Industry.

It is important to be in touch with our calling in order to live meaningful lives, lives that leave footprints behind us for others to follow. This is where the real adventure lies. This is where Alan has excelled. But life doesn't always move in a consistently rising arc of progress. Most of us have fallen along the way at times. We are all put in positions that force us to open our minds to learn and to grow, where we are challenged to match our talents with compassion, our achievements with humility and our intellect with wisdom.

Alan, I hope that I have enriched your life as much as you have enriched mine. I know that your story will allow us to glimpse the common seeds of humanity and to realise the promise of our precious lives, because ultimately we are all of infinite worth. I wish you and everyone reading your story, a life rich in compassion, humility and wisdom.

Namaste (I honour the divine in you)

Wendy Luhabe
August 2009

Wendy Luhabe was the longest-serving chairperson of Vodacom, from 2000 to 2005. Today she is a social entrepreneur and the chairperson and director of various companies, as well as the chancellor of the University of Johannesburg and a board and executive committee member of the International Institute of Management Development (Switzerland).

*'Do not follow where the path may lead.
Go instead where there is no path and leave a trail.'*
H.R. McAlindon

Killing me Softly
2006

All changes, even the most longed for, have their melancholy; for what we leave behind us is a part of ourselves; we must die to one life before we can enter another.
Anatole France

It happened again, just as I had started my workout at the gym. It was so unexpected, but then, it always is. I had only been on the exercise bike for a few minutes and I was feeling good. In fact, for a 54 year old I could proudly say that I was as fit, strong and healthy as I had ever been in my life. As I stepped up the pace on the bike, I reviewed the day's itinerary in my head. As Chief Executive Officer (CEO) of Vodacom for the last 13 years, I had experienced more than my fair share of heart-stopping, I-can't-do-this-any-more moments, but as I mentally ticked off the tasks for the day ahead, I was pleased to discover that today might well be, for a change, crisis free.

But it wasn't the constant pressure that irked me. My heart just wasn't in it any longer. I had been thinking for a while that it was time to move on. The only obstacle was that my shareholders were not keen to release me. Each time I had tentatively raised the issue with them, and there had been several such occasions, they had looked at me incredulously.

'How could you even entertain such a ludicrous idea?' they asked. I knew they would not easily or willingly let me go. My request had been rejected outright the previous year and I now knew I had to enlist the help of someone with more influence. My principal ally was Phil Williams, a Vodafone board member as well as my mentor and a close personal friend. Phil had never let me down in the past and he was the only person capable of persuading the shareholders to change their minds.

I adjusted my handlebars, still thinking about how to formulate my exit strategy, when my breath caught in my throat. Without any warning, I felt my chest start to pound. My heart rate was speeding up. I couldn't breathe, beads of perspiration broke out on my forehead, my limbs grew heavy and I felt a rising panic in my gut. Oh no, I thought, please, don't tell me I have to go through this again!

I was having a heart attack – a myocardial infarction, coronary thrombosis, angina pectoris, hypertrophic cardiomyopathy. I knew all the names for this unwanted intruder and the associated heart diseases, because this wasn't the first time. In fact, I knew everything there was to know about heart attacks. Since my first coronary in 2000, I had read everything I could lay my hands on about this dreaded killer. I needed to know more so that I could control what was happening to me. If I could successfully control the fortunes of a multi-billion rand company, then surely it was a simple enough task to take charge of my own health? At least, that is what I imagined.

Six years ago, I had collapsed in a hotel gym in London while the same sensations surged through me. Following my first heart attack, I had paid close attention to my physical well-being. I did everything by the book, taking care that I ate the correct foods and that I exercised regularly. But clearly I had not done enough, since I now found myself struck down once more and in urgent need of medical assistance.

I willed myself to stay calm and breathe slowly. I focused on carefully getting off the bike. 'Please God,' I rambled to myself, 'don't let me lose it right now.' I turned to my gym buddy and close protection officer, Gawie Hall.

'Let's go, we're leaving,' I muttered.

'What's up, sir?' he asked. He always insisted on calling me sir.

I slowly stumbled out of the gym, as Gawie hovered anxiously behind me. Those few steps to the car felt like a marathon. 'Just start driving, man,' I urged.

Gawie must have noticed the urgency in my tone and seen the desperate look on my face. He sped out the parking bay like a man possessed. I tried to breathe evenly in and out, pacing myself as if I were running a long-distance race. Gawie, however, was adopting a flat-out-to-the-finish approach. As he swerved into the first corner my heart started to gallop, as if trying to keep pace with the speeding car; and the thought crossed my mind that a car collision rather than a heart attack might prove my undoing.

'Where to?' Gawie yelled.

'The hospital – Unitas,' I croaked. It was the closest hospital that came to mind.

I gasped for breath as the pain engulfed my torso. A vice-like grip kept tightening around my heart, while a 400-pound gorilla did push-ups on my chest. With every breath I took the pain became more intense. I didn't think I would make it this time. It was so much worse and the pain had intensified so quickly.

I fumbled for my cellphone and with shaking fingers called my cardiologist, Dr Jeff King, at Sunninghill Hospital.

'Jeff, I'm having a heart attack. Gawie's driving me to the emergency room at Unitas. I don't think I have much time. Can you be there as soon as you can?'

It was an effort, but I punched in my fiancée Surina's number. She would worry about me if I didn't call. 'I'm on my way to Unitas with Gawie – heart attack,' I told her slowly, forcing my voice to stay calm. She got there minutes after I arrived.

I made one more call, to my assistant Rae van Zyl. 'Going to hospital, heart not good,' I managed to get out. By this stage I could barely speak.

Rae called my friend Ryan Noach, Deputy CEO of Netcare and one of our partners in the Vodacom Foundation. Ryan organised a medical team to be on standby at the hospital. Ten minutes later, Gawie deposited me at Unitas Emergency where a row of pristine white coats stood waiting for me. The nurses got me out the car and onto a trolley, pulling off my clothes as they wheeled me into the hospital. My heart kept heaving and the gorilla kept pounding. This is it, I thought, I'm not going to make it out of here. As many as one in three people who have a heart attack will die before they reach the hospital, and generally about half of the victims will be dead within a month. Now where had I read that?

'Leave his clothes on and move faster!' one of the medics yelled.

A dozen arms flew over me as they slipped an oxygen mask over my face and placed electrodes on my chest for an ECG. There was a sharp jab in my arm. Someone was drawing blood to test for the cardiac enzymes released into the bloodstream when heart cells die. There would probably be troponin in the bloodstream, usually an indication that there has been heart damage. I heard the doctor barking out more instructions. They gave me morphine for the pain, and then some more.

As they wheeled me into theatre, my eyes focused on the fluorescent lights overhead. We were moving so quickly that one blur of light after another merged into a dim smudge of white, into which I was drawn until the core of my being was located in my eyes. Nearing the point of greatest physical distress, I began to hear a buzzing noise. I wasn't sure if it was coming from the machines around me or from inside my head. I felt myself moving rapidly through my body. A euphoric haze engulfed me, as if I were on the brink of consciousness. It was not an unpleasant feeling. I felt an absolute inner peace, as if I were dead already; a feeling of tranquility that comes from knowing, instead of hoping, that we truly are immortal.

If this was what death was like, I remember thinking, I wouldn't mind it much. It was a rapturous moment and I let it take me away. I hovered outside of my physical self above the theatre, seeing my body from a distance as though I were a spectator. I watched the resuscitation attempt from this unusual vantage point, but didn't feel any emotional upheaval. I felt intensely alive and free of physical pain, unwilling to return to the confines of a physical body.

They shocked me back to life. My entire body lifted off the bed and I screamed full throttle. There was a chaotic energy pulsating through the room, generated by the team of men and women who were desperately struggling to keep me alive. Raised voices issued incomprehensible instructions; hands were thrusting at me.

A voice called out, 'Get out of my way, can't you see the man is dying.' I watched them from above with detached interest. When they brought the situation under control, there was another jab of pain and I floated away again.

Later, I tried to tell others what I'd experienced, but I had trouble doing so. In the first place, I couldn't find the words to describe the episode adequately. I was also afraid that people would scoff at me. I could imagine them saying to themselves and each other: 'What, one of South Africa's business leaders babbling on about an out-of-body experience? The stress must have taken its toll; time to put him out to pasture before he loses it completely.'

So I stopped trying to talk about it. Still, I knew with certainty that the experience had affected my life profoundly, especially my views about death, my purpose on Earth, the priorities in my life and my relationships with those whom I loved.

When I opened my eyes, I was surprised to be alive. I knew immediately I was in a hospital ward with an IV dripping chemicals into my veins, my heart attached to a monitor, and a pump inside me somewhere helping my heart along. I saw the steady pattern on the screen and I felt a rhythmic beat within my chest. And then I noticed the cardiologist who had tended to me, Dr Jacobs, at my bedside. I looked up at him, fearing what he might be about to say.

His face betrayed no emotion as he looked down at me, and his voice was cool: 'We almost lost you on that table. Your heart stopped beating for some moments. Do you know that for every minute the ventricles in your heart fibrillate, your chances of living are reduced by 10%? You're lucky to be here.'

Despite his neutral tone and manner, I immediately understood the awful significance of what he was saying. He might as well have said: 'Alan, your old life is gone. Welcome to your new one, and prepare yourself; you'll need a good roadmap for this one.'

The prospect of beginning a new life was daunting, to say the least, and downright terrifying if I really thought about it. And yet I would not be alone. I knew I could count on the steadfastness of my family. Surina's continual presence at my bedside was to carry me through those first few agonising days in hospital. The nursing staff was particularly superb – caring and considerate – and such was the bond established between us that we are still in touch to this day.

Leaving the hospital was a double-edged sword. On the one hand, I was relieved to be going home at last. On the other hand, I was nervous about being cut loose from the constant medical attention. It was as if I was entering a totally different world, one I was ill-equipped to handle.

It took me a long time to recover, not so much physically as emotionally. There had been a substantial amount of physical damage from the first heart attack, but this time round the pain and fear was almost entirely cerebral. For months after I was discharged, I experienced what I thought were severe panic attacks, brought on by the belief that I was on the brink of having another heart attack. It was, I realised, completely irrational of me to think this way, but there was nothing I could do to stop it. Whether sitting alone at my desk or at a conference table surrounded by people, it made no difference – my heart would start racing as the notion that I was about to die engulfed me. At home, I would wake up in the middle of the night, sweating profusely, short of breath, and my heart would be beating madly. I would get out of bed, take my tablets and wait for them to work while I watched the clock ticking from one second to the next, wondering at what stroke my heart would stop. I would stick my head outside the bedroom balcony door to get some fresh air, take a few deep breaths and try to convince myself that I felt a little better. But this hardly helped at all; I would return to bed in much the same state and so pass the remainder of the night in fitful sleep, tossing and turning until sunrise.

The truth was, though I was loath to admit it, I had no idea what was happening to me. I was not – and this was a wholly unpleasant revelation to me – in control of the situation. Whatever success I had enjoyed in my life, particularly in my business career, had been largely due to my ability to orchestrate events to run at my instruction. I was always in control. I decided upon a course of action and pursued it to its successful conclusion. But I couldn't apply the same formula to this current state of affairs.

During those long nights, Surina stopped me from going mad. She gently held me and comforted me, while I tormented myself with images of my last gasp for breath. I was like a child, helpless and vulnerable. Without her, I would have lost it.

And yet, as it eventually transpired, the problem was not psychological. I suspected as much when I felt my pulse quicken for no reason, often while I was driving. And it *did* quicken; it was not merely the fantasy of a troubled mind. Suppressing the rising dread I could feel welling up inside, I would drive to the hospital and request a check-up. Hooked up to an ECG, I would watch the doctors as they in turn peered at the monitor or scribbled notes on their clipboard charts, and listened attentively to their murmured conversations. But the doctors couldn't tell me anything. It was true that the tests they performed revealed an irregular heart pattern, but they could establish no reason, no *physical* reason for this. I suspected they believed the cause to be psychosomatic – it was, after all, my mind playing tricks on my body.

I understood their scepticism but didn't share it. The more I thought about it, the more certain I became that there really was something wrong with me. And I was right. The last time it happened, Dr King told me to check in to the Sunninghill Hospital where he and his colleagues spent six days doing tests to find out why I was struggling with a heart that didn't want to perform as it should. They finally decided to try ablation, a process that involves burning selected nerves in the heart wall in order to control an erratic heartbeat. They checked to see that I didn't have any ulcers and then pumped me with Warfarin to prevent any clotting. As I watched the ECG ticking along, from one minute to the next, my heart rate escalated rapidly, almost as if it were racing clear off the screen. By now, I was no longer scared of dying. I was just relieved that they could capture the event and analyse it. Finally, this was the proof I needed to convince the doctors that I wasn't imagining it all.

After analysing the test results, Dr King returned with the good news: the damaged part of my heart was fine; the origin of the racing heart rhythm was not coming from the ventricles, which is usually fatal. Fortunately, my condition could be controlled with appropriate medication. All I could think of was that I wouldn't have to be wheeled into theatre again and watch myself float away for good.

Dr Jeff King – physician, cardiologist, wildlife photographer extraordinaire and friend – was responsible for talking me back to good health. A heart patient is an inconsistent being: one minute I would be ready to run a marathon and the next I would be sitting at death's door. This emotional instability made it extremely difficult for me to believe that I had a future ahead of me. Jeff has the extraordinary ability to work from the inside out to get his patients whole again, and it worked for me too. It wasn't that I was afraid of death; it was the process of dying that I feared most, not the end.

I can understand why people go mad thinking about it. Although I can now say with absolute conviction that I prefer the option of living to dying, this is not how I had felt on the operating table when death had not seemed so bad after all, and I can credit this change of heart, a permissible pun in this case, to the sensitive ministrations of Jeff King.

The first time my heart gave in was early in 2000 at the gym in the Hyatt Regency Hotel in Knightsbridge, London – the gym that Princess Diana used to frequent. I was on my own on a Sunday afternoon and decided to kill some time at the gym while my colleagues, Andrew Mthembu and Graham Victor, went off shopping with their wives. We were flying back to South Africa that night.

The attack happened as I was running on the treadmill, my mind occupied by thoughts of the week ahead. In addition to the searing pain in my chest and the desperate struggle for breath, I remember how I still managed to dress myself. Absurd as it may seem, I felt that to be discovered dead with clothes on was important – as if a corpse would somehow look less dignified in a pair of shorts and a T-shirt. I can also recall the concern of the German manageress, not for me, I hasten to add, but for the possibility that I might die on her watch in her hotel.

An ambulance arrived and I was whisked away to Chelsea Hospital. Unbeknownst to me, an old friend and senior executive in Telkom, Rhynie Greeff, had been working out in the same gym. When I collapsed, Rhynie had seen it and followed me to the hospital. The first thing I saw when I opened my eyes was Rhynie's worried face. He wanted a contact number of someone who could come over to the hospital. I could barely speak for the pain and all I could think about was that I wouldn't need anyone because I would be dead soon. I managed to give my Good Samaritan the number of my assistant, Kevin Schmidt, who summoned my colleagues from their shopping spree.

Morphine was administered for the pain, and clot-busters for the clots. The pain subsided, but the blood clots wouldn't disperse. My colleagues arrived soon after. Andrew took one look at the heart monitor and walked out. As deputy CEO of Vodacom, Andrew was an articulate, well-read individual and clever strategist, as well as a trusted colleague and good friend. This was the man who would take over the leadership of the company one day. He was physically a giant of a man, but the hospital scene had left him visibly shaken. Eventually my colleagues left, but their wives stayed at my bedside in an unexpected vigil.

I was summarily transferred to the Royal Brompton, a renowned National Health Service hospital, though not before I had relayed the message that Kevin should take control of my personal finances. Specifically, I wanted him to ensure that my family would have immediate access to cash in the event of my death, which I knew he was capable of arranging with my bank.

Time passed, though in my delirious condition I could not tell if it was minutes, hours or even days that had gone by before I found myself being wheeled into theatre. A doctor's masked face appeared above me; I could detect a pair of grave eyes and nothing else. His voice, too, was sombre when he told me that I was very ill and that although immediate surgery was the only option, there was no guarantee that I would survive the operation. On this note of cheery optimism, the theatre doors swung open.

I survived the ordeal and a day later, in the early hours of the morning, I was taken aback at the sight of my younger brother Christopher standing in the doorway. This was my boyhood protector, coming in to take care of me again. The memories slipped in and out. I couldn't understand how he was here, and not in America where he lived and worked as a paediatric thoracic surgeon.

I learned later that Kevin had contacted him, whereupon Chris had done everything in his power to ensure that I received the best possible care before he boarded a plane for the UK. Having previously worked among the medical elite of London's Harley Street, he had urged his former colleagues and associates to monitor my situation.

Though his face betrayed concern, Chris managed to offer a wry smile.

'You're looking good Alan,' he tried to joke.

'Don't lie,' I retorted.

'The doctors saved your life. Do you know that?'

'I know. They said I was dying, but I'm still here.'

'I'm not totally happy though.'

'What's the problem?'

'They've done a good job, but the diseased artery has not been completely treated.'

There was a short pause, before I asked, 'So, what now?'

'You have to go back into theatre.'

The doctors didn't agree with Chris. 'Humour me,' he told them. 'Take him into theatre and just check it out again.' And of course he was right.

The recovery was slow, but I was cheered by all the get-well messages that arrived. One morning, a nurse came into the room with a piece of paper held out in front of her as if she bore a royal proclamation or holy relic, an expression of composed solemnity on her face. Probably some bloody awful test results, I thought.

Imagine my delight when I discovered that the piece of paper was, in fact, a fax from Nelson Mandela. 'We wish you a speedy recovery and look forward to your return to the country in good health,' it read. This short note, and the many others I received, buoyed my spirits enormously, helping me regain the confidence I needed to bounce back from so severe a setback.

Once I was discharged from hospital, I couldn't fly back home immediately since my heart was still weak. I was stuck in London. Not a bad place to be if you are in good health and high spirits. But I desperately wanted to return to South Africa for my son Nicholas's 21st birthday, which spurred me on to a quick recovery. I flew home with my wife, Janet, and the airline insisted that a nurse and an oxygen tank accompany me on the flight. I saw a cardiologist back in Cape Town and then went to our holiday house at Boggomsbaai.

I walked every day with my friend Peter Riha, the distance gradually increasing until eventually I could manage 10 kilometres. I even led a Bikers Rally to Vodaworld for Child Welfare and donated some of my shareholders' money to the charity, both of which I thoroughly enjoyed.

I was still incredulous that I had suffered a heart attack. I was fit, healthy and had never looked or felt better, which was hardly the profile of a typical candidate for heart failure. At the age of 48 I was bulletproof, for goodness' sake. I know now that both heart attacks were due to plaque breaking away from the artery wall, and the resultant blood clot was partly caused by medication that I was taking.

However, I also knew that this was not an entirely satisfactory explanation. There was another culprit involved – an adversary more dangerous than anything the pharmaceutical industry could come up with: Vodacom.

After the second attack I knew beyond a shadow of a doubt that the company I had launched, developed and cherished was now my own worst enemy – it was Vodacom that was slowly killing me. Unless I could free myself from its strangulating grip, I wasn't going to survive. The next heart attack, when it inevitably arrived, would be my last.

You don't get to choose how you are going to die or the hour that it will happen. You can, however, decide how you are going to live. I have few regrets as to the choices I have made in the life that I have lived, but it was now crucial that I discovered a new understanding of my life. I knew I couldn't go back and start afresh, but I could create a new ending. I had to make a choice: it was either me or Vodacom.

Endless Sunny Days in the Karoo
1952 to 1970

There is a garden in every childhood, an enchanted place where colours are brighter, the air softer, and the morning more fragrant than ever again.
Elizabeth Lawrence

If you drive south through the deep stillness of the Cango Valley towards the sea, you will reach the majestic Swartberg Pass where breathtaking views of the arid plains of the Karoo stretch out endlessly, punctuated by precipitous rocks, jagged and deep red. Then the road winds gently down to a fertile valley. Cradled by the Swartberg and Outeniqua mountain ranges, lies the town of Oudtshoorn, serene and unassuming beneath a cloudless sky. A town renowned for its opulent feather palaces, exceptional stone masonry bearing testimony to the feather boom spawned by the indigenous ostrich, Oudtshoorn boasts the most sunny days per year in the whole country, shielded as it is from the coastal winds by the mountains.

In the 1950s, picnics, swimming and general recreation were forbidden on Sundays in Oudtshoorn. The community was so conservative, it is said, that it blamed the miniskirt for the summer droughts that plagued the region. However, not all Oudtshoorn families were so doggedly conventional, and so for those more liberal-minded folk, the ban on Sunday entertainment was not to be borne out. Their response was simply to take their picnics further afield, away from the minister's judging eyes. Thus, on sunny Sunday mornings, there was an exodus to the coastal town of Wilderness, where the white, unspoiled beaches were dotted with families making the most of the sun.

On most Sundays, two little boys could be seen sitting shoulder-to-shoulder on the beach beside a long wooden surfboard, watching the waves rolling in. Alan, a pale, dark-haired child, longed to jump up and run into the foam-tipped surf. Thomas, ebony skin glinting in the sun, grabbed the tip of the surfboard and pulled his friend across the sand until his feet touched the water. '*Tlamo*, Alan, come,' he called out. Thomas splashed noisily with his feet until Alan, shrieking with delight and gasping at the coldness of the water, was drenched.

At the age of five, Alan had contracted Perthes, a disease of the hip joint in children caused by a temporary loss of blood supply to the hip. And, without an adequate blood supply, the rounded head of the femur dies, while the surrounding area becomes intensely inflamed and irritated, which can interfere with walking as the thigh muscles waste away. Alan was born on a wintry day in May 1952, and grew into an active, healthy child. But the sudden onset of Perthes had immobilised him, ultimately leaving him with a severe limp. Thomas's mother Elsie was the beloved housekeeper at the Komga home of Alan's maternal grandparents, Ouma Agnes and Oupa Tony, and it was Thomas's job to pull Alan around on a surfboard since he could not walk or run. Most summer holidays were spent with Oupa Tony and Ouma Agnes in Komga, and each December the entire family would set off to Queensberrybay on the Wild Coast.

A special treat on a Sunday afternoon was a leisurely drive around the countryside in the family's Chevy Impala. Alan loved listening to his father, Alan John Alexander, singing Irish ballads or the popular hits of Harry Belafonte and Nat King Cole. His father would choose a spot in the Karoo veld, stop the car, spread a blanket on the warm earth and set about making a fire to boil a pot of coffee. If it had been a good week, there would be watermelon. Alan's mother, Andronette, would slice up the watermelon, while the boys ate slice after slice, the delicious juice dripping down their chins, before hurtling into the sandy bushveld to explore the treasures it held. As the setting sun dipped below the horizon, the family would reluctantly return home again.

Second is Nothing

A legacy of those formative years is Alan's abiding preference for the music of the 1950s, which he continues to listen to during his weekends spent in the bushveld, courtesy of an old record player.

Home in those early days was a flat in a block called 'Evening Star', which had been a nightclub in its glory days, situated in Oudtshoorn's High Street. As the family grew, so did its home; a move to a larger flat in Powder Street was followed by the purchase of two adjacent plots in Victoria Street (the vendor being one Lionel Plotts, coincidentally) and the construction of the family's dream house. Around the corner from the Knott-Craig home was that of the late C.J. Langenhoven, named *Arbeidsgenot* (The Pleasure of Work). He died in 1932, and was perhaps Oudtshoorn's most famous citizen.

A legendary Afrikaans writer, poet, playwright and politician, Langenhoven penned the words for the original South African national anthem, *Die Stem* ('The Voice' or 'The Call of South Africa'), of which some parts can be found in *Nkosi Sikelel' iAfrika*, the country's post-apartheid national anthem. Alan's father used to speak of the writer's sharp wit, fiery speeches and quirky personality. Langenhoven's old newspaper, *Het Zuid-Westen*, was revived by Alan's father and renamed *Het Suid-Western*.

Newspapers, in fact, were the lifeblood of the family, a passion originating in the figure of John Ziervogel Craig, Alan's paternal great-grandfather, who worked as a compositor apprentice in the Cape Town print industry and further afield. During his early years as a journeyman printer he became acquainted with Cecil John Rhodes. It was at the start of the diamond-digging era in Kimberley and Rhodes suggested to John that they trek north to the diamond fields since there was a fortune to be made. John Craig was not too sure about digging for diamonds. He had just been appointed as government printer at Morija Mission Station in Basutoland, a stable, well-paid job. Why would he give up security to chase an elusive dream of making a fortune in diamonds? Common sense prevailed. John Craig went to Basutoland, while Rhodes went off to become a diamond millionaire. However, the Craigs did not perform badly. Through a series of takeovers and buy-outs they acquired a successful chain of country newspapers in the southern Cape. There may have been larger newspaper groups in the country boasting greater circulation figures, but none could match the Craig mini-empire for sheer gutsiness.

John Ziervogel Craig's seven children all bore the name Knott and Craig, a combination of his wife's maiden name, Elizabeth Jane Knott, and his surname, and thus the Knott-Craig name was born. Alan's paternal grandfather, Ronald Charles, was the youngest of the children. Grandpa Ronnie, a journalist who had witnessed the Worcester riots and who served as mayor of Graaff-Reinet, became the editor of the *Worcester Advertiser* and then bought the *Graaff-Reinet Advertiser*.

The Knott-Craig newspaper chain initially extended from Swellendam to Graaff-Reinet, and eventually from Riversdale to Beaufort West. Alan's father, Alan John Alexander, and his uncles, Arthur, Angus and Derek, were born with printer's ink on their fingertips. Even Elizabeth, their youngest sister, was a journalist in Cape Town. For a long time, Alan thought he would probably go into journalism and enter the family business. He became familiar with the old printing presses, spending many holidays cleaning the 'spacers', which were used between the lead type, getting high on the turpentine he used to clean them. It was a family business in the truest sense of the word since his mother was also involved, doing the accounts and running the stationery shop in Oudtshoorn (even though she was a qualified teacher), while his paternal grandmother, Granny Rae, ran the stationery shop in Graaff-Reinet.

One day, Alan's father came home smiling broadly. 'Alan, we are going to get you a new leg in Cape Town and when we come back you will be able to go to school,' he said.

Oudtshoorn's young doctor, Dr Botha (or Dr Boetie as he was affectionately known), had correctly diagnosed Alan's condition, but treatment was only available in the city. The road trip to Cape Town was a thrilling experience for the young boy, and the sights and sounds of the bustling coastal city made an indelible impression on him. While in the city, his father took him to see a miniature steam engine at the Cape Town station. Alan put a penny into a little silver box, and watched in fascination as it set the wheels of the steam engine in motion. If his father had allowed it, he would have put pennies in the box all afternoon to watch that steam engine chug.

The Cape Town specialist, Dr Bell, put calipers on Alan's leg and fed him calcium. Back in Oudtshoorn, he started going to school, just as his father had promised. His schoolmates, or at least some of them, were delighted to have someone new to tease and bully, especially when they saw his damaged leg, encased in its metal frame. The cruelty of children can be ferocious and in Alan's case his peers tormented him ceaselessly. They took great pleasure, for example, in pushing him to the ground, simply to watch him fall.

However, Alan had an important ally: Chris, his younger (by one year) brother. Chris was appointed Alan's bodyguard by their father. He made it his job to watch over his brother at all times. If Alan was on the receiving end of some rough treatment, Chris would make sure that the perpetrators got a dose of their own medicine. He was utterly fearless and was deterred by neither the size nor reputation of an opponent.

Eventually, as his leg grew stronger, Alan was able to dispense with the calipers and play and interact with the other boys as one of them. And yet the bullying continued. Alan felt himself demeaned and insulted by the constant barrage of physical and verbal abuse, and he became deeply troubled as a result. Unable to sleep and tortured by feelings of shame, self-doubt and anger, life for Alan became practically unbearable.

That was how things continued until, at the age of ten, Alan woke up and decided there and then to change his life. With absolute clarity Alan knew that until he took action, until he took control, he would never find peace. *He* had to put a stop to the bullying, not Chris, not his father, not anyone else. So, at the end of school that very same day Alan sought out the most notorious bully, who had made his life a misery from the start, and challenged him to a fight. He was not scared; he was simply committed to doing what he had to do. It was as cold, clear and simple as that.

The fight, if it can be called that, was over before it really began. Alan threw the first punch, much to his opponent's surprise, slamming his fist as hard as he could into the boy's belly. And with that single punch Alan was free. The bully, as is the way with all bullies, was a coward at heart; he had no stomach for a fight on equal terms, since he relied on intimidation to achieve his hollow victories. The boy hit back half-heartedly and then took flight. Alan didn't follow; there was no need to: both he, and the boy, and his school peers knew who had won.

Alan's success in conquering the playground bully gave him the confidence to tackle the town's roving two-boy bicycle gang, Coenie and Schalk, who scoured the neighbourhood looking to pick fights with whoever crossed their path. Alan had often been the target of their aggression. Convincing his friend Mark to come with him, Alan searched for, found and challenged the pair. And that was his second, and last, real fight. Coenie and Schalk were beaten, and gave no further trouble. It became safe to ride a bike in the streets of Oudtshoorn once more.

Life has mellowed Alan since. But his impatience and short temper are legendary, a possible result of the indignities he suffered in his youth. And though he may no longer raise his fists in anger, his tongue-lashings have administered many a verbal beating. But as quickly as his temper rises, it subsides. He bears no grudges and forgets an argument as soon as it is concluded, although those he has chastised concede that they find it disconcerting that he can recover his equanimity so quickly after his tongue has torn them to shreds.

Although Alan was free to explore the neighbourhood, there were also chores to be done at home. Since both his parents worked, Alan, being the eldest, washed clothes, cleaned the house, made supper and he and Chris bathed their two younger brothers, Terry and Tony, from the age of ten. When their homework was done, Alan and Chris would walk to the corner café to buy Wilson's toffees with one or two pennies clutched in their hands and a ball under one arm. On the way back, a soccer or cricket game would start up with the neighbourhood boys, which usually lasted until dusk. On lazy sunny afternoons, they lay under quince hedges and ate their fill of the fruit. Alan and Chris joined the boy scouts and often went out hiking in the Swartberg and Outeniqua mountains. They cooked over a fire and slept in the open under the stars. The boys made canoes out of zinc, sailing them down the irrigation furrows, and tunnelled caves in the veld where they lived imaginary lives. They were wonderful days.

Although the boys spent a great deal of time outdoors at play, there was a strict set of rules at home. Alan's father was a disciplinarian and would use the slipper as punishment on many occasions. His father's motto was 'First is first, and second is nothing', a creed that he expected his sons to live by. As a result, Alan was anxious to avoid disappointing him, and at school and home he pushed himself to excel at everything he did. But this desire to please his father did not stem from anxiety alone; Alan also knew that his father was a kind, generous man who wanted only the best for his sons, and the boy's efforts were as much in appreciation of these qualities as any other.

Alan's mother, Andronette, was a working woman, a rare phenomenon in a conservative South African town in the 1950s. Alan traced his maternal lineage to Champagne and La Rochelle in France where his eighth great-grandfather, Jacques de Villiers, escaped religious persecution in 1661. Jacques and two of his three brothers fled to Holland one night as the Catholic soldiers were approaching the farm. They were recruited by the Dutch East India Company for their wine-farming experience and set sail for South Africa as the only three passengers on the frigate *Zion*.

Jacques settled in the Cape and subsequently established the renowned wine farm, Boschendal, where the family lived until 1879. Eight years later, Cecil John Rhodes bought Boschendal, one of more than twenty farms that he acquired in the Drakenstein Valley, and established Rhodes Fruit Farms. After Rhodes's death in 1902, De Beers mining company continued to manage the farms for 40 years, after which they were sold to a syndicate. To this day, a plaque outside the Boschendal entrance pays homage to Jacques de Villiers, who laid the foundations for the farm's reputation as a renowned wine producer.

Although Andronette spent a great deal of time in the family's printing business, at home she instilled in her boys a love of reading, as well as an aptitude for disciplined study. Due to his mother's insistence that he read, courtesy of frequent visits to the local library, Alan spent hours devouring the *William* series, *The Hardy Boys* and even Shakespeare. Thanks to his love of reading and his Ouma Agnes's Maths and English lessons when his hip kept him at home, Alan skipped a standard when he eventually went to school and entered matric at the age of sixteen.

Evenings were spent around the kitchen table reading, doing homework or talking about the day's events. On Sunday nights, the Knott-Craig boys were allowed a treat of sugar on bread in a bowl of milk for their dinner, while they listened to Springbok Radio broadcasting a thrilling series called *Mark Saxon and Sergei* in *Operation Yesterday*, or LM Radio's top-twenty music hits hosted by Clacky McKay and John Berks. No one moved from the table so as not to miss out on a single second.

In later years, entertainment also came in the form of Uncle Derek, a favourite uncle with the boys since, as a wild teenager, he had stayed with Alan's family in Oudtshoorn. He would take the boys swimming early on Sunday mornings and introduced Alan and Chris to their first evening movie, *The Millionairess*, at the Plaza Bioscope in Graaff-Reinet. The only drawback to evening movies was having to don a suit and tie to see Tarzan swinging through the jungle or John Wayne swagger into town. When Elvis or the Beatles appeared on screen, the girls would scream in delight. The bioscope lights would be switched on to make them stop, but as soon as the movie resumed, the screaming continued. This went on throughout the entire performance, much to the boys' annoyance.

By far the best memories Alan has of his boyhood are the ones associated with holidays spent with his maternal grandparents in Komga, and the lifelong friends he made there: Pop, Katie and Frank Peters. In the 1950s and 60s, most people with the means to go on holiday went to Lourenço Marques; or LM as everyone called the then-capital of Mozambique. No one went to Cape Town; it was rainy and windy, and held no appeal as a holiday destination. But the boys preferred to spend their holidays with Ouma Agnes and Oupa Tony in Komga, near East London.

Oupa Tony was an imposing six-foot presence who wore a jacket and a bow tie even when he went fishing. The boys would go game-bird hunting with Oupa and his dogs, run wild in the surrounding mealie fields, and while away hours watching their grandfather tending his cattle and sheep.

Ouma was a teacher and published poetess of an anthology of verse titled *Under African Skies*. Other than the English and Maths tuition, the latter being a subject in which Alan excelled, she also introduced him to some beautiful books. He paged through Afrikaans classics such as *Hasie Jollieboy*, the *Trompie* series and *Groen en Goud*.

Their Komga holidays over, Alan and his brothers returned to school, first to Van Rheede Primary and then for a year to Oudtshoorn Boys' High, which is now a museum, and finally to the co-ed Oudtshoorn High School. Although Alan was a good student, his real interest lay in sport, particularly cricket, which he played for the first team. He met South African cricket heroes such as Graeme Pollock and Mike Procter, the latter having spent time with Alan and his brother Chris bowling in their backyard, while Athol McKinnon gave Alan a good grounding in the game as his coach. Swimming, athletics and even rugby formed part of his sporting curriculum. He was initially not permitted to play rugby, but eventually, in Standard Eight, his father relented. And it was actually in rugby that Alan won his only school prize, that of Most Improved Rugby Player, something he achieved despite knowing that each time he played he might damage his hip beyond repair.

Matriculating in 1969, aged seventeen, Alan was set to continue his education at the University of Cape Town (UCT). Before that could happen, however, there was the issue of compulsory military service. Alan decided to join the Navy for the year. After all, he thought, he could use this brief interlude as an opportunity to see the world. He stood alone on the platform waiting for the troop train, neatly dressed in his school blazer and a tie. With hindsight, the jacket and tie were a bad idea. As Alan stepped onto the train, he realised that the rowdy jean-clad crowd inside had been drinking since they had left home. He sat as inconspicuously as possible in the corner of his compartment hoping desperately he would survive the trip to Simonstown.

Not long after boarding, he looked up from his book to see five loud thugs, or so they seemed to him, laughing and jeering at the doorway. The only way to deal with this, he thought, was to pretend he was fearless. By some miracle, he wasn't beaten up. Johnny, the leader of the gang – and they were literally members of a gang from Port Elizabeth – made a friendly comment and they became good pals for the next year in the Navy. Alan had made his first Navy friend and acquired another personal bodyguard in the process.

The Navy turned out to be one of the most hellish experiences of Alan's life. Aboard *SAS Pretorius*, an anti-submarine frigate, he endured fierce storms, severe seasickness, cramped living conditions and hardly any time ashore. When the experience came to an end, Alan vowed never to set foot on a boat or ship again. The fact that sailing was to become one of his main passions many years later is, therefore, quite extraordinary.

Alan's boyhood in Oudtshoorn was idyllic. Even as his life moved away from his hometown, still it clung to him in a welcome embrace, in sepia-coloured images of carefree abandon and in snatches of Frank Sinatra's lyrics sung in his father's steady tenor: 'Our song I must admit still fills my hopeful heart, so please remember the words for I still remember the tune'.

Working in the Trenches
1970 to 1990

I will prepare and some day my chance will come.
Abraham Lincoln

In the grand scheme of things, Oudtshoorn was just a speck on the map, but from Barrydale to Uniondale, Abe Meyer was God. Uncle Abe was a senior technician at the local Posts and Telecommunications Office, a man who was revered and respected throughout the small town for the important position he occupied in the state behemoth. In the 50-rung hierarchy that was to become Telkom, Uncle Abe was probably comfortably ensconced on one of the middle rungs, but in Oudtshoorn he was king.

Alan had the privilege of calling him Uncle Abe because he lived around the corner from his house and was a good friend of his father's. Alan also had considerable contact with Uncle Abe because the older man was a regular visitor at the family home. As a teenager, Alan started dabbling in electronics, but his garage experiments often backfired and he would regularly blow up his handiwork. He would sadly pick up the pieces of his new invention and go off to Uncle Abe's house to find out why it hadn't worked.

Alan believed Uncle Abe to be God incarnate, who by the greatest stroke of good fortune just happened to be living around the corner. There was nothing the great man didn't know. Uncle Abe would painstakingly show Alan how to fix the botched creations and, in the process, formed an attachment to the boy. He enjoyed having his neighbour's son at his house, and was even more pleased that the boy was intelligent and showed an aptitude for engineering. Uncle Abe also knew about his father's ambition for Alan to study engineering and that this ambition would require funding. The Knott-Craigs could not easily afford the annual university and residence fee of R800, which would amount to R3 200 for a four-year engineering degree – far too much money for a newspaper editor and printer from Oudtshoorn.

One afternoon, Uncle Abe came to see Alan's father and told him about the Department of Posts and Telecommunications' bursary scheme. Alan, overhearing part of the conversation, was intrigued, especially when he heard his own name crop up. Eager to ask his father what the conversation had been about, Alan waited impatiently for Uncle Abe to leave. He heard the men exchange goodbyes and then, just as he was about to rush toward the door, his father's voice summoned him to the kitchen table.

'There is no way that you or your brothers will be going into the printing business,' his father announced when Alan entered the room. 'There may be ink on my fingers, but there never will be any on yours,' he continued. 'Alan, I'm going to send you to the University of Cape Town to study engineering with a Post Office bursary.'

'What about architecture?' Alan ventured hesitantly. It was an ambition he had harboured for quite some time.

'You can either become an architect and remain poor all your life, or turn your electronics hobby into a career and become an engineer – much better prospects in that,' his father insisted.

There was no further discussion, no arguments. If his father made a decision, there was no negotiation. Alan did not have any major objection to his father's plans for him, but even if he had, he would never have dreamt of questioning his judgement. As the patriarch of the family, Alan John Alexander Knott-Craig's word was final; Alan had no choice but to accept the fate his father had decreed.

However, there was one snag. To qualify for a Post Office bursary, Alan had to be an employee of the organisation. So, during the summer holidays of 1970, after completing his military service in the Navy, Alan went to work for Uncle Abe at the Post Office. For the princely sum of R110 per month before tax, Alan began his work as a pupil technician.

Among other responsibilities, a pupil technician had the unenviable task of inspecting the lines of telephone wires spanning miles across the country for any possible defects. His supervisor would drive down the road while Alan gazed up at the sky searching for errant wires held aloft by the tall wooden poles. He was required to fix any broken or damaged wires he discovered. He only did this once, since Alan feared heights. The idea of having to shimmy up the huge poles terrified him, so much so that on the single occasion he did, he was so nervous that he ended up wrecking the wires completely. He was not asked to climb again.

The part of his job that Alan loved best, however, involved repairing the telephone lines that spanned a farmer's land. Once the problem was out of the way, Alan and his supervisor would spend the morning chatting with the farmer and his wife over *koffie en koekies* (coffee and biscuits). There was no point in refusing; the farmer always insisted. It was his way of saying 'thank you' – a show of good neighbourliness that is practically lost today. Once the coffee had been slowly savoured and the farmer had had his fill of conversation, the boot of the supervisor's car would be loaded with fruit and vegetables, of which Alan would get a share to take home to his mother. Today, such a gesture would be misconstrued as a bribe, but back then it was a kindness.

The following year, Alan enrolled at UCT with the sought-after bursary signed and sealed by the Department of Posts and Telecommunications. He continued to work in the Post Office during his university holidays, as stipulated in the bursary conditions, and did so for the duration of his four-year engineering degree.

In order to gain experience at the Post Office, Alan was sent to work in virtually every discipline. This also involved a job that mainly consisted of overseeing two white foremen on stools watching a gang of black men digging trenches in which telephone cables would be laid. It was, Alan knew immediately, an absolutely pointless, mind-numbingly boring exercise and he dreaded having to do it. After a couple of days, he could not tolerate the inactivity any more; so, stripping off his shirt and grabbing a pick, Alan jumped into the trench to work alongside the diggers. The foremen shook their heads in dismay while the workers grinned broadly at the white man's pluck. Passers-by stared curiously at the white boy digging with the gang of black men and every once in a while a car would stop and its occupants would gaze in disbelief at what they saw.

During the apartheid regime, menial labour was reserved for black men. This was an unwritten law of the ruling white minority, and one which was seldom challenged from within. Alan had unwittingly broken this law. And in spite of the considerable respect he gained from the workers and the tanned, muscled torso he developed as a result of his labours, his time in the trenches ended quite abruptly. This new routine had been going on for some time when Alan made the mistake of telling his father that he was digging trenches for the Post Office. Mr Knott-Craig senior was not impressed. He summarily wrote to the Postmaster General demanding to know whether management was not embarrassed to be putting his son's university skills to use digging trenches. Without further ado, Alan was taken off trench duty.

He was then sent to the Post Office workshop in Prestwich Street in Cape Town, where he learnt to weld, braze and operate a lathe, among other useful skills. Alan was fascinated to learn that his grandfather had started his printing career in exactly the same place. His colleagues were varied and interesting, but the women were the most entertaining. Alan would watch them arrive at the workshop every morning chatting at the top of their voices about their domestic squabbles or complaining about their good-for-nothing husbands, their tiresome children and the trivialities of the day ahead. Still deep in conversation and gesticulating wildly, they would don their overalls, tie a scarf around their heads and remove their dentures, storing them in their lockers with the rest of their valuables. Alan was stupefied – they took out their teeth when they started their working day, and put them back in again when they stepped outside! The transformation from woman-next-door to toothless wonder had him agog every morning.

There were no people of colour employed in the workshop. The only black faces he saw were those of the men digging the trenches or perhaps the odd 'tea boy'. Everyone else was white, even the toothless women. Alan didn't think to question the Post Office's recruitment policies; coming from a small sheltered town such as Oudtshoorn, he had never even heard the word 'apartheid'. And there was no television in South Africa to inform him otherwise.

The time Alan spent climbing poles, fixing wires, digging trenches and welding in the workshops was time well spent, since it equipped him with skills and knowledge that would stand him in good stead in the years ahead. He became familiar with the workings of the Post Office's telecommunications infrastructure from the grassroots up.

Going to UCT was a big step for a country boy who had never been beyond Graaff-Reinet and Komga, which, given the short distances involved, could not be realistically classified as mind-broadening travel experiences. He loved life at UCT's Smuts Hall – he was served dinner, his room was cleaned for him, even his bed was made by someone else. All he had to do was concentrate on his studies, which he did, sometimes for up to eighteen hours a day. The reason he was so committed to his studies was simple – he was petrified of failing. If he did fail, the bursary would be revoked and he would have to face his father, a prospect that he feared more than anything else. If he did not succeed at university his father's anger would know no bounds, such would be the level of his disappointment. In other words, Alan dared not fail. He would occasionally go out with his friends on a Saturday evening, but socials, drinking sessions and student parties held no appeal for him. He mainly worked and studied, with the result that, among other things, he became even more accomplished in Mathematics.

It was at UCT that Alan first became aware of politics and the concept of apartheid. He was studying in his room one morning as usual when a group of friends barged in; they wanted him to join them at St George's Cathedral in Cape Town for a protest march. Alan didn't understand what it was all about and refused to go. Some time later the group returned, beaten and bloodied. The police had gone to work on them with *sjamboks* (whips) and one of the boys had been bitten by a police dog. This was one of the first demonstrations against apartheid organised by white students at UCT. Growing up in sleepy Oudtshoorn, politics was a subject that was seldom brought to his attention. And so, because he had been raised in an almost exclusively white community, the fact that UCT comprised only white students did not strike him as unusual.

He vaguely remembered when his father had come home with the news that Verwoerd had been assassinated in 1966. Alan had asked his father, 'What's Verwoerd?' Even though his father was in the newspaper business, he never wrote about politics; if he had questioned or criticised the National

Party in any way, he would have risked losing a substantial proportion of his readership.

Although UCT was overwhelmingly white, it was labelled a 'liberal' university in the 1970s. At that time, the term 'liberal' for a South African was understood to mean, among other things, opposition to apartheid rule. It also meant that the privileged white class should do what it could, collectively and individually, to empower the disadvantaged coloured and black classes that formed the overwhelming majority of the population. Alan witnessed an incident during his final year at UCT that perfectly illustrated this idea of positive intervention on behalf of another. The final-year students were told that those who had achieved the highest marks would be allowed to choose their thesis topic first. A coloured girl in his class chose the same thesis topic as Alan, although her marks had been inferior to his. The professor who was to decide the issue insisted that the girl be given first choice, despite being fully aware that on a purely academic basis it should be Alan's prerogative. Alan, in his state of political naivety, thought the professor had acted this way because the student was a woman – which in itself, of course, would have been no bad thing. However, reflecting on the matter years later, and with a much improved understanding of apartheid-era injustices, Alan realised that the professor's decision to intercede on the girl's behalf was because he wanted to give the coloured student the opportunity to do as well as she could academically, which would in turn increase her chances of success in a pro-white job market. The episode had been, in fact, Alan's first taste of affirmative action – he just hadn't known it at the time.

Alan's thesis entailed using a digital computer to control an analogue computer, which simulated a motor. Although unaware of this then, the thesis provided an important foundation for decisions he was to make later, when he had to select a cellular standard for South Africa. In the 1980s, analogue systems were about to be eclipsed by digital ones, but as with any new concept, people resisted making the change. Alan couldn't make his project work and his supervising professor couldn't shed any light on the matter. Alan was doing a thesis he didn't like and didn't understand, and he felt his lecturers were no help at all. He eventually approached another professor to talk over the problems he was experiencing. The professor in question was nicknamed 'Tweety Bird' by the students, based on his resemblance to the cartoon character of the same name. Professor 'Bird' helped Alan uncover the reason for his lack of success: Alan had been using a formula that, despite being taken from a Masters thesis that had been passed, was fundamentally flawed. With a rogue formula in place, Alan's own thesis was inevitably going to run into trouble.

Although Alan spent most of his time at UCT with his nose buried in his books, he did manage to get out and date occasionally. In his final year, he met a pretty school teacher on a blind date. Janet Schorn was also a talented singer and drama student with a contagious zest for life. Within a few months of graduation, on 22 March 1975, Alan and Janet, both aged 22, were married in Oudtshoorn. Their first home, however, was in Cape Town: a small flat near the Wynberg train station.

After graduating, Alan joined the Department of Posts and Telecommunications in Cape Town on a full-time basis and began to work back his bursary. He initially reported to a man who was to become his best friend. Americo Alberto Seixal Ferreira da Silva had come to South Africa from Angola to study at UCT. He had one of the most creative and brilliant minds Alan had ever encountered. Americo took one look at the long-haired youngster and was drawn to his enthusiasm and drive. Alan was a regular guest at Americo's home, helping him move house, planting his flower beds and almost setting his dining room alight during a fondue disaster. In the evenings, the two friends did a little moonlighting in the 'sweatshop', as they liked to call it, where they designed and built soccer pinball machines for a man named Jesus de Romão, a wealthy businessman who filled the boot of his huge Jaguar with the coins collected from his pinball profits. Alan ruined many of Janet's kitchen utensils etching the tricky little printed circuit boards for the pinball games, but the work was fun and he made a tidy sum on the side doing a relatively easy job.

Back in the office, Alan worked in the Pinelands branch for some time, where the underground cable network was managed. Whenever someone requested a telephone line, a technician would have to find a pair of cables that was not in use to be able to allocate a new telephone line. To be sure that non-allocated cables were selected, the technician had to consult endless paper records that listed allocated cables and those still available.

Mr Peter Henry, Alan's boss, and an imaginative engineer in his own right, asked Alan if he could computerise this paper system in order to provide quicker and more accurate access. Having acquired some computer programming skills while at university, Alan agreed to give it a go. Using one of the new mini-computers, Alan set about his work.

Of course, these incongruously named early computers were not 'mini' at all; they were probably about a hundred times bigger than one of today's laptops, while also being a hundred times less powerful. A huge disk, the size of the top of a washing machine, could store a maximum of two megabytes. It took about eight hours to compile a program. Sometimes Alan would walk into work in the morning only to be confronted by a 'crash' – a malfunctioning or inoperable program that needed fixing. Alan got busy teaching himself what he needed to know. He proceeded to write a program that successfully computerised a section of Cape Town's underground cable system, demonstrating how one could access cable network information in seconds. His boss proudly brought in a string of network experts to see what his youngster had done. And so it transpired that in the first half of 1975 Alan wrote computer programs for the Post Office network, and in the second half of the year he showed people how he had done it. There were people queuing at his door to see for themselves this miracle of computer technology.

News of Alan's feat reached the ears of Dr Charles Boyce, a respected world expert in the field of telecommunications technology and the Post Office's most senior individual in this sector of its operations. Alan's ability impressed him. He was keen to have the young man work at the company's newly constructed computer centre in Pretoria, for which he had overall responsibility.

'You're working in the wrong place, son,' he said. 'You need to be in Pretoria; we could use someone like you.'

'I can't go to Pretoria,' Alan replied. 'I'm a Cape Town boy.'

'You think about it,' Dr Boyce advised. 'You will go far if you're in the right place – and it's not here.'

In 1976, after much deliberation, Alan decided to take up Dr Boyce's offer. Janet was happy to follow him and embark on a new adventure. After all, Alan still had two years of his engineering apprenticeship to complete, after which they could, if they wished, return to Cape Town. In Pretoria, Alan was given a small desk stuck behind a door and left to his own devices. Furthermore, there was no one suitably qualified to whom

Alan could report, which left Dr Boyce as his direct mentor. Alan hated his first year at the Pretoria computer centre because there was nothing to do. The Post Office didn't seem to know what to do with him. Alan was earning only R120 per month, and while Janet earned twice as much as this, they struggled to make ends meet. However, they managed to acquire a flat in Sinoville in Pretoria from their lifelong friend Lena Beale, where they contentedly settled in.

Two years later, in 1978, the Knott-Craigs moved home. They became house parents at Pretoria's Louis Botha Children's Home, an institution that cared for orphans and children from broken homes. A colleague of Alan's, also a house parent at the home and aware of Alan's financial difficulties, had suggested the idea. The transition proved a success; as well as benefiting from rent-free accommodation, the couple also enjoyed living among the children. Janet's teaching skills, allied to her naturally warm and sympathetic nature, meant that she was well-equipped to deal with the ten or so demanding youngsters in her charge. Alan took over the maintenance of the pool, did renovations to the house and arranged the entertainment for the children – simple activities that didn't cost much, such as picnics and games in the garden.

Money, however, was still in short supply. This is when Alan began writing course manuals for Wits Technikon, where for each manual he was paid a princely sum of R1 500. The job, though lucrative, had two drawbacks: first, the course subject material was often deadly dull (there is only so much one can say, for example, about the thread patterns of a hexagonal bolt); second, the course subject material was often beyond Alan's understanding. The first disadvantage Alan endured; the second he solved by doing research, mostly a great deal of reading, then structuring the course around the knowledge he had gained. Once the manuals were written, he was commissioned to translate them into Afrikaans. One of Alan's bosses, an Afrikaans linguist called Doep, sat on a panel that 'invented' Afrikaans words. If he got stuck with a word, Doep would simply create an appropriate translation, and the word became official. It presumably found a place in the Afrikaans dictionary and no one was any the wiser regarding its dubious origin.

Alan Thomas, the couple's first child, had been born in 1977. Baby Alan spent his second year with the ready-made family at the Louis Botha Home, but by the time Nicholas was born two years later, Alan and Janet decided it was time to create a new home for their own children. They moved into their new house in Wingate Park, where they lived for the next 22 years. At the age of 26, Alan was already a father of two and still earning less than R200 per month. If it weren't for his writing projects, they would have been close to destitute. Their financial position became even more precarious with the birth of their third son, Matthew, in 1982. Janet started a crèche at home while Alan busied himself converting their garage into a classroom. Despite the financial stress, Alan and Janet had all they needed. They were happy.

Charles Boyce knew that he had to move Alan or risk losing him. He assigned a man called Eric Wood to mentor him. Eric, a well-loved and respected engineer, had the task of setting up a data communications network for South Africa. It was pioneering work and exactly the sort of challenge Alan had been waiting for. From his hideaway behind the door, Alan emerged into the open and rapidly set about making a name for himself in South Africa's nascent telecommunications industry.

Aside from building the country's first X.25 packet-switching network, which was inaugurated in 1982 and marked the beginning of data communication technology, one of Alan's most interesting challenges during this time involved Beltel, a videotex system that provided a primitive form of electronic banking, a postal code search facility, extensive telephone directories, teleshopping, movie schedules and client 'web pages'. In essence, it was a forerunner to the Internet. However, it had never taken off, and was considered a costly failure. It had also attracted a considerable amount of bad press. It had around 10 000 customers, and kept breaking down. In 1988, Dawie Malan, a senior management executive and brilliant engineer, called Alan into his office.

'Alan,' he said, 'I'm going to give you Beltel to fix. If you can't do it within the next year, I'm going to can it.'

Alan was delighted to be given the chance to prove his worth and gladly accepted the challenge. He soon discovered that Beltel didn't work partly because the system equipment being used could not meet the demands placed upon it. However, new equipment could only be obtained via a long and arduous procurement procedure. Alan could not afford to wait for the red tape to run its course. He therefore took the matter into his own hands and approached the Managing Director (MD) of Olivetti South Africa, Mr Virgilio Zaina.

'I need you to give me the biggest computers you have,' was Alan's opening gambit upon meeting Mr Zaina.

'Oh, really!' the other man replied. 'I must give them to you just like that?'

'Yes, on trust,' said Alan.

'And what do I get out of this deal?' Mr Zaina wanted to know.

'If it works,' said Alan, 'we will buy the computers, and probably more. If it doesn't work, you lose out. I can't give you any guarantees that this project will be successful, but I am confident.'

It was a huge risk, but Mr Zaina agreed to supply Alan with the computers he required for his new venture. That the deal had been secured upon a handshake and a sense of mutual trust, defined Alan's approach to business. Some might call it old-fashioned, but for Alan it was an essential component of all his business dealings, and he was to maintain this approach throughout his career. Years later Mr Zaina wrote to Alan from Italy saying, 'I was always convinced that one day you would be the top man in the South African communications business.'

Alan then presented a ten-point business plan to the business community and media explaining how he was going to resuscitate Beltel.

Mr Zaina was true to his word and the new computers were installed. Alan built up a new team around Americo, who was summoned from Cape Town, and Pieter Uys, a bright young engineer from Stellenbosch University, who had some years earlier waited hours outside his office to convince Alan to hire him. Alan liked the spunky young man; besides being a brilliant engineering mind, which strengthened Alan's team considerably, he was a daredevil on a motorbike and a madcap on the ski slopes, matching Alan's sporting prowess every step of the way. The three men made for a formidable team, leaving in their wake a trail of successful projects.

They would sit each day and strategise how to get Beltel working. One of the key factors was the need for a new software package to be distributed free to all Beltel users. This software package would be far superior to its market competitors, and would resolve many of the problems currently plaguing the system. The decision to have bespoke software written was made one evening just before they left the office. The next morning Pieter walked in and gave Alan a disk that featured the required software, written overnight on coffee and adrenalin. His colleagues were suitably impressed.

The package, which Alan rated very highly, was duly distributed under the name PCBel. Beltel's trajectory changed direction and the system enjoyed a period of sustained growth. At one point it boasted more than 100 000 active users and approximately 150 service and information providers. But as the Internet became more popular, one of the service providers on Beltel, Interlink, offered a portal onto the net. It was through these pages that people had their first glimpse of the World Wide Web. Beltel's days were numbered; its user base shrank as people left to join the net and its end came on 31 December 1999, when it was shut down for good.

At the beginning of the 1980s there were murmurs of change, not only politically, but also within the telecommunications industry. Alan, having successfully completed an intensely stressful four-day management training course, was encouraged to enrol for a four-year Masters in Business Leadership (MBL) degree at the University of South Africa, which he subsequently did in 1984. The course necessitated part-time study after hours, but Alan revelled in it, particularly since it gave him new insights into financial management. As far as finances were concerned at the Post Office, there were only two possibilities: the budget was spent on paying people or buying equipment. Profit never entered the equation. 'He who spends the most, gets the most,' was the organisation's mantra. The MBL changed Alan's attitude to money and the concept of profit. It also meant that he spent a further four years in the same occupation tied down to the same employer.

Alan graduated in 1988 with an MBL tucked under his belt. He was subsequently promoted to a bigger office with the new title of Assistant General Manager, Corporate Strategy. He was not too certain what the title entailed, but he created a niche for himself, one that would eventually take him way beyond his expectations. The country was moving toward radical change, just as Alan was on the brink of embarking on an unchartered course, and with this momentum, there were new and exciting opportunities beckoning on the horizon of a new decade.

The Rise of a Giant
1990 to 1992

After climbing a great hill, one only finds that there are many more hills to climb.
Nelson Mandela

He walked with distinct poise through the throng of people with a beatific smile upon his face. He looked old, older than he should be, but that didn't seem to matter. The smile, his height and the grace of his movements, marked him out as a leader of incomparable stature. Cries of 'Viva Africa! Viva ANC!' filled the air as the crowd, which had waited for hours in the blistering sun for their leader to emerge, gave vent to the joy, excitement and relief they felt, now that he was finally returned to them. It had, after all, been 27 years.

Alan leaned forward in his chair, his eyes drawn to the television screen to get a closer look at the world's most famous former political prisoner. As Nelson Mandela walked out of Victor Verster prison to be greeted by his adoring public, Alan gazed upon the face of the man who had been considered so dangerous, so subversive that he had been kept hidden away on Robben Island for 18 of those 27 years. It's about bloody time, thought Alan, shuddering at the thought that a person's life could be taken away so brutally, and at all the wasted years that could never be recovered.

The release of Mandela in February 1990 marked the beginning of the end of apartheid and the slackening of the shackles of racial division and suppression. Elsewhere in the world other barriers crumbled, tyrannies were exposed and new freedoms were claimed. The Cold War was almost at an end and Russian hegemony in Eastern Europe was being challenged. The previous year had seen the pro-democracy movement in China gain international recognition following the Tiananmen Square massacre; it had also seen the destruction of the Berlin Wall, that most potent and hated symbol of ideological oppression. Worldwide, there seemed to be a revival of reconciliation, appeasement and hope.

As South Africa bravely took its first teetering steps toward democracy, another quiet revolution was underfoot – one that would forever change the way society communicated and exchanged information. It took time for the seeds to take root, and it started with a man who, for the moment, continued to labour deep within the labyrinthine structures of the civil service.

Alan had worked his way up the state ladder of the Posts and Telecommunications hierarchy. In 1991, the organisation was divided into two separate entities, one of them was the Post Office and the other Telkom SA Ltd – the sole provider of telecommunications in the country, which had issued its 5-millionth telephone that year to its predominantly white market.

The new telecommunications entity needed someone to commercialise its operations and transform one of the country's largest state enterprises into a profitable business. That person was Jack Clarke, one of South Africa's top businessmen and recently retired as the chief executive of the leading information technology group, IBM South Africa. Jack was a uniquely talented individual; he was not only respected for his business acumen but also admired for his innovative way of thinking. As chairman of Telkom, Jack was to have a defining influence on Alan's life, both professionally and personally.

One morning, and without warning, Jack walked into Alan's office. Not quite knowing how to address Telkom's most senior figure, Alan stood up to shake his hand and settled for a polite, 'Good morning Mr Clarke.'

'Call me Jack,' replied the chairman, before adding, 'I've heard about some of your projects at Telkom and I think you and I will have a lot to talk about.'

'Yes, sir,' replied Alan, the ever-respectful public servant.

'There are some exciting developments in the cellphone industry happening right now,' Jack continued. 'You and I need to discuss how we are going to get that technology to work here. Let's make a time, OK?'

And in that brief conversation a relationship was forged, one that was destined to continue for many years as the two men's understanding of and liking for one another developed.

Several months later, Jack came to Alan with a proposal. As before, he wasted no time with unnecessary preliminaries and got straight to the point.

'Listen Alan,' he said, 'I need someone who can think strategically, who understands technology as well as business, to explore the overseas telecommunications market. I think you can do it. I want you to take a team and go overseas to investigate this new cellular technology. See if it's something we should be doing.'

Although Alan was vaguely familiar with the term, he was not remotely qualified to speak about cellular technology with any authority. Still, if Jack believed he could do it that was good enough for him. His younger self's obsession with the need to avoid disappointing his father had never entirely disappeared; Jack was not his father, of course, but he was a man of comparable worth in Alan's opinion.

When Jack had gone, Alan sat thinking about the brief he had just been given. He knew Jack wanted to provide telecommunications services for millions of South Africans who didn't have access to a telephone. The landline telephones (there were only 9 lines per 100 people) were mainly owned by the white population. But erecting poles and stringing wires to provide landlines to those millions who didn't have telephones was not a viable option – the distances involved were too great and the user base was too scattered and remote. And, when Alan considered the forms of mobile telecommunications available at the time in the country, he could only come up with Telkom's own car phone network, which was based on the outdated C450 analogue technology.

'The car phones are hopelessly inadequate as an alternative option,' Alan informed Jack when they next met.

'Too expensive and too clumsy,' agreed Jack. 'No one really believes it to be more than a toy for the rich. A larger investment in this network won't work. The technology has become dated and the man in the street will never be able to afford it.'

Starting in June 1990, the government lifted the state of emergency and scrapped apartheid laws; in a corresponding act of conciliation, the African National Congress (ANC) suspended its armed struggle. Negotiations were underway to establish a much more inclusive government – one that was truly representative of the country's demographic make up.

As transformation swept through the country at every level, Alan's efforts to transform Telkom's cellular services gathered pace. His first task was to set up the team that would travel with him on his fact-finding assignment around the world, covering Europe, Australia, the Far East and the United States (US). The three people chosen were all senior Telkom executives: Frankie Vian, a human resources expert; Stuart Scott, chief-in-charge of compiling the huge tome that was known as the Yellow Pages directory, a daunting task that he accomplished with meticulous efficiency; and Dr Gabrielle Celli, an Italian engineer with a passion for red wine and good food, introduced to Alan by Americo. No one in the team could claim to know a great deal about cellular technology, but Alan had known that this was likely to be the case. In all other respects, each team member possessed the experience, professional expertise and dynamism that he anticipated would be essential to the success of their mission.

Alan had known for some time that a key component, perhaps *the* key component, to the successful introduction of cellphones to South Africa was the adoption of a common standard, a digital one at that. This requirement was the same for all countries who wanted to introduce, or already had, cellular technology; it would be no different for South Africa.

The first generation of mobile telephony (known as 1G) operated as an analogue system using primarily the Advanced Mobile Phone System (AMPS). It appeared first in the US, in 1976, and then in Australia. The main problems with AMPS were that it was very susceptible to static and other noise, and that it offered no protection against eavesdropping. The European version of AMPS was the Total Access Communication System (TACS), which could also be found in Hong Kong and Japan. The C450 standard was used in Germany, Portugal and, as mentioned a little earlier, South Africa. The three systems (AMPS, TACS and C450) were not only completely incompatible with one another, but also even when used in adjacent countries, they provided no continuity of communications.

The Europeans were the first to tackle the problem of incompatibility. In 1982, Groupe Spéciale Mobile, an association of public telephone bodies, was specially convened for the purpose, ultimately rendering the analogue systems obsolete by crafting the fully digital second generation (2G) cellular telephony standard, which became known as the Global System for Mobile Communications (GSM). The system's unique, even revolutionary, feature was that it offered a service that crossed national boundaries and provided encryption of conversations. In other words, an Italian wanting to travel to Britain, for example, could take his or her cellphone on the journey, safe in the knowledge that GSM would mean the phone remained operable. For this system to work, however, all handsets and networks had to be identical and the GSM standard had to be rigorously enforced. The new system rapidly gained popularity and spread across the continent, with Germany and France leading the way in terms of network building. By 1993, GSM had 1 million subscribers in Europe and 70 networks in 48 countries. Today there are close to 4 billion GSM cellphones in the world.

At the end of their European trip, the team convened in a St Katharine's Dock pub on London's River Thames the day before they were to return home. The group of men reviewed everything they had learned during their time away, which had been a great deal. As the evening drew to a close, Alan summarised their position.

'It's pretty obvious,' he said, 'we have to recommend that South Africa must go the cellular route, and that it should adopt the GSM standard, digital as opposed to analogue. And what's more, we must insist on a competitive environment, with at least two cellular players – we don't want to create another Telkom.'

The others were in full agreement with this position statement, which Alan would then use as the basis of the report he had to submit to Telkom's chairman. This he did within a few days of his return, despite being thoroughly exhausted by the demands of the trip overseas.

After reading the report, Jack met with Alan to discuss its implications. He had liked the report and was in broad agreement with most of the recommendations the group had made.

'I agree with your preference for digital, Alan,' the chairman began. 'Analogue technology could become even more expensive in the long run. And if it becomes cheap it usually implies nobody wants it, which means you can't get rid of it and it's impossible to get spares even if you wanted to keep it running. Besides, you can't get kids excited about old technology. If we are going to persuade the best engineers to come and work for us, we must go with the latest technology.'

Alan was immensely relieved, as well as pleased, to know that Jack was on his side, since securing his backing had been a priority right from the start. However, this was only half the battle. As Jack pointed out, 'The choices may be obvious to us, but that's not enough. We have to convince a number of key people that they need to do this our way. In fact, the real work starts now.'

'Well, at least there's a shift in thinking taking place; we just need to build momentum,' said Alan. 'Look, at the moment telephone penetration is at a 9% low in the country. Cellular will give people easy and affordable access to communication and it will be the most practical means of introducing telephones into areas with no infrastructure. Either they choose cellular or Telkom will have to spend R120 billion in the next couple of years providing telephones for the masses.'

Jack did not doubt Alan's commitment to cellular-phone technology or his determination to see the ideas they were discussing become a reality. However, he also knew that the radical nature of what Alan proposed could well alienate people, and that if his plan was to progress any further, Alan simply had to secure their support.

'I like what you're saying,' he commented as the meeting ended, 'but you should save it for the trenches. You are going to have to put on the performance of your life to get this idea off the ground.'

Jack was right: most people were not at all enthusiastic about the proposals Alan and his team had put forward. Many thought the trip had been a completely hare-brained, unnecessary waste of time, since the anticipated costs of the new technology would make it unaffordable for the overwhelming majority of South Africans; therefore, only an elite sector of the population would benefit.

And, in a sense, this was a valid criticism. Although GSM phones were considerably cheaper than existing cellular motor phones – R3 000 as opposed to R11 000 – this hardly classified them as low-cost products. But, as Alan repeatedly tried to convince the doubters, cellular technology would become progressively more affordable as its popularity grew. And

Alan had no doubt that demand would rise—at least to the level of 75 million users worldwide by the year 2000.[1]

Demand would rise, Alan insisted, because cellular technology was far cheaper and easier to install and maintain than fixed-line telephony. And because cellular technology did not need new extensive (and expensive) infrastructural support systems, it should be possible to achieve a very high penetration rate much more quickly. In addition, a common standard would create the economies of scale necessary to bring down costs and make cellular telephony available to everyone.[2]

When it came to choosing between the TACS or GSM standard, TACS was the more popular technical standard. Perhaps its single most important advantage was the size of the handsets; these were relatively small and certainly much smaller than the brick-like GSM alternatives. However, GSM's functionality was better and had several features that its rival lacked. Alan's preference for GSM was to be vindicated in the near future as the system's technology reached a level of technological sophistication that its competitor could not hope to match. It was GSM, not TACS or AMPS, which was able to accommodate the high-tech digital offerings spawned by the arrival of the Internet.

The temptation to stay with the cheaper analogue technologies, however, was strong. If analogue was good enough for the world's premier superpower, America, then surely it should be good enough for South Africa? This was the line of reasoning many anti-digital campaigners took. This view frustrated Alan, who was convinced that although America led the rest of the world in many areas it lagged behind in the field of communications technology since the regulators' break-up of Ma Bell. If South Africa clung to analogue technology it would lose out in the long term, since the more progressive-minded nations—the ones who 'went digital'—would simply see the country as a convenient dumping ground for old (analogue) technologies that nobody wanted any more. For Alan, this was a dreadful prospect. If South Africa genuinely wanted to participate on equal terms in the global economy, it dare not take such a retrograde step. He was adamant that this was not going to be another disastrous Third World venture—one where donor nations were happy to supply African countries with technologies, tools and equipment of diminished value and negligible long-term viability. Alan wanted South Africa to be a pioneer in cellphone technology. He wanted to put Africa on the map like never before.

In 1992, Alan achieved an important breakthrough. With the help of Telkom's media manager and long-time friend Amanda Singleton, he made a video that showcased his ideas. The South African government, keen to keep abreast of Telkom's investigative work in the area, studied the video and debated its content. Eventually, it agreed with Alan's assertion that GSM would be the preferred technology for South Africa and that there should be at least two operators. Then the fun and games started. Alan wasn't sure if GSM wanted to be in South Africa, but he desperately needed the association's backing in order to purchase the GSM technology.

Kari Martinnen, chairman of GSM at the time, needed more information on South Africa's licence conditions and frequency allocation – issues that had not yet been finalised. At the same time, there were still international boycotts against South Africa, despite the country's imminent move to a multi-party democratic system of government. The official view from the International Telecommunications Union was that South Africa remained out in the cold, and it cautioned Martinnen not to expect its backing should he decide to support the country.

The union's attitude reflected that of the global community generally. The world was unsure what this 'new South Africa' would look like. There were fears that the country might descend into chaos, even civil war, if a militant sense of injustice caused the formerly oppressed to take drastic action. The country had no democratic tradition, so there was no precedent to suggest how the new government would fare. In short: South Africa was a high-risk country for any potential investors. Alan knew this; so did Martinnen. The odds were stacked against both men.

Alan decided to throw South Africa's hat into the ring by sending Martinnen the South African Minister of Posts and Telecommunications' press release announcing the government's intention of issuing two cellular network licences in 1993. It was not an official document and it didn't specify all the information that the GSM office needed. Nevertheless, Martinnen decided to trust his instincts and he therefore proposed conditional approval of South Africa's membership. Martinnen had for some time wanted GSM to have a global presence and regarded South Africa as a potentially important new market, providing entry into Africa as a whole. Alan, for his part, was encouraged by Martinnen's decision. It was true that if GSM's requirements were not satisfied its support would be withdrawn, but at least South Africa was in for the time being.

Telkom's monopoly of the telecommunications industry was absolute; the prospect of having to compete with other operators was thus its worst nightmare. Jack Clarke was the only person within the organisation who saw the benefits of competition and he lobbied tirelessly with the politicians for the introduction of cellular on a competitive basis. He received substantial support from two individuals: the Minister of Finance, Derek Keyes, and the Minister of Public Enterprises, Dawie de Villiers.

The Telkom board was, predictably, upset with the notion of competition and insisted that Alan remove mention of this from his report. De Villiers wanted almost the exact opposite of this: the introduction of competition without Telkom's participation. He felt that the introduction of mobile telephony to the country held huge benefits and that strong competition was essential to protect consumers.

Jack was devastated by De Villiers's statement. He had lobbied so intensely, not only to insist on the introduction of a new competitive cellular industry, but also to secure Telkom's presence in that market. He felt that Telkom had a right to operate a network or own a percentage of one because it had invested considerable time, money and effort in the research and development of a cellular network.

It was tricky. The government was the sole shareholder of Telkom, and it could hardly act against the company's interests. In addition, Coopers and Lybrand pointed out that in most countries where GSM had been implemented, it was standard practice for the existing fixed-line telephone operator to operate one of the cellular networks.

The resolution to this complex issue came after further intense discussions between Derek Keyes, Jack Clarke and Danie du Toit, Telkom's MD. The Minister was persuaded that if Telkom owned 50% of the mobile network it would enhance its value as a government asset. The three men agreed that licences would be issued to two cellular operators, and that Telkom could form part of one consortium that would bid for the cellular licences, but that it could not have more than a 50% stake in the group. However, if that consortium lost out in the envisaged tender process, then Telkom would not be involved in the cellular industry at all.

There was also the issue of money. Telkom was debt-ridden and was itself in need of funds, ideally from foreign investors. Even if it wanted to own a 100% investment in a cellular network, it simply couldn't afford it. Dr Piet Welgemoed, Minister of Posts and Telecommunications, was sent overseas to source companies that might want to invest in South Africa's telecommunications industry.

While in the UK, Dr Welgemoed met with Sir Gerald Whent and Sir Julian Horn-Smith, Vodafone's CEO and Director of International Investments, respectively. Vodafone, which was listed on both the London and New York stock exchanges, operated the largest contiguous telephone network in the world and had a market capitalisation of £4.5 billion (almost R60 billion). It was debt-free and was widely acknowledged as one of Britain's most successful enterprises. Vodafone also had an interest in the operation and construction of cellular networks in ten other countries, where it worked in tandem with host-nation companies. Discussions were positive and the three men shook hands on the possibility that Vodafone would do business in South Africa.

Locally, Johann Rupert, head of the luxury group Richmond and the tobacco giant Rembrandt, expressed an interest in investing in the new cellular company. Two of his executives, Dillie Malherbe and Thys Visser, met for preliminary talks with Alan and Ben Bets, senior general manager at Telkom. The discussions went well and a short while later Johann confirmed that he was willing to become a cellular shareholder. However, his participation was subject to two conditions: one, that the Chief Financial Officer (CFO) of the new group would be his appointment; and two, that he would provide advice on the marketing and branding expertise. Alan was reluctant to proceed on such terms. However, with the benefit of hindsight he was glad that he did, for it led to the appointment – Johann's appointment – of Leon Crouse, a financial genius and Alan's future right-hand man. The chemistry between Alan and Leon was instant. To this day, Alan credits Vodacom's financial success to Leon's formidable financial expertise, his level-headedness and leadership qualities. Vodafone's Sir Julian approved of Johann's choice and Leon was welcomed into the fold. When Alan announced his retirement some fifteen years later, Leon decided to return to work for Johann Rupert, and also retired from Vodacom.

The Rise of a Giant

At long last, Alan's vision was beginning to take shape. Just how important the advent of cellphone technology in South Africa would be was still a matter of conjecture. Alan, however, had a clear vision of what cellular would mean to ordinary people. 'The widespread introduction of cellular phones to South Africa will impact on our lives more dramatically than television has.'[3]

Little did he know at the time that he would be credited with shaping the cellular revolution in the country.

Chasing the Dream
1993

All you need is the plan, the road map, and the courage to press on to your destination.
Earl Nightingale

Every year, Alan had organised the annual telecommunications conference hosted by Telkom. He had done this with his customary élan and this year it would be no different. The conference was planned to be held in Cape Town in February 1993. Alan's frenetic energy suffused the event from the start, issuing instructions thick and fast – so much so that he was nicknamed AK-47. He could be seen everywhere, solving problems, answering questions, motivating others, making sure every detail adhered to his exacting standards. His team, committed though they were to executing his plans to perfection, found the pace and volume of work exhausting, yet still they kept going, working round the clock to ensure that the Telkom93 conference was even bigger and better than its predecessor.

The conference's Regional Head of Operations was Reuben September, today the CEO of Telkom. For Telkom93, however, Reuben reported directly to Alan, who had been promoted to senior general manager. Alan rated Reuben highly. 'Even then,' he remarked, 'Reuben had drive, talent, ambition and charisma.' The late Alvin Scott, Alan's friend and colleague of some twenty years, was his right-hand man in organising the conference, and went on to become Vodacom's Western Cape Regional Manager.

Alan had plans to position cellular technology at the top of the conference agenda. And, since a central theme of the conference was the review of emerging technologies and strategies to ensure a faster and cheaper penetration rate of telephones in South Africa, he was feeling cautiously optimistic. As it turned out, nearly a quarter of the papers presented at the conference concerned cellular telephone systems.

Cape Town's Civic Theatre and the foyer of the Nico Malan Opera House (now the Artscape Theatre Centre) were transformed into a huge telecoms exhibition. With over 1 000 delegates, 21 overseas speakers, and 36 exhibitors, including Panasonic, Siemens, Nokia, Ericsson and Alcatel, the conference attracted national and international attention.

One of the main attractions was the cellphone handsets on display. The delegates were fascinated by these new gadgets that appeared at stand after stand. Small groups gathered to discuss the new devices, held the handsets to their ears and marvelled at how 'small' the brick-like items were.

To demonstrate the 'brick's' capabilities, a trial GSM base station and a 4.5 m satellite dish had been set up in advance. Johan Engelbrecht, who would eventually become the Network Control Executive at Vodacom, was in charge of the demonstration, which included the processing of some 5 000 calls as evidence of the system's potential. Johan watched as some of the delegates eagerly made calls and were swept off their feet by possibilities they could scarcely imagine, while others considered it little more than an expensive yuppie toy. Many scoffed at the notion that anyone would actually want to walk around with a telephone in their hand all day. Today, it is easy for us to see how misplaced this scepticism was, but, at the time, many people genuinely thought that the cellphone was a dead-in-the-water idea.

MD of Telkom, Danie du Toit, stalwart of the old-school telecoms dispensation, a good communicator and a people's person, referred to Telkom as a giant ocean liner that couldn't be turned around at a whim. It would take time, but he assured the delegates that the organisation would change from a rigid bureaucracy to a sleek business model. 'We live in hope,' said most.

Second is Nothing

The keynote address of the Telkom93 conference was delivered by Andile Ngcaba, Head of Information Systems for the ANC. Andile's passion for telecommunications emerged as he watched, intrigued, while the technicians manipulated the mass of wires and switches at the East London Post Office, where his father had been postmaster for over twenty years. Armed with a Philips bursary, Andile studied in Umtata, before leaving the country in the 1970s to join the ANC military wing. Nelson Mandela had praised Andile as 'our bravest young commander', in reference to his military career within the ANC, much of which had been spent in Angola and the then Soviet Union. While abroad, he had received training in specialised military communications technology, which led to his current appointment following his return from exile in 1990. Andile was to become the Director General of the Department of Communications in the new South Africa. Today he is chairman of Dimension Data.

Andile's message at the Telkom93 conference was that the ANC was firmly opposed to privatising the public telecommunications network. He warned against using foreign consultants who would rush into obtaining cellular licences before there was sufficient planning and consultation, and before clear licence conditions had been set by the regulator.

Whether or not the nationalist government intended it, the effect of commercialising telecommunications would have been to take the parastatal, Telkom, out of the hands of a newly empowered black majority in a democratic dispensation. The ANC announced that, though it was no longer wedded to nationalisation as a matter of general policy, public corporations and state business enterprises that were privatised prior to political negotiations would be prime candidates for re-nationalisation. This attitude took the wind out of the sails of the telecoms commercialisation gambit.

Andile explained that the telecommunications policy framework was still under discussion, and in the interim, a mobile licence was not on the cards. The ANC didn't know how to handle a new player in the telecommunications arena when it hadn't even got to grips with the status quo – they needed more time. The debate was picked up by the media, which reported that Andile Ngcaba didn't want cellular to be introduced to South Africa. In refuting this claim, Andile declared: 'It's not about introducing cellular to the country as such; it's about how it should be done. The concern is for black involvement and how black empowerment will fit into the bigger telecoms picture.' In contrast with the robust pro-capitalism tone of the conference, which supported privatisation of the telecommunications industry, Andile's words went against the grain.

Alan had already put in eighteen months of legwork to justify the introduction of cellular as a means of providing universal access and he was determined to show everyone that the concept would succeed. He had made a short film about how mobile telephony worked since no one seemed to be able to grasp the idea. The film showed the cellphone being used in a car, on the street, on the ski slopes, and even in a rural hut. Andile particularly disliked the shots of a rural hut dweller using a cellphone, because, he said, such a person would never be able to afford a luxury product of this nature. Alan understood the ANC's stance, but he was not giving up hope that his vision of cellular technology for everyone in the country could be achieved by the end of the year. Although Andile and Alan differed on the application of cellular, they became firm friends. Fourteen years later, the *Financial Mail* reported Andile as saying, 'I accept now that Alan was right and I was wrong.'[1]

And, despite the ANC's anti-commercialism stance, the buzzword that was on everyone's lips was 'cellular'. At the close of the conference, the Minister of Posts and Telecommunications, Dr Piet Welgemoed, announced that the South African government would be granting two licences to cellphone operators through a tender process. He observed that it was 'the cheapest and quickest way' to offer South Africans access to a telephone. The new technology, coupled with the expected competition, would force down costs and improve service delivery, which would benefit the consumer. This decision would encourage overseas investment, create jobs and ultimately lead to a larger market. However, Telkom's involvement would be limited to a 50% shareholding of one of the tendering consortiums.

In effect, Telkom would be losing control of the telecommunications network, a state of affairs it was bitterly unhappy about. The nationalist government seemed to view commercialisation as a step toward ridding itself of what had become a complacent, top-heavy parastatal. It was keen to push Telkom toward a market-oriented corporate culture. In place of the command structures of state-owned enterprises, market incentives would induce the parastatal to operate on a proper business footing, which would in turn encourage the development of a customer-oriented organisational culture in what was widely perceived as a slothful civil service bureaucracy.

But who would oversee the tender process? The decision would undoubtedly be a contentious one, since relationships between the National Party government and the newly empowered ANC were fraught with tension. At the Convention for a Democratic South Africa (Codesa) held at the World Trade Centre in Johannesburg in December 1990, telecommunications had been high on the list of subjects proposed for discussion. Negotiations had ground to a halt with accusations of government involvement in the right-wing plan to sabotage the talks. Evidence emerged that the spiral of violence was indeed orchestrated by elements in the security establishment trying to derail the negotiations. The ANC and unions launched rolling mass action, involving strikes and marches demanding majority rule. It was agreed at Codesa that Codesa II would try once again to get the political ball rolling.

The assassination of Chris Hani in April 1993 brought proceedings to an abrupt halt, and propelled South Africa to the brink of disaster. Hani, the popular leader of the South African Communist Party (SACP), was shot and killed by a far-right Polish immigrant who had been given the gun by the Conservative Party Member of Parliament, Clive Derby-Lewis. Mandela's speech shortly after Hani's murder helped stop the country from plunging headlong into civil violence, as the nation responded positively to his call for calmness and restraint. There were riots, but the scale of violence was nowhere near as bad as it might have been. More positively, the tragedy focused minds, and the two negotiating parties renewed their push for a peaceful settlement with renewed vigour.

The job of formulating the R1.2 billion cellular tender was given to Eugene van Rensburg, an adviser at the Policy Unit for Public Enterprises and Privatisation. He had been appointed in the interests of speeding up the process since South Africa did not yet have a telecommunications regulatory body in place. The provisions of the tendering process were complex and wide-ranging, covering aspects such as performance guarantees and the penalties attached to non-performance, cash guarantees, and the need for the tendering companies to provide evidence of their ability to reach the widest possible community.

Overseeing the tender process would be Ters Oosthuizen, former Eskom general manager, who was appointed Postmaster General and eventually regulator of the cellular industry. Ters had a huge presence – he was a big game hunter, Springbok marksman and respected advocate, feared in court and respected by his colleagues. He had a reputation for being 'tough but fair' and he was someone with the requisite authority and experience to manage what would inevitably be a fiercely contested affair. His supporting technical team was made up of South African, British and Australian experts. Ters didn't want any suspicions shadowing the process. No one was going to derail the process with him at the helm. In order to attract foreign investment, a credible tender invitation had to be compiled to ensure that the best international players would be keen to respond. The tender had to be a well-structured document, especially in terms of the business obligations that it imposed on the licencees.

In April 1993 the tender was issued. Bidders had until July to submit their proposals. Alan wondered whether it was possible to put together a coherent document within such a short space of time that would provide the impetus required to establish a national cellular company. The tender documents listed several conditions: an initial licence fee of R100 million; an ongoing licence fee of 5% of the operator's net revenue; annual radio fees of R5 million payable to the Postmaster General and a R50 000 submission fee.

The message was clear: don't bother applying unless you are absolutely serious and have the resources to back your bid.

The tender document was unique in two other respects: first, the bidders had to show how they would generate R1 billion in economic activity outside the mainstream business; and second, the successful applicants had to sell airtime on community phones in underserviced areas at a third of the normal price.

Alan and Jack discussed the document at some length, which they agreed was 'tough but fair', just as Ters Oosthuizen would have wanted it.

'The cleverest thing they did,' Alan said, with a wry smile of appreciation, 'was to specify the 5% fee of revenue. It seems like nothing, but once the operators start generating billions, which will happen, that 5% will become a huge money-spinner for the government.'

'That's for certain,' replied Jack. 'No other country has introduced this fee before and it's an important criterion in the long term. It's smart because they cream off the one line that can't be fudged – revenue.'

'The second clever concept,' commented Alan, 'is that of community phones. That is an excellent idea; we just have to work out how we can provide them in underserviced areas at subsidised rates. I believe that the commitment to community service is something that the selection committee will look at very closely.'

Alan was correct in thinking that the community-service telephones would figure strongly in the selection panel's deliberations. What was the point, after all, of providing something beyond the reach of most South Africans? If that happened, Alan thought, then the doubters would have been right all along: the cellphone would be no more than a rich man's plaything.

As if reading his thoughts, Jack said: 'Remember, by the time we're up and running, the ANC will be in power and they are going to scrutinise your commitment to helping disadvantaged communities. We have to become the new government's partner in eradicating disparity and poverty.'

There were five consortiums bidding for two licences: the Telkom group, M-Net, Anglovaal, Barlow Rand – all strong, well-established outfits – and the relatively unknown Suntel organisation. At the outset, however, over 60 groups internationally had expressed an interest.

With the cellular network licensing process well under way and the tender documents distributed, Alan left Telkom, taking a salary cut and giving up his pension rights, and, with no other contenders for the job, became CEO of a brand-new, no-name cellular company on 19 May 1993. His package as the new CEO was R330 000 per annum, which was a great deal of money for Alan, but they could have offered him half that amount and he would still have taken the job.

At that stage, the future Vodacom consisted of a handful of people crammed into three offices in a corner of the 24th floor of Telkom Towers in Pretoria. Alan headed up a team consisting of Shane Hibbard of car-phone fame; Johan Engelbrecht, as technical specialist; Barry Vlok and Pieter Uys, as senior engineers; Loodt van Aardt and Willem Swart in charge of finance; Anthony Bold, as human resources expert; Lionel Naudé, as head of marketing; and Ben Higson, Vodafone's shadow man and project manager. Rob Pasley, financial wizard of note, did the number crunching on the business plans.

Alan had not been the first choice to run the new cellular operation. Ben Bets, senior general manager at Telkom, had been offered the job before

Alan, but had turned it down. Considering his seniority, it had seemed the logical choice. It was generally accepted that his refusal was due to the fact that he was holding out for Danie du Toit's job as CEO of Telkom. Besides, the new position as head of Vodacom was a risky move; no one knew where the new company was headed, whereas Telkom provided ongoing security.

Despite his appointment as CEO of the new cellular company, many people at Telkom still considered Alan an upstart. He was the *Engelsman* (Englishman) from the Cape who didn't quite understand the company protocol. Or perhaps he did, but didn't care to abide by it. Ben Bets, himself no meek, biddable civil servant, had taken it upon himself to show Alan how to do things 'the Telkom way', which included not directly addressing a senior member of staff, following the correct reporting procedures to the letter, and knowing his exact place within the bureaucratic set-up. Alan, who had become friends with Ben, thought it a complete load of hogwash and blithely ignored all such advice during the years he spent with the company. Of course, in the eyes of some, this made him something of a maverick and, when he left, they were glad to see the back of him. Alan could detect in their attitude towards him a reluctance to support him in his new job: 'You're on your own now buster; don't expect any help from us,' was what they seemed to say. But Alan had not expected anything else. Besides, it was all water off a duck's back as far as he was concerned – he'd been self-reliant for so long that their jibes carried no sting. He always did things on his own terms anyway.

Alan made no bones about the fact that he only wanted the best engineers to join him at Vodacom. Ultimately he recruited about 500 top-level engineers from Telkom, which caused a further rift between Alan and the Telkom faction. Those who refused his offer were, in Alan's opinion, missing the opportunity of a lifetime: the chance to be at the forefront of a cellular revolution that would dramatically, and permanently, alter the technological landscape.

Alan's first major decision as CEO was to come up with a name for the company. Weird and wonderful names were being bandied about – Livewire, Bright Blue, Starfone – but there was nothing that held any strong appeal. Alan, together with Johann Rupert's marketing team from Rembrandt, were somewhat constrained by the fact that both Telkom and Vodafone wanted their names used in the new cellular company. 'Vodakom' was proposed, and, although the name had a certain 'ring' to it, it was felt that the 'k' was too Afrikaans-sounding, which would seem out of place in the new dispensation.

The final choice – 'Vodacom' – was only agreed on after several more months of deliberation, by the end of which Alan was thoroughly fed up with the whole process and no longer gave a damn what name the company was given. The name, of course, was merely a re-spelling of the discredited 'Vodakom'. However, replacing the politically incorrect 'k' with a 'c' was not entirely insignificant. Alan liked the fact that 'Vodacom' could be read as an acronym for 'Voice and Data Communications'.

Subsequently, the storm of conspiracy theories that surrounded the 1994 elections cast doubts on the political neutrality of the name chosen by Alan and his associates. The idea began to circulate that Vodacom could be interpreted as 'vote a com', meaning 'vote for a comrade' or 'vote for the communists'. And then there was the observation that in many African languages the word 'voda' means something dark or sinister. Alan and the team sensibly chose to ignore these alarmist objections. 'So what if the comrades, communists or whoever think they have Vodacom's vote,' Alan remarked, 'at least all this conjecture keeps Vodacom top of mind and raises our profile.'

The logo was also created. Alan learnt from the Rembrandt marketing team that the colours of the company logo were very important. Alan, being colour-blind, did not attach much importance to the colours chosen, but he had to make allowances for the rest of the nation. They settled on blue, denoting hi-tech, and green, with its Earth-friendly associations. There was some insistence on giving the brand an international flavour and thus the spinning globe atop the Vodacom logo came into being. In the end, Alan just wanted something to brand. As he saw it, it wasn't important what you called something; it was only important what you did with it. 'Regardless of the name, the branding will build it,' he told his team.

Shortly afterwards the Vodacom team moved to offices in Hatfield where, under Alan's leadership, they worked feverishly night and day to prepare their documents for the cellular licence tender. Eventually, on the last day of June, Vodacom's CEO and his senior colleagues strode into the Postmaster General's office pushing a trolley of tender documents before them.

Ters Oosthuizen received five bids, one of which had to be discarded because it had been handwritten on a single sheet of paper. The remaining four bids were heavyweight consortia with international partners. The M-Net stable comprised the M-Net subsidiary Multichoice (30%), the UK's Cable & Wireless (30%), Transnet's Transtel (10%), and black business organisations Fabcos (5%) and Naftel (25%). Another 5% siphoned off the current shareholding would later go to a pension fund aligned to the Congress of South African Trade Unions (Cosatu). The next bid, that of the local group Barlow Rand, was made up of Barlow Rand (35%), Deutsche Bundespost Telekom (34%), and a black share-holding earmarked at 32%. Cellstar Cellular Network put together Grintek (51%), Telkom Finland (11%), Finnfund (11%), and a black shareholding at 27%. And of course there was Vodacom, which consisted of Telkom (50%), Vodafone (35%) and Rembrandt (15%), later offering 5% to a black empowerment group.

Vodacom's bid highlighted the following aspects:

- The local cellular market was projected at 320 000 subscribers after five years and 500 000 after ten years. (It reached 320 000 in eight months and 500 000 in two years.)
- Cumulative capital expenditure in the first ten years was estimated at R625 million, of which shareholders would fund the majority. (Vodacom exceeded capital expenditure by February 1995 with huge network roll-out costs; by August 2003, the capital expenditure was R17.5 billion.)
- Within three years 65% of the population would have Vodacom coverage and 70% within five years. (By 2003 Vodacom's coverage extended to 95% of the population.)
- Vodacom would provide a community-phone service at call costs of less than half the contract GSM tariff and at a third of the prepaid tariff. It promised to provide 1 million people with 22 000 community phones within six years. (An estimated 3 to 4 million people would eventually make use of the community phones, generating subsidised call traffic of some 100 million minutes per month.)
- Vodacom would employ about 250 people within two years and 400 after ten years. (By October 2003 Vodacom employed almost 4 000 people in South Africa alone.)
- Vodacom undertook to generate an estimated R1 billion in the South African economy within the first five years of operation. (This was

achieved well within the five years, and at Vodacom's financial year end of March 2003, the company had paid a total of R2 billion in direct licence fees alone.)

Each bidder's team was then questioned by a five-member tender committee. Alan was surprised at how thorough the panel's evaluation process was. His team was interrogated on every last aspect of the bid and the panel refused to accept vague or unsubstantiated answers. Alan, despite finding the experience something of an ordeal, was impressed and reassured by the committee's hard-line approach, which showed great integrity and seriousness of purpose.

The tenders submitted and the interviews completed, the panel had until September to make a decision. Now it became a waiting game...

At long last, on the afternoon of 22 September 1993, the result was announced: Mobile Telephone Network (MTN) and Vodacom had been awarded the two South African cellular licences. The news created a flurry of media activity. This was a big news story and the press was quick to react; the newspapers carried headlines like *The Star*'s, which proclaimed: 'Cellular phones ready to take SA by storm'. Other publications claimed that the new technology would empower black communities as it opened up 'a new world of opportunity that would propel them into the 21st century'.[2] There was also a great deal of excitement about the R100 million Vodacom investment in a community cellular phone service and the estimated 4 000 jobs that this would create.

Not all the press coverage was positive, however. Some reports derided the prediction that the cellphone would directly benefit small business. The idea of a roadside stallholder, a mobile vegetable trader or a plumber conducting his business via a mobile phone was ludicrous. 'Come off it!' they said. 'Those cellular phones cost thousands of rands. Even in America they are considered ridiculously expensive. Most South Africans won't waste that type of money on a phone, for goodness sake.' In the opinion of the more cynical members of the press, the cellphone was a pointless and costly yuppie toy, on a par with the 'hula hoop, the yo-yo and battery-operated luminous socks'.[3]

The negative press reports affected Alan very little; he had, after all, heard it all before. He was, instead, delighted that all the hard work the team and he had invested had paid off. But there was no time to relax or bask in the glory of their accomplishment – there was still a tremendous amount of work to get through. The next task, an arduous one, was to negotiate the licence conditions between all the parties. Telkom had a monopoly on fixed-line telephony protected by law, while Vodacom and MTN were licensed to operate cellular networks. Ters Oosthuizen gave them a week to negotiate the licence and the multi-party agreement, covering issues such as Telkom's provision of fixed links required by the cellular operators to connect calls between cellphones and fixed lines. Since this process had to be completed by the end of September – otherwise the tender would lapse and they would have to start all over again – the negotiations continued day and night almost without a break. Each party brought along its phalanx of legal experts, and the meeting room became a whirring vortex of energetic discussion as each group sought to tie up the best possible deal.

Sitting apart from the hubbub was a young woman whose job it was to record the decisions, queries and contested issues of each day's work for Vodacom. In the evening she would type up her notes, which she would then take with her to the office the following day. Perhaps her job was not the most glamorous or prestigious, but it was nonetheless an essential one, and without her quiet contribution the negotiations would have been unmanageable. The woman's name was Surina Larsson. Surina would go on to head up Vodacom's bursary initiative; she would also gradually become part of Alan's personal life and, eventually, his wife, following their marriage in September 2008. But that was still in the far-distant future.

At 8:30 p.m. on the last night, Ters dropped his pen, leaned back in his chair and said decisively, 'You've already buggered up my dinner, you've got 30 minutes to wrap it up.' And they did: half an hour later the documents were signed and dated, and the matter concluded.

Vodacom and its three shareholders – Telkom (50%), Vodafone (35%) and Rembrandt (15%) – were poised on the brink of creating a new cellular industry. The Vodacom board would be formed from candidates proposed by each of the shareholders, with representation to be based on the percentage of shares held. Rembrandt nominated Dillie Malherbe as its representative. Vodafone put forward Sir John Peet, David Henning and Sir Julian Horn-Smith (who would later become Chief Operating Officer [COO] of the Vodafone Group). Telkom proposed Jack Clarke (to be

Vodacom's chairman, since Telkom had acquired this right), Danie du Toit, Ben Bets and Reuel Khoza. The first three Telkom appointees were from within the organisation, the fourth, Reuel Khoza, was a prominent South African businessman who ultimately held directorships with the Black Management Forum, Nedbank and Munich Reinsurance, amongst others. His appointment came amidst calls from black-owned telecommunications companies, such as Suntel, for the government to stop the unilateral restructuring of the industry. Suntel also criticised the 'excessive' licence fees, which it said the majority of black-owned local companies could not afford, adding that the government was aware of this but was more interested in attracting foreign investors – investors for whom the fee would not be a deterrent.

'As the fourth corner of the board that reflected its three shareholders,' said Reuel, 'I was the sole black voice and I gave my point of view without flinching, effectively setting the tone for the way Vodacom would do business in the new South Africa.' He then added, 'My presence was a token one, but my point of view was not.'[4]

Vodafone's role would be a pivotal one within the new set-up; it had the experience, technical expertise and distribution know-how that could only benefit the newcomer. Alan experienced Vodafone operations at close quarters when, in July 1993, he had spent a month-long sabbatical at the company's headquarters in Newbury, England. Phil Williams, Vodafone's Human Resources Director, was in charge of Alan's induction. 'Does the man have to schedule every bloody minute of my day,' Alan muttered to himself as he was escorted from pillar to post through Vodafone's training process. Once he got to know him, Alan grew to admire and respect Phil for his sharp business acumen, his intuitive observations of human nature and his ability to defuse conflicts with tact and calculated logic. More than anyone else at Vodafone, Phil would become the person who Alan relied on for support and advice; they formed a friendship that Alan would value in years to come.

The Vodafone induction process was rigorous. Every Monday morning there was a Business Review Meeting (BRM). All the executives would gather around the CEO, Sir Gerry Whent, in the boardroom. Sir Gerry chain-smoked cigars, and as the room steadily filled with smoke, the others would try to hide their discomfort by shifting uncomfortably in their seats and taking frequent sips of water. But no one dared open a window. Sir Gerry was the boss and he did as he pleased. Eventually Sir John Peet, the founding partner and, in Alan's view, 'the only one with big enough balls', would get up and open a window. Sir Gerry ran the company from these BRMs. He was something of an autocrat. He was quite prepared to let others talk, but what they said very seldom affected what he had decided to do in the first place. No one argued with him – there was very little point in doing so anyway since his mind was better and he did business more effectively than anyone else.

In one of his personal meetings with Alan, Sir Gerry offered the younger man a piece of advice: 'If you want to control the money in your company, then you have to sign every single cheque.' Sir Gerry signed all cheques over £100. So Alan did the same, he signed every cheque over R100; in doing so, he achieved a level of control over Vodacom's finances that, prior to meeting Sir Gerry, he might never have believed possible.

Sir Gerry's approach to annual budgets was similarly forthright. He was only interested in budgets that were clear and to the point, and distrusted anything overly long and complex. Assessing Vodacom's annual budget took him no more than half an hour, whereupon he would wave Alan and his CFO, Leon Crouse, away with the warning, 'See you next year and make sure you don't screw up.' His tone was friendly enough but Alan was quite certain his life would be over if he did indeed 'screw up'. Ever since then, however, Alan has believed that if you cannot assess a budget within half an hour, you have no business trying to assess it in the first place.

Vodacom lost R180 million in its first year of operation, but Alan was not perturbed. It was early days yet. If he was going to make money, he would have to take risks. The trick was to stop thinking about it. He willed himself to stop worrying about what he could lose and concentrated instead on making cellular work. He resolved to focus on the vision and to hire the best people to look after the detail. He would leave the financial woes to Leon Crouse and use his energy to build his dream.

It's a Deal
1993

Courage and perseverance have a magical talisman, before which difficulties disappear and obstacles vanish into air.
John Quincy Adams

The best-laid plans often go awry just before the final breakthrough, and so it was that Alan's hopes were put on hold while a political drama complicated the launch of the new telecoms era. As the cellular deal started gathering momentum during the course of the year, a major dispute was brewing between the ANC and the prospective operators. The cellular operators had already met with the ANC and the outgoing government at Shell House in Johannesburg, though nothing of substance had been forthcoming. The ANC accused government of trying to push through a strategic project of national importance in the dying months of its reign. The government had, for example, recently tried to rush through parliament an amendment that, if passed, would have given the Postmaster General the power to legalise the licence. The ANC wanted the bidding process to be suspended, at least until such time as the Transitional Executive Council, of which it would form part, had been established. The fact that the cellular licences made no provision for black empowerment was another issue that deeply troubled the ANC. As an indication of how seriously it regarded the matter, the ANC said it would revoke any licences granted without its approval should the government choose to ignore its demands.

Alan sought out Jack; he had to let someone know how he felt about this. And what he principally felt was frustration.

'There go several years of my life down the tubes,' he said gloomily, once he had found his colleague. 'This is going to be a long, drawn-out process with no happy ending.'

'Alan, remember this is the new government in action. It's your future partner,' was Jack's comment.

'Whatever government comes into power in 1994,' Alan insisted, 'it will still have a 50% stake in Vodacom through Telkom. And what about the fact that we are going to give millions of black people affordable access to phones for the first time in their lives – can't the ANC see what a great idea that is?'

'Convince them,' was Jack's advice.

The shareholders got wind of this new development and would not invest another cent until the fiasco was sorted out.

As a first move toward reconciliation of the affair, Alan, Jack and Dillie met with Andile Ngcaba and Lyndall Shope-Mafole (who eventually succeeded Andile as Director General of Communications). They made a formidable team, and could employ the 'good cop' (Lyndall), 'bad cop' (Andile) routine to devastating effect. MTN had similar meetings, its representative being Dr Ntatho Motlana, Mandela's personal doctor. They met in a conference room at the ANC's headquarters in Shell House on a floor controlled by Pinky Moholi, current MD of Telkom South Africa.

According to *The Star*, quoting Dr Piet Welgemoed, there had been an exchange of letters between F.W. de Klerk and Nelson Mandela in which Mandela was quoted as saying, 'Stopping the project now would threaten South Africa's reputation as a venue for investment.'[1] The fact that De Klerk and Mandela were discussing the matter gives a good indication of how critical the cellular network issue had become to the country's political fortunes. If this initiative was a success, it would show the rest of the world that South Africa meant business, but if the network were to fail, then South Africa's bid to resume its place on the international stage would lose momentum since it would then be all too easy to view the country as one more 'Third World' country trying to run before it could walk.

The chief negotiator for the ANC, Cyril Ramaphosa, and the National Party's lead negotiator, Roelf Meyer, called a meeting on 1 October 1993 at the World Trade Centre in Kempton Park, Johannesburg, to which they summoned all the relevant parties: Vodacom, MTN, the Postmaster General, the ANC, Cosatu, and the Posts and Telecommunications Workers Association (POTWA). The cellular issue had moved to centre stage amidst the political negotiations.

It was Meyer who set the tone for what was to follow when he said: 'We approached the cellular issue in the same spirit of trust that has been built up in the constitutional negotiations. We could see it was in the country's interests to get the industry going and to overcome the obstacles.'[2]

Meyer was as good as his word, for both he and Ramaphosa approached every issue with the attitude that there wasn't a problem that could not be solved through negotiation. Ramaphosa calmly reiterated the ANC's wish to be involved fully in a matter that would have a profound impact on the country's future – a request that, since the ANC was *already* engaged in talks about the country's future, he suggested was reasonable enough.

The two issues that dominated the talks were Black Economic Empowerment (BEE), and competition. For the first, the need to have trade unions involved in the ownership of networks was something the ANC insisted upon. For the second, Dr Motlana, chairman of MTN, was adamant that the industry would grow faster and would put more cellphones into more people's hands if competition was allowed to flourish.

The debates at the World Trade Centre were way beyond anything Alan had imagined. What surprised and pleased him most was the manner in which the negotiations were conducted. For two groups that had, until very recently, been directly and often violently opposed to one another, the mutual respect that now pervaded the proceedings was remarkable. As Alan watched and listened, he knew that the country would be in safe hands. The way Meyer and Ramaphosa handled the telecoms issue boded well for the negotiations on South Africa's future. This was the most positive and unexpected result of the cellular drama for Alan. South Africa was being guided by competent, rational, highly intelligent people who understood the meaning of mutual respect. It was a lesson he observed and applied to his advantage in Vodacom's success.

For three long weeks, the suspense at the World Trade Centre was tangible as the various parties tried to structure a telecoms deal that was acceptable to everyone represented there. Sir Julian Horn-Smith and Chris Nightall from Vodafone flew in from Britain to assure the future government of South Africa of their good intentions to help rebuild the country and to secure their investment in Vodacom. Dillie Malherbe did the same on behalf of Rembrandt.

At the end of October 1993, Alan received a call from Ramaphosa summoning him to the World Trade Centre for a meeting with himself and Andile. Alan knew at once that this was going to be *the meeting* that decided Vodacom's fate. Now that the moment had arrived, he felt curiously calm and relaxed; the tension of the previous three weeks slipped away in the knowledge that the suspense would soon be over.

Ramaphosa wasted no time in delivering his ultimatum. 'We want you to increase the equity held by black business in Vodacom,' Ramaphosa said, looking directly at Alan. 'The shareholders in your company have to give up 5% of their shares for black participation, but the 5% cannot be extricated from the Telkom share. If you manage to do this, we will recognise the validity of your licence and we have a deal.'[3]

Alan had no objection to Ramaphosa's demand, but he had no mandate from his shareholders to make a decision of this nature on their behalf. Furthermore, Vodafone and Rembrandt might raise strong objections to the proposal that they had to contribute the full 5% while Telkom was not required to give up anything. In those few seconds of silence, while Ramaphosa waited for an answer and Alan sat deep in thought, Vodacom's future hung in the balance.

And then his mind cleared and the answer was obvious. To hell with it, thought Alan, this is our opportunity, right here, right now, to clinch the deal, and he leaned forward to offer the other man his hand.

'Of course we'll do it,' said Alan with conviction as he, Ramaphosa and Andile sealed their momentous agreement with a handshake and nothing more – the agreement was never reduced to writing.

Alan's feeling of well-being lasted for the time it took him to meet with the shareholders and break the news to them shortly afterwards. All hell broke loose. Vodafone was furious that he had made such an agreement without its consent. Alan could do very little to placate the company; all he could do was ride out the storm as best he could. He was certain that his days were numbered and that Vodafone would fire him. This was the first of many occasions that Alan came close to being booted. It was, as could have been predicted, Jack Clarke who stepped in to save him. His ultimatum had an even more uncompromising edge to it than Ramaphosa's.

'It's a no-brainer guys,' he said, 'either you give 5% away or you call it quits. End of story. In November we start rolling out the network.'

And that settled it.

Dillie Malherbe was instrumental in facilitating the black empowerment deal, which took almost three years. Vodafone was not keen to give up its shares, but eventually relented on relinquishing 3.5% of its 35% shareholding, while Rembrandt, the smallest shareholder, gave up 1.5% of its 15% share. The two trade unions that had been earmarked for the deal were POTWA and the National Union of Mineworkers (NUM).

The problem was that empowerment groups were reluctant to accept the shares. There was a great deal of money involved (some R50 million at the time) and the risks were high since cellular telephony was a new industry and a very risky one. And obtaining a bank loan would be difficult, since not many financial institutions would be prepared to sink capital into an unknown company offering an obscure, untested technology. This proved to be the case towards the end of 1994, when the South African Clothing and Textile Workers Union (SACTWU) and the NUM agreed to buy the 5% Vodacom shareholding, which was valued at R120 million – not a single bank was prepared to finance such a high-risk deal.

Dillie was at his wits end by this stage. In desperation, he suggested that the three existing Vodacom shareholders collectively finance the union deal. This didn't fly either and the stalemate continued. In the end, Rembrandt financed the deal on its own, buying Vodafone's 3.5%, adding it to its own 1.5%, and placing it in trust until the money was raised. In 1996, SACTWU and NUM bought the controversial 5% share of Vodacom for R118 million. Six years later, Vodafone and Rembrandt bought back their original shares for a total of R1.5 billion, making it one of the most lucrative black empowerment deals in South Africa.

MTN also agreed to increase the public holding of Transtel from 10% to 20% and to provide a 5% shareholding to a Cosatu-affiliated pension fund. The network operators also agreed that 50% of their service providers would be represented by black business.

The cellular networks were back on track. The ANC officially recognised the licences, the shareholders were content with the financial arrangements, and Alan couldn't wait to get started. But Christmas was approaching and Alan, like the rest of the country, had to slow down for a while. He appreciated the break, since he knew that the new year would bring with it a whole new set of challenges for him to engage with. With his Telkom pension pay-out and leave pay, he bought a plot of land at Boggomsbaai on the southern Cape coast for R50 000, on which he would build his 'retreat'.

As the new year was ushered in, Alan faced the daunting task of launching a new product, a new company, a new industry. With no relevant experience and a non-existent track record, he was going to have to rely on a combination of instinct, common sense and luck to make this venture work. The road ahead was clear and the race had begun. There were six months left before the commercial switch-on of the cellular network and Alan was determined to get there first.

Connecting the Dots
1994

A dreamer is one who can only find his way by moonlight, and his punishment is that he sees the dawn before the rest of the world.
Oscar Wilde

The stage was set for a new democratic dispensation in the country and the telecommunications industry was about to host a new player that would revolutionise communication, not just in South Africa, but across the entire African continent. To Alan, it was quite remarkable that the two events seemed to be mapping the same trajectory – that the sense of nervous, yet hopeful, anticipation surrounding the soon-to-be elections also accompanied the imminent launch of the cellular network.

The country's transformation was not something Alan could challenge, change or avoid, even if he had wanted to – and there seemed little point in worrying unduly about something so inevitable. But that was not the case with the new technology he was to launch. Alan was acutely aware of the fact that what he did or didn't do would directly influence the success of the cellular network, and it was this awareness of his own responsibility that made him slightly apprehensive. The fact that he had no previous experience in running a company didn't bolster his confidence. He was a civil servant, not a businessman; but he had a deep desire to be something much more. In moments alone, Alan would say to himself, 'You know you can do this. You've seen the future and you *are* going to be part of it, and that's all there is to it.'

He didn't dwell on doubts. There were endless tasks to be completed before the tentative launch date of the cellular networks on 1 June 1994, a date chosen by MTN, courtesy of the regulator. One of the first items on the agenda was setting up the base stations and the design and construction of an internal core switching network. The plan was to install 500 base stations across the country, covering the main highways in the process. The regulator allowed MTN to roam on Vodacom's network for as long as it liked. MTN used it until September 1994, which created a certain amount of tension for Alan since he could hardly cater for all his own customers, never mind theirs. But base stations were erected in record time and both networks functioned as well as could be expected.

It was important to have the best billing system possible, a system that would seamlessly itemise every call at the prescribed tariff and send out an invoice to every customer every month. The system had to get every item right every time – no errors were permitted. It was an additional free service that had to be convenient for the customer. Alan knew that the billing system was complicated, but Vodafone provided expert advice. Alan spoke to Vodafone's billing guru, Ian Maxwell, on how to proceed.

'What would you suggest Ian?' asked Alan. 'Is your system the way to go?'

Ian said tongue-in-cheek, 'Off the record, don't use Vodafone's system. But if anyone else asks, the Vodafone billing system is the best system in the world.'

Alan purchased a tried-and-tested billing system from Germany, which was successfully deployed in Vodacom for the next ten years under the eagle eye of Allan Beets.

A financial system also had to be fine-tuned and a Subscriber Identity Module (SIM) card manufacturing operation had to be set up. South Africa was going to be the only country in the world that manufactured its own SIM cards under the relentless drive of Leon Shirk. Service provider contracts had to be finalised and the distribution network had to work like a well-oiled machine. A customer help centre had to be established and staffed with people trained to assist Vodacom's customers, even though they themselves had never used a cellphone. Tariff plans had to be worked out.

A marketing strategy had to be compiled and implemented. Commercial agreements with Telkom for transmission lines had to be hammered out. Premises had to be found and fitted out for the new company and its recent recruits. And so it went on.

One of the first decisions Alan made early in the new year was to spend R10 million on advertising right away, several months before Vodacom opened for business. This pre-emptive move was a crucial aspect of his vision to establish Vodacom as the brand leader at the start of the cellular race. If he could position Vodacom in such a way that it became the first name people picked out when they thought of cellular technology, he was convinced that the next step, persuading the public to buy Vodacom's products and services, would be that much easier.

The first advertisement, which Alan decided to broadcast countrywide, was a television commercial produced by The Whitehouse, a national advertising agency. It showed a series of black plastic cellphone bricks falling from the sky amidst puffy white clouds. There was nothing exceptional about the advertisement; it was merely a message to the public that the advent of cellphones was nigh, with the Vodacom logo appearing in the bottom-right corner of the screen as a discreet prompt – it let people know where they could find the new technology, but it did so without any overt attempt to 'sell' the Vodacom brand.

Alan's bold marketing ploy dismayed Vodafone, which sent Jack Clarke a rude letter pointing out that Alan couldn't advertise something to an audience who had no idea what he was selling.

'You have no money and you are already wasting it,' the company accused Alan.

Alan's response was, 'If you want to compete with the best, you have to achieve top-of-mind awareness with the consumer, and that costs money. Period.'

Vodafone's retort was that Alan should be fired. Vodacom wasn't even up and running and Alan was, for the second time, convinced he was about to lose his job. Jack had saved his bacon over the 5% black empowerment share issue, but this time round he didn't think he'd be so lucky. He was mistaken: Jack was even more vociferous in his support.

'Back off,' he told Vodafone. 'I like what Alan's doing. If you don't like it, then leave.'

This did nothing to improve the situation. Fortunately, the timely intervention of Phil Williams rescued the relationship from possible collapse. In his diplomatic, subtle manner, Phil managed to convince the two sides that there was more to be gained from working together. His crisis-management skills were second to none. To Alan's mind, if it were not for Phil, Vodafone might well have replaced him with someone far more conventional. When he talked with Alan, Phil reminded him that there would always be opposition to new ideas that did not fit the accepted mould.

'Your ideas are always going to be too radical, Alan,' Phil said. 'They'll always be too risky, too expensive, too off-the-wall for most people. You are going to have to find a way to live with that, because it isn't going to change.'

Although Alan understood and could accept what Phil was saying, the thought of having to justify his decisions in similar situations in the future was not a pleasant one. He told Phil as much.

'Look on the bright side,' Phil replied. 'If your ideas were immediately understood and accepted, there wouldn't be anything innovative about them. It's the ideas that come up against strong resistance that make the biggest impact.'

But it would be unfair to Vodafone to say that it made no attempt to reconcile matters. In 1995, the day before the Rugby World Cup started in Newlands, the various shareholders met at Rembrandt's Fleur du Cap chateau in Somerset West. It was a crucial board meeting. 'Were there any other sort?' Alan wondered. The tense atmosphere made conversation extremely difficult. And then Sir Gerry Whent, Group CEO of Vodafone, spoke and the mood lightened considerably.

'Gentlemen,' he said, 'what we have here is a touch of Newbury arrogance and a dose of South African pride.'

With those few well-chosen words, Sir Gerry was able to chastise the two warring factions without either side taking offence or questioning the truth of his assertion. The tension was defused and the board members settled down to an amicable discussion. It was the only Vodacom board meeting Sir Gerry ever attended, and Vodafone subsequently became a staunch ally of Alan's for many years thereafter.

Alan's relationship with his smallest shareholder, Rembrandt, had none of the troubles that plagued the one he had with Vodafone. He considered

Rembrandt to be the ideal shareholder. Johann Rupert performed and contributed when he was required to do so, he did not interfere with the way Alan ran his business, and he made no complaints as long as Rembrandt was making a return on its investment. The relationship between Vodacom and Rembrandt was one based on trust, which as far as Alan was concerned was the best type of business relationship to have. Alan wished that all his business dealings could be this straightforward.

Regardless of the gripes and gremlins that tested Alan's patience, he was pleased to note that public interest in the new cellular phenomenon was growing by the day. People were particularly keen to know what the tariffs would be, since this would largely determine the affordability of cellphones.

On 3 February 1994, *Business Day* and the *Cape Argus* reported that Vodacom's business tariffs (before VAT) would be 99c per minute for local peak-time calls and R1.50 per minute for long-distance calls. On weekends and weekdays between 8 p.m. and 7 a.m., the tariff would be 60c per minute. A week later, Vodacom dropped its long-distance peak rate to 99c per minute and its off-peak rate to 49c per minute in response to MTN's tariff release. The rates were well received, since a rate of around R1.30 per minute had been anticipated. Of that 99c, about 27c of each call went to the service providers, and 4c of every call went to the government as part of its licence fee (in addition to the initial R100 million licence fee and the annual radio licence payment of R5 million). This left Vodacom with 68c per minute with which to pay its bills and offer further discounts to corporates. These rates were accompanied by a connection charge of R70 and a R122 (before VAT) monthly subscription.

Because Vodacom and MTN had to pay 21c per minute for each call connected to the Telkom network, it would not be possible to undercut Telkom's local tariffs for calls from a cellphone to a fixed line. However, long-distance calls would be highly competitive and often cheaper, with a Johannesburg–Durban call costing half if it was made through Vodacom's network rather than that of Telkom. In addition, neither Vodacom nor MTN could charge customers less in peak periods than what Telkom paid for calls terminating on their networks.

The general consensus was that the tariffs were far lower than expected because the market was far bigger than expected. Six months before switch-on, in June 1994, cellphones were already selling around the clock. Advertising on TV and radio and in newspapers was paying off, whilst the additional layer of competition provided by service providers made the idea of buying a cellphone that much more attractive to many people.

The tariffs announcement had served to fuel a price war between the operators. Vodacom published its tariffs first; MTN followed days later with lower prices. Vodacom responded in kind a few days later still.[1] The regulator finally stepped in and instructed the two rivals to put prices back to the level they had been lodged at initially, arguing that an early price war could kill the industry. The whole idea of applying regulation to a competitive market environment was anathema to Alan at the time and remains so today.

The positive reaction to the tariffs created even more heat around the subject of cellular technology. The advertising campaign had done its job, and with each day that passed, it became increasingly obvious to Alan that he may have seriously underestimated the demand for the little black bricks drifting down through the clouds. On 22 March 1995 Alan told *Die Burger* that it was conceivable that in five years time there would be more cellphones in South Africa than Telkom phones. By 2000 there were some 5 million cellphones in South Africa and less than 5 million Telkom phones.

There was another event on the horizon that was to provide the ideal launch pad for the cellphone – the first democratic elections to be held on 21 April 1994. The government needed cellphones to ensure communication between the polling stations, the police, the media, the Independent Electoral Commission and government officials. Vodacom and MTN were each to provide 1 250 cellphones for the event.

On 1 March 1994 Vodacom and MTN were each allowed to connect 4 000 subscribers in a 'trial' phase. A further concession was made to each network to connect another 2 000 subscribers apiece during this period. During May 1994, each network could connect another 10 000 in a further limited test phase. Vodacom connected all 10 000 of its May allocation on the first day of that month. While the distributors stirred up a frenzy of demand, the regulator had created a false shortage with its trade limitation, and the cellular networks were set up for immediate success.

'Interest has exceeded our expectations,' Alan said in an interview to the press, 'and we have doubled our call-carrying capacity. While initial estimates showed that there would be 120 000 subscribers in the first year, it is now believed that this figure will exceed 200 000.'

When Vodacom opened for the test phase of its commercial service, Alan spent the first day at the Customer Care Centre. The centre was managed by Ibeth Coetzee, who had assigned Francois Theart, known to everyone as Naki, to run the help desk. Naki was a quadriplegic who had been severely wounded in Angola. When Alan arrived at the centre the scene was one of complete chaos. Customers had to be told to switch on their cellphones before they could dial a number; they were demanding refunds on phones whose batteries they had not charged; others had not inserted their SIM cards. The help desk operators could barely cope with the uproar. Alan took a step forward, then stopped, wondering if his presence might be more of a hindrance than a help.

At that moment, out of nowhere, Naki appeared; tearing towards him in his wheelchair at high speed and shouting out instructions. Alan nodded quickly and followed Naki back into the crowd. There were no job descriptions at the help desk; everyone did everything. Alan swung into action and did as he was told. Naki was the boss here and Alan fully respected it. Later, when an air of at least partial calm had been restored, Naki came to apologise.

'Sorry man,' he said with a worried frown. 'I didn't know you were the CEO.'

Alan smiled. 'No problem,' he replied, 'we're all here to pitch in and this is your territory. I was happy to be of service.' Alan and Naki, as well as all those first customer care operators, were to enjoy a special relationship in years to come.

Ibeth built up customer care into a well-oiled machine manned by over 1 000 people. Other than providing crucial assistance to its customers, it became a valuable source of information whenever a new product was launched. Just by determining the pattern and content of the calls, a potentially insidious error could be prevented from developing into a full-scale malfunction.

And then election day arrived. Millions of South Africans queued for kilometres in the blazing sun to cast their vote. Alan dashed from one polling station to another to make sure that the cellular system was working. Each time he saw the tall cellphone masts rising into the sky on top of the polling stations, he experienced a small surge of pride. But he was not about to get ahead of himself. The future was still terribly uncertain and though the initial signs were promising, the project was still in its infancy – it was much too early to say what the future held in store for cellular technology.

The run-up to the election had been largely trouble-free and the voting process had been pronounced 'substantially free and fair', while the response of the international community had been encouraging. But the new ANC-led government had yet to be tested in action. Could the government deliver on its promises? Could Vodacom? Alan believed that Vodacom would become what he wanted it to be: a market leader in cellular communications technology. He also felt personally responsible for making this happen.

On 1 June 1994, the cellphone industry exploded into the market. The numbers multiplied rapidly: within five months Vodacom had increased its customer database by 540% and signed on 100 000 customers, making it, after Germany, the second-largest GSM network in the world at the time.[2] The demand had been vastly underestimated. Vodacom started rolling out base stations at break-neck speed. At two base stations per day it could scarcely keep up, initially investing R250 million more than expected. The media headlines tracked the network's every move and mapped its progress across the country.

The question now being asked was no longer 'Can cellular succeed?', but 'How successful will cellular be?' Alan was about to find out.

With a Little Help from my Friends
1969 to 1994

Take up one idea. Make that one idea your life – think of it, dream of it, live on that idea.
Swami Vivekananda

On 20 July 1969, 2:56 a.m. GMT, Neil Alden Armstrong, Mission Commander of the Apollo 11 spacecraft, became the first human to stand on the surface of the Moon. Millions of people all over the world sat before their TV screens, transfixed by what they saw. Theo Rutstein, however, saw nothing. Instead, he listened to his radio as the momentous events unfolded, sitting with his head pressed against the speaker to hear Armstrong declare, in a faraway voice that struggled to get through: 'That's one small step for man, one giant leap for mankind.'

Theo did not have a TV set because nobody in South Africa at that time was allowed one. The National Party considered television a pernicious evil and so it was banned. Theo cursed his *verkrampte* (conservative) leaders for their decree, for it meant that the momentous moonwalk – and here Theo wondered in what way the walk could be termed 'evil' – passed him by unseen, if not unheard.

Theo's frustration was shared by the majority of South Africans, for whom the government ban made little or no sense. They, like he, dreamt of the day when the government would repeal the unwanted legislation and allow South Africans access to televisual technology. Theo's engagement with the issue didn't end with dreaming about it; he decided to find out if he could turn the dream into a reality. If the government wasn't going to bring television to South Africa, he would.

To research his subject, Theo went to the UK, where TV was a well-established medium (black and white TV had arrived in 1946; colour in 1968). On his return to Johannesburg, Theo placed an advertisement in four major Sunday newspapers. The advert said: 'When TV comes into the country there will be two million people wanting a set. Will you be able to get one?'

This intriguing opening line was followed by an explanation of how Teljoy (the name Theo had chosen for his new enterprise) would guarantee delivery of a set when television arrived in the country – and Theo was sure it was a question of 'when' not 'if' it arrived. No money was necessary; all a person had to do was to sign a contract that legally obliged him or her to rent a set from Teljoy when the time came.

The advertisements were a phenomenal success: following the first weekend's print run, Theo received calls from 5 000 individuals wanting to take him up on his offer.

Theo then began campaigning for the introduction of broadcast services to the country. The campaign received overwhelming support from the general public and eventually the government could ignore the issue no longer. Theo met with the Minister of Posts and Telegraph, Albert Hertzog, who gravely informed him, '*Dit is nog 'n spyker in die doodskis van die volk*' ('This is another nail in the nation's coffin'). The Minister's priggish response was seized upon by the public as further evidence of a government hopelessly out of touch with modern-day realities.

The government reluctantly agreed to establish a commission of inquiry to look into the matter. It took another five years for Theo's efforts to bear fruit. However, when the ban was finally lifted in 1976, Teljoy was firmly entrenched in people's minds and the company's order book immediately started to fill up.

The success of Teljoy encouraged Theo to look for further business opportunities. The idea of introducing cellular technology to South Africa came to him during a visit to London in 1992. He was walking along a crowded Oxford Street with Dennis Kennedy, Teljoy's CFO, when both men were nearly knocked off their feet by a bicycle courier who shot out of a side street, narrowly missing them. Theo was about to send the man on his way with a choice phrase or two until he noticed the mobile phone pressed against his ear.

'That's it; that's it Dennis; that's the answer,' Theo said excitedly as he turned towards his companion, grinning like a madman.

'What is?' asked Dennis, completely taken aback.

'Mobile phones, that's what,' answered Theo, still beaming broadly. 'South Africa needs mobile phones. It's so obvious – why didn't I think of it before?'

And that is how, quite by chance, Theo decided to channel all his energies into bringing cellphones to his home country.

Back in South Africa, Theo approached Telkom – the country's only licensed provider of telecommunications. At a meeting with some of the company's senior executives, including Alan, Theo discussed how he could become involved in the introduction of mobile phones to South Africa. Telkom had at this point in time already broached the same subject with Vodafone in the UK, and discussions were some way down the line. Theo could not have known this beforehand, of course, so perhaps it was simply a case of being in the right place at the right time. Lucky or not, Theo's outstanding success with Teljoy was certainly a factor in Vodacom's subsequent decision to award him the first service provider licence.

Once Vodacom was up and running, Alan soon found Theo's contribution invaluable. Having overseen the introduction of one new communications medium to the country, television, Theo was well placed to support Alan in the introduction of another – cellular telephony. Theo became a service provider exclusively for Vodacom and the two men became close friends. Alan admired Theo's ability to take a product to market on a grand scale, his sharp legal insights (the product of his time as an advocate), and his instinctive grasp of marketing.

'Look at what Theo did with television,' Alan would say. 'Well, he did the same for cellular. He led the growth of an entire industry in this country on our behalf.'

One of Theo's main concerns for cellphones was the need to broaden their market appeal as far and as widely as possible. The perception that many people had of mobile phones – and this was something Alan was aware of, too – was that they were only intended for the corporate business sector. The implications of this were that the general public only ever thought of the cellphone as a yuppie toy or business tool.

Theo and Alan acknowledged the need to overturn this perception if they were to have any hope of securing a future for Vodacom. As Alan remarked to Theo during one of their many brainstorming sessions, 'We need to make cellphones a mass item. People need to know that they can buy a cellphone like they would buy toothpaste off the shelf.'

Both men were firm believers in the use of pre-launch advertising as part of a marketing strategy, and both believed it was necessary now. Theo's newspaper advertisements, published when there wasn't a single television set in the country, had shown just how effective a pre-launch campaign could be. The fact that televisions were nowhere to be seen at the time made no difference; people had bought into the *idea* that Teljoy was offering them and that was enough. Theo and Alan had to do the same with the cellphone: they had to make the idea of owning or using a cellphone a realistic possibility in the minds of the general public. But how?

'The takeaway cellphone' was Theo's idea. If Vodacom wanted people to know that buying a cellphone was an easy and convenient process – as easy and convenient as buying a tube of toothpaste, using Alan's example, then presenting the phone in the guise of a takeaway product might be the key. Theo suggested that marketing the cellphone as a hamburger – perhaps the best and certainly the most ubiquitous example of a takeaway product to be found – would be the best way to go. Alan thought the idea was absolutely superb – completely bizarre but, still, superb – and the two men set about putting Theo's idea into action.

The takeaway cellphones were launched at the Rand Show in Pretoria in April 1994, before any network had started operating. Theo and Alan 'served' their cellphones in a hamburger box to curious people who were keen to 'taste' the new item. The 'cellphone burger' was examined, handled, experimented with and discussed, which for Alan and Theo was the whole point of the exercise. They were certain that once people had had an opportunity to see and touch the phones for themselves, the aura of exclusivity and inaccessibility that surrounded them would fade away.

The 'burgers' were also delivered to the CEOs and other senior management figures of various corporates. Nobody was asked to pay anything; all they had to do was use it for a month and then either keep it, if they had liked it, or return it, if they hadn't. Those that kept the cellphones would then be subject to the terms and conditions of a pre-discussed Vodacom client contract.

The response to the 'cellphone burger' concept was very encouraging. People began to look at the product in a new way, just as Alan had hoped, and now saw it as a device that could enhance their business and social lives in ways they had never previously imagined. Alan and Theo's next step was to find a way of getting the product to the people; in other words, they had to set up a distribution system.

Theo, working on the principle that it's always better to work from the top down, took Alan to meet Hymie Sybil, chairman of Prefcor, which included the retail chain, Game. The day before the meeting (to which a further twenty company directors came), Alan set up a temporary base station in the basement of Prefcor's premises in Durban to pick up and transmit cellphone signals.

The next day, Alan gave a cellular presentation to Hymie and his colleagues. It was going well and Alan sensed that his audience was definitely interested, if not fully convinced. It was at this point that he pulled a cellphone out of pocket, handed it to Hymie and said, 'Go ahead, make a call.' There were one or two exclamations of surprise but the room became absolutely silent as Hymie punched in the numbers on the keypad. In the second or two that it took for the signal to get through, Alan wondered how he would recover – how Vodacom would recover – if the phone failed to work and Prefcor's chairman was left listening to the sound of silence and cursing the fact that he had let some fool waste his time.

Then Hymie lifted his head and, looking straight at Alan, said in a cool calm voice, 'Hello Mom, I'm speaking to you on a phone with no wires.'

Alan's stunt proved to be the coup d'état: Hymie agreed to distribute the Vodacom cellphones, which led to Theo negotiating a deal between Teljoy and Game in which the retail giant became Vodacom's exclusive distributor of cellphone products and accessories.

'He was a damn good salesman and believed totally in his product,' said Hymie of Alan's presentation. Alan spent the next couple of months convincing top retail executives to come on board as exclusive dealers for Vodacom.

Alan also approached Raymond Ackerman – 'Mr Pick 'n Pay' – courtesy of a meeting arranged by Theo, hoping to tie up a similar deal. At first, Ackerman was sceptical of Alan's big plans for cellular in the retail sector.

'Why should we be involved?' he asked.

'Simply because it will be the best exposure to market you'll ever get,' Alan responded. 'We will be providing 22 000 telephones to townships throughout the country. The easiest, quickest and most effective way to do this is to set up communication kiosks in refurbished shipping containers. Imagine each container branded by Pick 'n Pay. Your company's visibility in the market would rise dramatically and people would associate Pick 'n Pay with positive development in their community, adding to your already enviable reputation.'

Ackerman agreed to Alan's proposal. The men shook hands and they parted ways. Nothing was written down and no contract was initially signed, but the deal stood and Ackerman was as good as his word – the Pick 'n Pay containers were to become a common sight in townships the length and breadth of the country. In addition, the company stocked its stores with Vodacom cellphones and airtime. Alan heard nothing from Ackerman until, some thirteen years later in 2006, he received a personal 'get well soon' message after suffering his second heart attack.

From the launch date in June, community phones would be distributed primarily to black entrepreneurs, who would earn commission on calls made. Sites where the density of human traffic was high – taxi ranks, railway stations, garages and spaza shops, and so on – would serve as locations for the new kiosks. Pick 'n Pay would sell phone cards in units of R20, which consumers could use to buy airtime, while Teljoy was appointed as Pick 'n Pay's exclusive provider of Vodacom airtime. Vodacom supplied all the equipment the phone-shop operators would need; it also established a training programme for operators where basic bookkeeping skills and management principles were taught. However, it was the entrepreneur's responsibility to take care of the safety and security aspects of his or her operation.

Vodacom opened the first community payphones in Evaton, while MTN focused on the township of Alexandra. As Vodacom rolled into Evaton on a cold day in July, the entire community descended on the colourful steel structure to see for themselves what their new phone shop could do. Mothers with toddlers tugging at their skirts; a young man in the middle of his shaving regime with razor in hand; a woman waving her long wooden spoon after abandoning her cooking; they all came to witness Vodacom's promise come to life. The phone-shop concept was a world first that provided millions of people with access to a communication tool and created thousands of much-needed jobs.

Alan soon discovered that setting up the containers in the townships only worked if the community became involved. He learnt that the chief of the community had to be approached for permission to set up the containers in his area, whereupon an ox would often be slaughtered to celebrate the occasion. Each township had its own rules and codes of conduct regarding how it did business. The local businessmen and -women often worked within strictly defined territories, beyond which they were not allowed to trade. A container could not be placed randomly, anywhere in the township, or simply where it was most convenient for Vodacom, since it could lead to the outbreak of hostilities in territories where the trespassing had taken place. Vodacom, therefore, had to be careful that the containers were placed in such a way that their presence offended neither the existing traders nor other phone-shop operators.

A community phone, because it used radio waves and not cables, could usually be set up within 24 hours, which represented a huge saving in time and money.

But the community phone's biggest selling point was that it gave potentially millions of people access to telecommunications technology for the first time. The days of a single telephone being used by hundreds, sometimes thousands, of people were over. Before cellular was introduced, the people of Morokweng in Limpopo had one phone line that served 80 000 people and, more often than not, that line was out of order. Cellular brought them back into the country, and more importantly, back into the economy, as people explored the countless possibilities, opportunities and advantages the service placed at their disposal.

However, one problem remained that troubled Alan: the cost of the handsets. He knew that in the long term, as the market became more competitive, the cost of the handsets would drop significantly, but at the moment they remained too high for many people. Alan realised that the cost issue was one that had to be solved, and solved quickly, if the Vodacom bubble wasn't to burst. The anti-cellular brigade would waste no time in pointing out the fact that, after all, they had been right: the cellphone was an expensive luxury and no more than that.

Alan and Theo explored the problem from every possible angle to see what options they had. They both agreed that the handset, though an important part of the cellular package, was less important than its function, which was, naturally, to make calls. The solution they arrived at necessitated a completely different approach – one that placed the use of the phone at the centre of the picture instead of the instrument itself. As Alan describes it, 'We felt that if we thought in terms of generating income through calls made, rather than cellphones bought, we might be able to get around the price problem.'

The idea was for Vodacom to subsidise the price of the phones and then offer customers a contract in which Vodacom would effectively lease them the unit on pre-agreed terms. In this way, the negative connotations of offering a product with a high price-tag could be overcome and the promotion of the phone's purpose, its call-making function, would regain the public's attention. The cost of subsidising the cellphones was enormous, but it had the desired effect – sales rocketed.

Alan's bravado inevitably received a cool response from Vodafone. Chris Nightall from Vodafone in the UK called Theo and asked him to have a chat with Alan because he was making some 'insane decisions'. And Theo, though he supported Alan all the way, had some sympathy for his bemused colleague.

'Alan must have driven Vodafone crazy,' Theo recalls. 'I mean, subsidising the cost of the cellphones and giving away SMS (Short Message Service) and voicemail probably doesn't make obvious financial sense, does it? But Alan had guts like you wouldn't believe. He knew what he was doing and, anyway, things turned out pretty well.'

Theo was right. Nine months later, Chris called Theo to tell him that Vodacom had exceeded all expectations. He also offered Theo the chance to run Vodafone's operations in Spain, which he declined.

The Vodacom-Teljoy relationship, meanwhile, underwent a major transformation. Teljoy, initially much bigger than Vodacom, came under unexpected strain as a result of the rapid growth of the cellphone market. Theo had originally aimed for 20 000 subscribers within a year; instead, he captured 100 000, which brought about administrative problems and losses due to fraud. Since tracking mechanisms were inadequate at the time, airtime fraud spiralled out of control. Teljoy was struggling to fulfil its role as Vodacom's service provider. By 1995 Vodacom's financial position was strong enough to allow it to buy a R75 million share of Teljoy. The much-needed cash injection eased Teljoy's position considerably; it also saw Teljoy become part of the Vodacom Service Provider Company.

Alan had his hands full running all the facets of Vodacom, and unexpectedly, he had Teljoy and three other external service providers, which Vodacom had recently purchased, to oversee. He needed a good business brain to oversee their operations.

There was a young man in Leon Crouse's financial division who had an uncanny knack for putting together business deals and making money. Shameel Joosub had impressed Alan with a deal he had made with Siemens a few years earlier, negotiating a 30% reduction on the wholesale price of the handsets and then selling them the same afternoon at a tidy profit. He created a virtual equipment company within Vodacom that carried no stock. Thousands of cellphones were bought and sold before having to pay for them, making a handsome profit that was passed on to the customers.

Alan knew that Shameel was the right person to oversee the integration of the four companies. He gave him six months to turn the companies around from a loss to a R200 million profit target. It was a tall order, but Shameel had already carved a reputation for himself at Vodacom as the man with the best business head in the company. After six months, the Vodacom Service Provider Company had made a R240 million profit and the size of the company doubled within two years. Today, Shameel is MD of Vodacom (Pty) Ltd, a company with over 6 000 employees, almost 12 000 retail outlets and 8 000 base stations.

Service provision was, for Alan, at the centre of the entire cellular system. The network operators, Vodacom and MTN, could only be as good as their dealers and Alan had staked his company's reputation on being the best in this regard. The dealers had a direct relationship with cellphone customers; they sold phones and SIM cards to them, of course, but they did much more besides. A dealer was responsible for marketing new or modified products and services, and offering after-sales service and technical support. But it wasn't just about the *quantity* of work the service provider had to manage; it was the *quality* of the service given that was of even greater significance.

The dealers were the 'face' of Vodacom; they were the people who would set the standard, good or bad, upon which the company would be judged.

This is why Alan devoted so much of his time to learning how the dealers carried out their work, what obstacles they encountered and how he could help remove these, what suggestions they had for raising service standards, and so on. Each service provider had its own distribution network, which incorporated a chain of retail outlets offering all the products and services just mentioned. Alan would visit these outlets to fact-find, discuss, observe, listen – whatever it took to help them perform to the best of their capabilities.

'You can get away with not liking your shareholders or your colleagues or business partners,' says Alan, 'but you must look after your distributors. You have to understand their hardships and help them overcome them. Forget about your distributors and you can forget about having a business.'

The time Alan spent nurturing Vodacom's relationship with its dealers was time well spent, since many of them are quick to acknowledge his input. Many of his distributors became good friends – they were people he liked and enjoyed spending time with.

Selwyn Chatz, of Chatz Cellular, forged a partnership with Alan that led to the establishment of the Vodacom 4U franchise stores, which both men concede they could not have achieved without each other. Selwyn added the competitive edge that drove not only Vodacom's market share, but became a force that Shameel delighted in taking on.

Gavin Varejes, founder of Richmark and co-founder of Blue Label, displays a photograph of Alan in each of his buildings because, as he says, 'I don't sell a Vodacom product, I sell an Alan Knott-Craig product.' Blue Label became Vodacom's best-selling prepaid channel for three years running before Alan retired from Vodacom, garnering three Vodacom CEO Awards for Excellence in the process.

Mark Attieh, creator of Supercall and Cointel, decided to move from exclusively selling MTN airtime to becoming an exclusive Vodacom supplier after meeting Alan. As Mark says, 'I liked his manner: direct, open, friendly. There were no hidden agendas or silly mind games. The deal was done in an hour.' Mark's successful companies contributed in a large measure to Vodacom's success, becoming its mainstream drive into the prepaid market and WASP (Wireless Application Service Provider) market (developing and offering services using the Vodacom network, for example, SMS voting, competitions, games, etc.) before Vodacom bought both companies.

'More often than not, the real innovation, the real work, was done by our dealers and service providers on our behalf. They were the soldiers and generals of our success,' says Alan. 'People like Dan Barret, MD of Game, and his Chief Buyer Alan Herman, masterminds behind Game and Dions, who were ultimately responsible for Vodacom's retail success; Robert du Preez, innovative businessman who built one of the most successful dealer chains in Cape Town; Karin Mostert who built a massive dealer chain in the area between Somerset West and Plettenberg Bay and became a driving force in the whole franchise chain; Paul and Gill Finlayson, who initially converted half their house into a cellphone shop before their business took off; Blaise Sommerville who went from gym instructor to successful franchisee in Pretoria; Guy Morris who runs the biggest franchise store in the country from Menlyn; Sean Joffe, who secured cellular kiosks at all the airports in the country exclusively for Vodacom airtime; Piet Fourie, who built a mini Vodaworld in Bloemfontein with the emphasis on mobile data; Barry Wolmarans, ex-Springbok flyhalf, who runs a chain of Vodashops in Bloemfontein; and Doc (Yusuf Carrim), co-owner of Metro, who provided innovative incentives, becoming the biggest single dealer in the country.'

Alan's attitude towards his dealers and service providers was based on a genuine wish to see them succeed. But, as Alan also points out, Vodacom benefited, too.

'We were all in this adventure together – if one of us went down, so would the others,' says Alan. 'So it was in everyone's best interests to make sure we all did well. I was just doing my bit to make it happen.'

Covering the Nation
1994 to 1995

*The world is changing very fast. Big will not beat small any more.
It will be the fast beating the slow.*
Rupert Murdoch

If you arrive at Cape Town International Airport and drive into the city centre on the N2 highway, you will see a huge billboard spanning the road that reads, 'Welcome to Cape Town, where a cloud covers the mountain and Vodacom covers the rest.' It is a message that always makes Alan smile, not only at the clever wordplay involved but also because the message is, in fact, true. The slogan cannot be dismissed as a typically over-the-top sales gimmick, which would have diminished its impact. Alan really covered the entire country with the Vodacom network to the astonishment of his shareholders and competitors alike.

Alan had decided to roll-out the Vodacom network on all the country's main highways in time for the 1994 December holidays. It was a move that surprised everyone. There seemed no need for Alan to jeopardise Vodacom's current run of good form by diverting time, money and other resources to a far riskier-sounding project. Alan, of course, had to persuade the shareholders to part with more money so that he could fund the project, despite the fact that Vodacom had just started operating and barely made ends meet.

He first met with the Telkom board chaired by Dikgang Moseneke, who had succeeded Jack Clarke. An advocate by profession and holder of several honorary doctorates, Moseneke was an imposing presence. Neither the Telkom chairman nor the board shared Alan's enthusiasm to spend more money on covering the highways.

'How can you ask us for more money when you haven't made any yet?' Moseneke demanded. It was the same question Vodafone was to ask.

Alan was not about to back down. 'Almost every South African will be driving to either Durban or Cape Town these December holidays. If we cover the highways our customers will be able to use their cellphones everywhere they go. This will gain us market share, which in turn will generate the revenues we need to justify the expenditure. I promise you, we will never look back if we make this move now. Believe me, it will be money well spent.'

'But Alan,' Moseneke insisted, 'the bulk of your market is in the metropolitan areas. Covering the highways won't help Vodacom at all; it isn't something you should be thinking about.'

'Sure,' Alan admitted, 'the density of cellphone users on the roads isn't that high, but that misses the point. People need to know that, if they want to, they can use their phones anywhere, any time – including when they are in their cars, and that applies to metropolitan customers as much as anyone. Even if they never use their phones on the roads, just knowing that they can will make them choose Vodacom as their preferred network.'

'Well, it sounds no more than a public relations exercise to me, and a damn expensive one, too,' Moseneke retorted.

'Not at all,' Alan replied quickly, warming to his theme. 'Think about it. There are hundreds of thousands of sales reps, company agents, technicians, truck drivers and farmers on the roads. Imagine what a cellphone might mean to them: they can phone clients, get help if they have a breakdown, ring the boss if they're running late, and so on. I'm telling you, if we cover the highways we secure a whole new market, and also increase our market share in the metropolitan areas. But it has to be done right now.'

Moseneke considered Alan's request. 'There is no rational reason for me to give you more money,' he told Alan. 'But I'll recommend that the board approve your request.' Alan has always admired Moseneke for sticking his neck out and making an unpopular decision, which in the end proved to be essential for Vodacom's lead in the cellular market.

Alan's idea of extending network coverage to include thousands of kilometres of national highways was to Vodacom shareholders one more example of the Vodacom CEO's peculiar approach to business. They had appointed an unknown civil servant who concluded deals with the ANC without consulting his board and threw money at advertising campaigns before he had a product to sell. Spending more money on covering isolated stretches of road on the off-chance that Vodacom subscribers may want to use their cellphones, was an idea that had 'Knott-Craig' written all over it.

Even the competition was unconvinced. MTN's John Beck scoffed at the notion of highway coverage, 'It just doesn't make economic sense to put in coverage for 1 400 kilometres of nothing,' he said. 'This technology is a production tool which is needed by people in metropolitan areas.'[1] Eventually, MTN had to follow suit, and build parallel coverage on the highways, but it was too late to blunt Vodacom's initiative.

Despite their by-now habitual reluctance, the shareholders gave Alan R200 million to cover 3 000 kilometres of roads, which was completed in three months – another world first. The network was extended along the highways between Pretoria and Cape Town, and Johannesburg and Durban, as well as all the towns along these routes. The result was that Vodacom's market share rose from 48% to over 60% after coverage of the highways was completed. When the summer holidays came to an end, Vodacom was besieged with calls from new subscribers and from MTN customers wanting to switch their network provider.

Alan referred to the need for network coverage as the 'parking lot syndrome'. He told *Business Day* in an interview: 'You can build the best shopping centre in the world, and market it everywhere – but if you don't have a good parking lot, nobody will come.'[2] Retailers, as the theory goes, attach a great deal of importance to the car parks next to their supermarkets. The car parks are often free and those where a fee is payable do not make vast sums (although this may have changed over the years), representing an extremely unproductive use of space. But without a car park the supermarket is doomed. The point Alan was making was that although Vodacom would not generate much income from a solitary base station on the side of the road, a subscriber's need to make a call would make it an essential structure. Subscribers needed to know that coverage was available everywhere they went and they could make a call whenever they had a need to do so. Thus, regardless of its location, base stations were an essential part of a network operator's business.

Highway coverage benefited cellphone users in a number of ways, most of which Alan had envisaged. The fact that motorists could immediately call the emergency services in the event of an accident or breakdown was particularly useful. And, because the drivers of the police, ambulance and fire vehicles had cellphones with them, the call centre personnel could contact them and direct them to the scene much more quickly and efficiently. The country's rescue services reported that cellphones enabled them to halve their response time, which in many cases resulted directly in saving lives that otherwise would have been lost. And, as Alan had predicted, the sales representatives, delivery drivers, car and motorbike couriers, and so on, used their cellphones to talk to clients, rearrange schedules, report delays, receive messages from office-based colleagues, and much more. But there were indirect benefits, too. For example, farmers with land adjacent to the highways received electricity for the first time when Vodacom had to introduce, and pay for, the new electricity supplies needed along these routes.

When Alan targeted the December 1994 holidays for the completion of the initial highway coverage programme, he knew this meant he had to work fast. The company he chose to provide the infrastructure for the highway cellular network was Brolaz, a Johannesburg-based company that supplied infrastructure for Telkom. Alan knew the organisation to be disciplined and reliable, with a focus on exceptional quality. Brolaz provided a comprehensive one-stop service, including site acquisition; lease agreement with the landowner on whose land the tower would be erected; design and engineering; tower construction; and electricity connection. Alcatel and Siemens supplied the equipment destined for the base station's interior.

Ivo Lazic, Brolaz MD, had been used to constructing base stations for Telkom that took twelve to eighteen months to complete. Alan wanted his highway base stations completed in ten to twelve *weeks*. The absurdity of the demand bordered on the ridiculous; there was absolutely no way he, Ivo, could do what Alan wanted in the time available. But, as it turned out, he could. Whenever Alan asked the impossible, Ivo delivered time and again.

'Telkom was like a big, slow-moving machine,' says Ivo. 'It was so cumbersome it couldn't move quickly even if it wanted to. And then along came Vodacom, which was a much smaller, more streamlined operation. Alan started talking and I began thinking to myself, Hey! Maybe this guy's right; maybe it can happen. I immediately liked his style of management: he knows what he wants and he wants it fast, whatever the cost, and it has to be the best.'

So Ivo and his team set about seeing how they could cut back the construction time by standardising the engineering processes involved in the tower construction. 'Working with Alan is a challenge; there's no doubt about that,' Ivo says. 'But it's a challenge that seems to bring the best out of people. You find yourself working harder and harder to meet his demands, but the satisfaction you get when the job's done, and done on time, is incredible. Alan had lots of these crazy demands, which I call AKC Specials, and there wasn't one of them I refused to take on.'

As the network roll-out progressed, Alan would drive around Johannesburg with Pieter Uys, usually on a Saturday or a Sunday, trialling the Vodacom network, searching for gaps with cellphone in hand and Bryan Adams in the background belting out 'Can't Stop this Thing we Started'. If a call was dropped at any point, Alan would contact Ivo and request an additional base station on the spot. Ivo's team would start working on the same day Alan's call came in and the base station would be up and running within a couple of days. Alan's demanding schedule gave Ivo the opportunity to pioneer innovative engineering techniques for Vodacom and other companies worldwide, which raised Brolaz's profile nationally and internationally.

'Alan's motivation was to keep Vodacom users talking and he'd do whatever it took to make sure this happened. So, if your cellphone broke he'd deliver you another one to use while it was being fixed. This way, you'd keep making calls and that's where the revenue was. It was the same with the network; it had to be perfect at all times so that subscribers never had to worry about whether they'd get a signal or not. It was the right approach, for sure, even if it meant a helluva lot of work.'

During 1994 and 1995, Vodacom built at least two base stations every day to cover major national roads, 60 additional towns, shopping centres, office blocks and townships. By December 1995, expenditure was up to

R2.5 billion and the roll-out was three years ahead of schedule. At this rate, 70% of South Africans would have coverage within a year, a target originally set at five years. Vodacom beat GSM networks across the world with the speed of its roll-out, a pace that has not been matched since.

To understand the importance of coverage, one needs to understand the basic principles of cellular technology. Cellular telephony's most obvious distinguishing feature is that it uses radio waves, instead of wires or cables, to transmit data and sound. The word 'cellular' refers to the division of an area providing the service into units, or 'cells'. Each cell has its own base station, comprising tower-mounted antennae and accompanying equipment shelters, to allow radio waves to be sent and received within the base station's operating range. In metropolitan areas the operating range may extend up to 5 kilometres in any direction, while in rural areas the operating range may have a radius of up to 50 kilometres. Every cell uses a set of radio frequencies to provide service in its specific area. South Africa only has 55 radio frequencies per operator in the 900 Meg band, which have to be continually re-used. Each cellphone call needs one radio frequency each time it makes a call.

A base station handles all call traffic in its area and signals between a mobile phone and the network-switching subsystem. The radio frequencies of each base station overlap, so that the cellphone user can continue to use his or her phone without interruption as the caller moves along the network. The wireless network senses when a signal is getting weaker and hands over the call to a base station with a stronger signal.

Even when a user is not talking, the cellphone communicates with all the nearest base stations. In this way, it's ready to connect a call at any time. Because the shape and size of cells vary, there may be empty spaces between the coverage areas of two or more cells. These gaps or dead spots can also be caused by trees, tall buildings or other obstructions that block a wireless signal from reaching a nearby antenna. If a site is overloaded or obstructed, then the call is dropped. Not only does the cellular company lose revenue, but it also loses a customer.

'Alan wanted to make sure that every single customer had a perfect cellphone experience with every call,' comments Ivo. 'Therefore, the base stations' reliability was a key factor. He wanted to make it easy for a customer to buy a phone, insert a card and get connected. Everything had to be easy and convenient. Alan's vision was clear, not just in black and white, but in amazing technicolour.'

The most visible evidence of cellular technology to millions of subscribers must be the towers that are dotted throughout the landscape. A tower is usually 55 metres tall with an internal climbing ladder to the platform and feeder cables running to the top. The poles, painted in the trademark red and white, weigh 8 tons and are affixed to a concrete foundation weighing 80 tons, which means there is no chance of them falling over. Towers have to be lined up perfectly because antennas must be able to 'see' each other at exactly the right spot. The amazingly innovative designs that imitate nature were to come later.

Putting up a tower takes time, which was the one thing Ivo did not have. The problem was that the municipality required plans for any structure needing a foundation, and the tower required an 80-ton concrete base. Drawing up these plans, submitting them and then waiting for council approval, *if* it was forthcoming, meant Ivo had no chance of meeting Alan's deadline. Ivo's solution was to design a temporary base-station site that did not need concrete foundations, and so obviated the need for council approval. The base consisted of a strong steel container that held the tower; the container itself was set upon railway sleepers set into the ground and held in place by a system of high-strength steel ropes affixed to its corners. The new base station could be set up in under eight hours.

Says Ivo, 'We worked through weekends; we did all-night sessions; we worked ourselves to a standstill. Because the roll-out needed to happen at the speed of lightning, we did hundreds of millions worth of business on a handshake. And that's how we've always done business.'

Towards the middle of 1995, however, Vodacom came under increasing pressure from the environmental lobby and the general public to improve the aesthetic appeal of the growing number of towers visible across the country. Alan acknowledged this concern and asked Ivo to design something new.

The result was the palm tower, a cleverly disguised cellular tower that, as the name denotes, looks like a palm tree. The materials used for the tower had to be aged up to five years within a 24-hour period in Armscor's laboratories using military technology, while the bark was created using special colourants applied to the steel trunk. The tree tower was designed with an internal ladder accessible through doors at the bottom and top of the structure for easy access to the platform. The palm towers were so lifelike that the leaves even moved in the wind.

The reaction was overwhelming – people loved them. The environmentalists were also appeased. The 'tree' tower cost twice as much as its 'steel' counterpart, but the additional cost involved was not an issue for Alan. He knew that Vodacom's reputation could have been irreparably damaged if he had done nothing.

In February 1996, the first cellular palm tower was erected in Durbanville in the Western Cape – a queen palm 55 metres high with leaves 11 metres wide. The queen palm tree soon gave rise to new designs, such as the wild date palm, pine tree, the yellowwood tree, the buffalo thorn tree and cypress tree. In some cases, the Brolaz camouflaged trees became regarded as works of art in their own right. In the Kruger Park, for example, the towers appear as petrified trees and the base stations are hidden inside hollow boulders; in the Drakensberg, they have been turned into working windmills; and in Port Elizabeth, the antenna was set up as a lighthouse with a children's playhouse alongside. Ivo's trees are now in demand in Europe, the Middle East and Australasia. He has set up windmills in Mykonos, date palms in the Arab Emirates and he has even used the masts on a ship to camouflage antennae.

The partnership between Ivo and Alan was a synergistic one – a joint effort that produced spectacular results that neither man could have achieved alone. Alan's pioneering vision of a cellular South Africa, harnessed to Ivo's groundbreaking engineering work, propelled Vodacom forward at an even greater speed and garnered Brolaz international acclaim. But it is the fact that this commercial success was not achieved at the expense of sacrificing public goodwill that pleases Alan most.

'I believe in progress,' he comments. 'If I didn't, I wouldn't have gone anywhere near Vodacom. But I don't believe in progress at any price. Ivo and I did what we could to reassure people that Vodacom cared about the environment. The camouflaged trees weren't cheap, but you have to put your money where your mouth is. I like to think that we managed the base station roll-out programme pretty well.'

The public's acceptance of the disguised tree towers suggests that the programme was indeed well-managed. However, acceptance has also been forthcoming from another, quite unexpected quarter – the tree towers are so lifelike that some bird species have chosen them for their nesting sites. In the Northern Cape near Upington, an endangered Martial eaglet was raised on one of Vodacom's masts and, on another occasion, black eagles settled on top of three towers in the Free State and the Northern Cape.

Vodacom currently has over 8 000 base stations and is constantly expanding its network, not necessarily for coverage, but for purposes of capacity. With the continuous demand for airtime, the camouflaged towers are here to stay, complete with management procedures for nesting sites.

Rollercoaster Ride
1994 to 1999

When performance exceeds ambition, the overlap is called success.
Cullen Hightower

'Vodacom is not, and has never been, just a telephone company. Vodacom transacts hopes, dreams and aspirations... We are changing the way that people communicate,' wrote Wendy Luhabe, Vodacom chairperson from 2000 to 2005.[1] Millions of people in Africa have been isolated from the mainstream economy, but the advent of cellphones brought opportunities that made a substantial contribution to improving their quality of life. Various studies have found that cellular telephony has had a pronounced impact on improving Africa's economic prospects, which include growth in per capita Gross Domestic Product (GDP) – for every 10% increase in cellular penetration, an estimated 0.6% growth in GDP is achieved – an increase in employment opportunities, direct foreign investment and small business development.

However, years ahead of independent studies Alan had said, 'Providing all South Africans with affordable access to telecommunications is crucial to the economic prosperity of South Africa,'[2] since 'Communications allow people to participate in the country's economy to a far greater extent.'[3] Alan never lost sight of his vision, driving Vodacom to become an explosive force in the multi-billion rand cellular industry, and in the process, empowering a new generation of entrepreneurs.

With cellular technology came economic emancipation and it was Vodacom that propelled the process forward at an incredible rate; it was the fastest growing GSM cellular network operator in the world. Alan was committed to providing the best network service in the country; he wanted Vodacom to be the primary source of 'phone power' for the country's cellphone subscribers. In order to achieve this, he knew that Vodacom's products and services had to be the best. So he established a Product Development Division run by Leon Shirk, a man Alan refers to as 'the best innovator in the world'. An electronic engineer by profession, Leon left Anderson Consulting to join Alan's revolutionary brigade at Vodacom. Leon never forgot Alan's words to him at the end of their interview: 'You can have the job, but if you screw up, you're fired. I'll give you all the chances in the world, but I take no prisoners.' Leon liked a challenge and started a week later.

The first thing Leon was tasked to do was create a South African SIM business. A SIM card, also known as a 'smart card', acts as an identity card for a cellphone user's handset and ensures that the call billing is directed to the correct user. Embedded in the card is an electronic chip that stores all the relevant information required to operate the cellphone.

Leon visited Germany, where SIM technology was first developed (originally by the Munich-based firm Giesecke and Devrient). His fact-finding mission over, Leon returned to South Africa and, in February 1995, a smart card production plant was opened in the Cape with the capacity to print up to 6 million cards per year. The chip was developed by Motorola, and programmed and packaged in Cape Town, creating hundreds of jobs in the process, as well as contributing to Vodacom's R1 billion economic development programme.

Once Leon was satisfied with the SIM card design, he had to figure out a way of getting people to buy them. As Alan had already established, the cellphone itself – the handset – was of secondary importance to the technology that powered it. People had to *use* the phone for it to be of value to them and, of course, to Vodacom. But it was the SIM card that made the cellphone usable – a tiny piece of plastic card that, on the face of it, looked entirely inconsequential. Why would anyone be interested in buying anything so... *uninteresting*?

The solution Leon proposed to Alan was the Vodacom Connector Pack. The 'pack' consisted of an oversized box that held the SIM card as well as an instructional video and manual. The 'too big' design was intentional. Leon wanted to draw attention to the tiny SIM card, and the best way of doing this was to package the card in a totally incongruous manner. As Leon says, 'We basically put fresh air in a box. It was our way of putting airtime on the shelf, and it got people interested.' As well as adding an element of fun to the purchase of a largely excitement-free product, the 'pack' made buying a SIM card a tangible exercise.

With bulky Vodacom Connector Packs dominating the retailers' shelves, Vodacom's cellphones stole a march on MTN's offerings. But Alan and Leon didn't stop there. Investing some R26 million, Vodacom's market share rose further with the launch of a whole host of value-added cellular services, including information services such as: weather reports, traffic updates, and stock market figures; increased voicemail capacity, call waiting and call forwarding functions; directory enquiries, time-check and operator assistance facilities; a satellite vehicle tracking service; call timing, call barring and caller identity functions; TwinCall – two cellphones operating on the same number; a fast-dial service for the flying squad; and a free SOS line for medical and other types of emergencies.

Crime prevention received a boost with Vodacom's CellWatch project. Vodacom subscribers dialled 112 to report a crime and their cell numbers and locations were automatically identified and forwarded to the appropriate emergency number. Thanks to the innovative deals signed by Vodacom with its international partners, customers could pack their cellphones along with their toothbrushes on their trips abroad. International roaming enabled subscribers to use their existing cellphone and SIM card in other countries (today Vodacom is connected to 411 international networks spread across 185 countries). Vodacom was the first network operator to introduce international roaming, fax and data communications, voicemail and emergency services. In many cases, its services were world firsts.

As the novelty of making and receiving calls wore off, SMS became all the rage. Initially, it was a slow starter, but it soon became the most active cellular service in the world. In January 1996, it cost 80c to send an SMS. Alan decided to make the first fifteen SMS messages each month free for an entire year to create a demand for the service. He was convinced that once subscribers got into the habit of using the SMS facility, they would never look back. This new offering held great appeal for the teenage market and revenue soared. Although limited to 160 characters, a new language was born. It gave rise to a new short snappy vocabulary that had kids glued to their cellphones. Once the free offer had expired at the end of the year, the SMS usage dropped for only one month, but then it continued to grow exponentially. It has boomed ever since. Today Vodacom's non-voice revenue is 12% of total revenue – a R6 billion business. Since the introduction of MXit and Vodacom's own version, known as The Grid, teenagers have been tip-tapping crazy as 500 billion cellphone messages criss-cross the globe each year.

The Please Call Me idea happened by chance. Alan was leaning over the railing of the Vodacom building chatting to a colleague, Phil Geissler, when Phil pointed out one security guard trying to attract another's attention, and because his buddy didn't see him, the security guard called him on his cellphone. Alan immediately spoke to Leon about creating a Please Call Me service. Because the Please Call Me SMS sent was free, Vodacom made money by adding short advertisements just below the message, but the real money came from the return call. This concept generated hundreds of millions in revenue. By 2008, Vodacom generated 20 million Please Call Me requests daily.

It was Vodacom's launch of prepaid airtime in 1996 that signalled the company's arrival on the international stage. Vodacom had signed up 600 000 contract subscribers in the first two years, which exceeded everybody's expectations. But Alan knew that these subscribers only represented a small section of the South African public – specifically, those individuals who had been vetted by a credit bureau and declared creditworthy. Of course, a credit check can only be done on someone who has a credit history, uses a bank account, earns an income, and owns assets; in other words, white South Africans. For the far greater number of black South Africans – unemployed or low-waged, without a bank account or any valuable assets – the credit check had no relevance.

Prepaid airtime was designed to redress this imbalance. If airtime could be bought separately, without the need for a contract or credit check, and if it was readily available in affordable amounts, the market for cellphones would increase exponentially. Millions of less privileged South Africans would then be able to join the cellular revolution, which had always been one of Alan's main objectives.

Today, prepaid airtime is a worldwide phenomenon and it seems almost impossible to think how the cellphone industry survived without it. But, back in 1996, Alan had to work very hard to convince the Vodacom shareholders that the plastic packaging wrapped around a tiny SIM card brightly branded as Vodago would bring the next wave of subscribers. In fact, it might not have happened at all. Bob Chaphe, MD of MTN at the time, was concerned that Alan was destroying the classic cellphone business model. He approached Brian Clarke, the then-MD of Telkom, and urged him to veto the launch of prepaid. Brian apparently shared the MTN chief's anxiety and put the matter to Vodafone. Perhaps it was a case of 'better the devil you know', but Vodafone refused to intervene; the UK company had seen enough of Alan's supposedly crazy schemes take off successfully to know that he deserved its backing.

It took a year to develop, but on 1 November 1996, with Siemens' Intelligent Network Platform, Vodacom commercially deployed prepaid. The prepaid concept, marketed as Vodago, was a no-strings-attached package.

'Subscribers don't have to sign contacts and they don't have to qualify for credit,' Alan explained to the public. 'It is essentially a free telephone service since it requires no installation cost and no fixed cost per month. If you make no calls, you have no cost, while emergency calls are free.' A *Business Day* article on 2 December 1996 reported that Vodacom expected to attract 250 000 prepaid users within the next year.[4]

The network was initially designed to carry a capacity of 60 000 subscribers. Today there are 33 million Vodacom prepaid subscribers in Africa. Vodacom was arguably the first in the world to implement commercially the breakthrough technology of an intelligent network platform for prepaid products. The floodgates opened up to a whole new market and today millions of people buy their SIM cards and airtime from their local grocery store, supermarket or petrol station as they would a loaf of bread. The cellular 'takeaway' as envisioned by Alan and Theo at the beginning of the cellphone era is now an everyday reality.

In May 1998, Vodago was recognised as the best marketing success worldwide by the GSM Association, comprising 239 networks in 105 countries. Alan flew to Cannes where he accepted the Marketing Success Award on behalf of Vodacom from the GSM Association chairman, Adrian Nugter. He also delivered a paper at the GSM World Congress on Vodacom's prepaid concept, which was considered a marvel. Delegates crowded the conference room to hear how Vodacom had made the cellphone accessible to Africa's people.

The success of prepaid also led to Alan's induction in 2001 as one of only eight Gold Members worldwide of the GSM Association's inaugural Roll of Honour for 'his determination to introduce mobile communications to the masses in a community where many had never made a phone call in their lives'. It is due to prepaid that cellular telephony is not the elitist phenomenon that many initially feared it might be. In fact, it gave those less privileged access to the economic playing field and provided millions of people an opportunity to earn a living.

Vodacom quickly moved from one innovation to another. Leon Shirk proposed the development of a Vodacom Internet service. At Alan's request, he personally presented the business idea to the board and asked for R100 million so that Vodacom could beat one of its shareholders in product development – Telkom. It was very arrogant, but they agreed to it even without a business plan. The business was built in just over six months and 50 000 clients were signed up. Leon put the Internet in a tin, and called it Yebonet. The customer would rip the top open and all the software was inside. The same 'takeaway' branding was repeated once more. In 1998 World Online approached Vodacom to buy a share in the service. The following year, the balance was sold at a peak price for a R40 million profit just before the computer bubble burst.

'Vodacom's Internet era was short-lived, but it was a good experience and we made a great deal of money out of it. When you have nothing to lose and you want to be the best, you do extraordinary things,' remarked Leon.

In July 1998, the cellular industry was turned upside down by another of Alan's controversial decisions. The *Sunday Times* reported: 'In one of the most controversial salvos fired in the battle for cellphone subscribers between network operators Vodacom and MTN, Vodacom announced free access to voicemail for its 1.1 million subscribers.'

The giveaway was worth about R1 million a day. Jacques Sellschop, MTN's corporate relations executive, claimed that Vodacom had no choice but to offer free voicemail because its service was so poor. 'Perhaps they feel compelled to do this in anticipation of the KPMG-audited comparative quality tests,' he added.[5] He would come to rue those words when *The Star* published a story on 28 July 1998 with the headline: 'How MTN shot itself in the Foot'. MTN also insisted that it had no plans to do the same and would always remain price-competitive. Alan, of course, begged to differ. Market research, he maintained, suggested that free voicemail would act as a powerful incentive for people who were considering buying a cellphone. Many of the prepaid subscribers, who made up almost two-thirds of Vodacom's new business, could now also rely on voicemail to keep in touch since it was free; sometimes it was their only reliable address.

Known as 'Vodamail', Vodacom's R6 million initial voicemail system was launched to great critical acclaim. The highly sophisticated service was provided free of charge, although the standard call rate fee did apply when messages were retrieved. Voicemail proved an instant hit; the service initially registered some 30 000 calls per day.

However, Alan had expected the voicemail service to be even more popular, and wondered why this was not the case. The answer, when it came, was quite simple: he realised that subscribers did not want to pay a fee to retrieve their voicemail. It was like having to pay a fee each time you opened your letterbox, or each time the postman delivered a letter – and of course, nobody would agree to that. It was the sender who had to bear the cost of the voicemail service, just as it was the letter sender who paid the postage fee; the retriever should pay nothing. When Vodacom, at Alan's insistence, introduced free voicemail retrieval, the call-completion rate rocketed from below 50% to more than 80%, driving revenues up. Free voicemail became so successful that MTN had to follow suit. Today it is international best-practice.

The 1990s witnessed a titanic struggle between Vodacom and MTN over which would emerge as the country's preferred network provider. For the most part, the competition between the two companies was both open and amicable. Alan had repeatedly expressed his belief in the benefits of free-market competition and his MTN counterpart was of similar mind. Alan said to the press tongue-in-cheek, 'Competition is great. What we fear most is that we will beat MTN out of business and then we won't have any competition.'

On one occasion, however, this good-spirited rivalry turned into something rather unpleasant. In July 1998, MTN's Bob Chaphe challenged Alan to pit the quality of Vodacom's network coverage against that of his own.

'We'll organise the whole event,' Bob said. 'The idea is to gather an entourage of technical experts and journalists, including consumer guru, Isabel Jones, to drive through Johannesburg to see which network performs the best. Of course, it will be audited by KPMG to ensure the veracity of the results.'

'No way,' said Alan. 'I'm not playing it by your rules. I would rather not be part of a one-sided game. You go and play by yourself. We'll sit this one out.'

'Scared of the competition, Alan?' Bob laughed.

'Not even a little, *Boet* [Brother],' Alan assured him.

Alan wanted nothing to do with the event, which to him appeared little more than a cheap publicity stunt that MTN wanted to engineer to its own advantage. But the event went ahead anyway. With two heavyweights in the ring, the media couldn't wait for the contest to get started and reported the event in the newspapers at length. Alan was not surprised to hear soon after that MTN had come out on top, but still resolved to think about the matter no further.

Then, a few days later, a serious-looking stranger was ushered into his office. The man was a private investigator and he carried with him a series of documents and photographs that he wanted to show Alan. Bemused, Alan studied the material that lay before him. He was particularly intrigued by several photographs showing the inside of a helicopter packed with sophisticated electronic equipment in the place where the rear seats would usually be.

'What's all this?' he asked the investigator.

'A jamming device,' the man replied. 'It can be used to interfere with a network's radio waves – all high-tech stuff.'

'I can see that, but why show me? What have I got to do with this?' Alan queried.

Before replying, the man walked across the floor and shut the door to the office. He returned to Alan's desk and then, in a low, even tone said, 'MTN hired that helicopter, stripped the insides and installed the jamming equipment before the trial with those journos began. Your network never had a chance; they completely messed it up.'

Alan was astonished. He knew that he and MTN were playing for high stakes, but this was ridiculous.

'How do you know it was MTN?' Alan demanded, reluctant to think that this might be so.

The investigator handed Alan the proof of payment record for the hiring of the helicopter. He had also obtained the helicopter's logbook that recorded the details of its flight path that day. It had traversed exactly the same route the car filled with journalists had taken through the streets of Johannesburg.

Alan was angry and disappointed to discover that MTN might have taken such unprincipled, not to mention illegal, action. But he did not believe for a moment that Bob would have allowed himself to get caught up in such deviousness. He would never have agreed to go along with such underhand tactics. Alan had to pay a seven-figure sum for the evidence, which he then took to Bob.

Bob was incredulous, just as Alan had expected him to be. On investigating the matter, Bob admitted that MTN had used a helicopter on the day of the trial, but assured Alan that the equipment on board had been used for monitoring the networks only, even though it had the capability of jamming a network.

But Alan was not going to let the issue go away quietly. If Bob was right, why had it been kept quiet from KPMG and the media? He presented his evidence to the press. He felt they had a duty to report the behind-the-scenes behaviour that had compromised the authenticity of their MTN versus Vodacom story. He received apologies and it was clear that the affair had caused the press a great deal of embarrassment, but no major exposé of the affair was forthcoming. There was only one extensive story published by *The Star* on 28 July 1998, accompanied by an amusing black-spy versus white-spy cartoon. A senior director at KPMG also called Alan to apologise and to tell him that the company had withdrawn its 'clean' audit.

Alan had a further opportunity to reveal what had happened when Joan Joffe, Vodacom's marketing manager at the time, told him that she was due to be interviewed on Radio 702 along with her MTN counterpart, Jacques Sellschop. The helicopter saga had left relations between the two network giants delicately poised, and Joan wanted Alan's advice on how she should approach the interview.

'Give them hell,' he told her. And she did. Joan was not a street fighter, but she was not about to retreat into a corner. The interview was vicious: Sellschop denied all the allegations; Joan called him a scheming liar. She wasn't comfortable with the interview, but she kept her poise. And the interview could not be judged a failure because of this, since the general consensus was that Vodacom had emerged as the moral victor. 'The media played the story like a well-tuned fiddle,' says Joan. 'We got so much mileage out of a situation that we hadn't wanted to be part of in the first place.'

Still Alan was not satisfied. No one was taking responsibility for the mess that had damaged Vodacom's reputation. He decided to take MTN to court for defamation. He didn't give a damn about the repercussions; MTN had to be held accountable for what it had done to his company.

Not long after, before court proceedings had begun, Alan received a call from then President Nelson Mandela inviting him for tea at the Union Buildings in Pretoria. Alan knew him well enough at this stage for the president to call him by his first name. He had first met Mandela in 1995 through a well-connected entrepreneur and mutual friend, Yusuf Surtee. Alan thought at the time that the meeting with the president would be a case of shaking hands and leaving. However, when Alan arrived, Mandela graciously greeted him as if they had been friends for years. Alan was initially tongue-tied and hovered in awe. He remembered the afternoon he'd watched the old man leave Victor Verster prison on TV without an inkling of their meeting just five years later. From the minute Mandela shook his hand, he could have asked Alan anything and he would have gone to the ends of the Earth to do it for him – and he often did. Madiba, the clan name by which Mandela is affectionately known, built schools and clinics with private sector money because the government didn't deliver as fast as he would have liked. Alan often used his shareholders' money to fund these initiatives.

However, it was not a common occurrence that the president invited him for tea so he must have something important to discuss, thought Alan. Alan surmised that he wanted to discuss a potential project for Vodacom to take on. When he arrived, he bumped into Bob Chaphe in the foyer. The two men were not on speaking terms and were clearly unhappy to be meeting under such circumstances.

Second is Nothing

'What are you doing here?' asked Alan, as politely as he could.

'I've been invited for tea,' replied Bob. 'And you?'

'Same,' said Alan.

They exchanged puzzled glances. But before they had time to discuss the matter further, they were taken to see Madiba. After a minute or two of general conversation, Madiba outlined the reason why he had invited them.

'Gentlemen,' he said, 'I believe there is a court case pending between MTN and Vodacom. I am sure that you both have good reasons for the court case, but I don't want to know what they are. However, it doesn't look good for the country to have our top mobile network operators at loggerheads. There has to be another way. Why don't you go into my private study and see if you can come up with a solution to all this. Come back and let me know what you decide.'

Alan and Bob left the room gulping like guppies. When they got to the study, neither knew what to say. They were both mortified to have been rapped over the knuckles. In utterly gracious terms, the president had told them to stop their petty squabbling, to remember their civic responsibilities, and to resolve their differences in a dignified, reasonable manner.

Neither wanted to disappoint Mandela, but since there was a court case pending, both were wondering how to go about resolving the matter in the absence of their lawyers. They sat in silence in the presidential study for a while, contemplating a way forward. They were offered drinks. Alan felt he needed a gin and tonic considering the situation, but settled for a glass of water instead.

Eventually Alan said, 'I don't know about you, but I don't want to go back in there and tell the old man that we couldn't come to an agreement.'

'Well, let's get this sorted then,' Bob responded.

And so Alan withdrew the court action and all claims for damages. In return, Bob agreed to offer an apology to Vodacom, since he too was eager to put an end to any further damage to MTN's already beleaguered reputation. In less than half an hour the matter was settled and Alan and Bob sought out the president.

Madiba smiled broadly, but before they could tell him that they had resolved the situation, he said, 'I knew you wouldn't disappoint me; thank you for sorting out your disagreement.'

Alan wondered how many other crises Mandela had solved by simply allowing his presence to be the catalyst for resolution. When Mandela asked you to do him a favour, Alan contemplated, you would rather disown your own mother than disappoint him.

In 1997, on behalf of Vodacom, Alan accepted the Unlisted Company of the Year Award. The award recognised entrepreneurial skill, leadership and innovation. The company was also commended for its consistently excellent level of service, innovative marketing strategies, and recognition of the importance of developing people. By its third year of operation Vodacom had connected over 1 million customers and delivered on its promise to the government to become a partner in rebuilding South Africa. The *Sowetan* reported that in three years the cellular industry had created over 7 000 jobs, contributed over R15 billion to the South African economy and paid R2.7 billion in taxes, licence fees and additional revenue for Telkom – seven times more than had been expected.[6] By the end of the year, Vodacom and MTN's networks covered 80% of the population – quadrupling initial growth projections.

'Those were incredible days,' remarks Leon Shirk. 'Everything we touched turned to gold. With Alan's support and passion, we felt we could make the world come alive. Alan has this instinct for putting the right things in the hands of the right people, which always seemed to work. He also played a huge role in protecting our ideas. He knew from his Telkom days how easy it was to kill innovation so he watched over us like a hawk until we were ready to fly; and when we did, we were untouchable.'

The Yebo Gogo Brand
1994 to 2007

It is not slickness, polish, uniqueness, or cleverness that makes a brand a brand. It is truth.
Harry Beckwith

Vodacom is not just a marketing success; it is a branding phenomenon. Alan cut his teeth on branding under the guidance of his shareholder, Rembrandt. He wanted to position Vodacom in the marketplace as soon as possible, which meant he had to learn a great deal in a very short space of time. The experience was as demanding as it was rewarding and, as Alan recalls, 'The learning curve wasn't steep; it was vertical!'

But the hard work paid off and Rembrandt's expertise rubbed off, since Alan's marketing campaigns – bold, innovative and personal – proceeded to capture the hearts and minds of the general public. In the same way that the Hoover® became synonymous with vacuum cleaners and Kleenex® with tissues, Alan aspired to make the public see Vodacom in every cellphone.

'I believe that branding can either make or break a company,' says Alan. 'It can take years to build a brand, but once you have a dynamic vital brand that connects with consumers, it has to be nurtured and protected. The brand is who we are; it has to remain current and relevant in the hearts and minds of every customer or it will fade away before you know it.'

The Yebo Gogo Brand

Six months before cellular's commercial launch, Alan was already advertising his product on television, intent on establishing the Vodacom brand as the generic term for the product. Long before Vodacom made its official appearance, he had already signed exclusive distribution deals with the major retailers to sell his airtime. Paying substantial connection bonuses, which enabled service providers and their retailers to discount cellphones, was another innovative marketing strategy that saw cellphone prices plunge to among the lowest in the world. And, because Alan had a vision of transforming cellular into a fast-moving consumer item like bread or milk, the Vodacom brand had to be made available like any other off-the-shelf item. From day one, subscribers could connect to the Vodacom network via retail stores such as Pick 'n Pay and Game. Today, amongst the 12 000 distribution outlets where subscribers can buy cellular goods, there are hundreds of corner cafés, garages and small retail outlets, making Vodacom the most recognisable and sought-after cellular 'takeaway'.

Branding Vodacom as an 'available everywhere; usable anywhere' cellular service explains why Alan insisted on making a huge capital investment in covering the highways. As he repeatedly told anyone who would listen, and quite a few who wouldn't, the whole point of cellular technology was that people should be able to take their cellphones *and use them* wherever they wished. A base station, regardless of its location, became an essential part of a network operator's business as soon as a subscriber decided to make a call in its vicinity. If a subscriber couldn't make a call whenever he or she wanted to, what was the point of having a mobile phone? Highway coverage was, in Alan's estimation, an absolute necessity.

'It was,' he says, 'one of the best business decisions I ever made. You just had to see the bigger picture, that's all. And in the long run, it was good for our brand. After all, we gave our customers a service they could access anywhere, any time, without fail.'

Another bold marketing move was Alan's decision to build Vodaworld – a R50 million retail complex in Midrand, which opened in March 1998. Cellular customers are generally removed from the cellular operator by a layer of service providers responsible for retailing airtime contracts, which can have the effect of diluting customer loyalty to the brand. Vodaworld's purpose – apart from being a one-stop shop where subscribers could access anything cellular – was to remind its customers that Vodacom was about *people* not just concepts, products and technology. And it was 'the personal touch' that would ultimately determine the level and intensity of brand loyalty among cellphone subscribers.

Marketing something as amorphous and abstract as cellular technology was, Alan knew, never going to be easy; but if Vodacom could take the intangible and make it as real, human and personal as possible, customers might be persuaded to come on board. Within twelve months the mall had paid for itself and a new generation of brand-loyal users had emerged.

In the interests of improving the one-on-one relationship Vodacom had with its customers, Alan hired Interactive Africa, a company specialising in relationship marketing and the development of loyalty programmes for corporate clients such as Reebok, Nedbank and Sun International. Ravi Naidoo, the company's MD, suggested that the range of products and services that Vodacom offered was not well-suited to a standard single-page advertisement – there was simply too much information involved. From this initial observation the idea for *Vodaworld*, the Vodacom magazine, was born. The magazine 'belonged' to Vodacom subscribers in the sense that it was a free, customised publication that catered exclusively for their needs. And it was an essential tool to monitor subscribers carefully and tap them for feedback.

And then, of course, there were the advertising campaigns. A Sandton advertising agency, Draftfcb (then known as Lindsay Smithers), was hired to design an advertising campaign to launch Vodacom. MTN's radio campaign, already up and running, was extremely effective, which persuaded Alan to avoid using the same medium. Instead, he instructed the agency to focus exclusively on television advertising. The aim of the first batch of commercials was to promote Vodacom's road coverage service, which was at that point in time the company's one distinguishing feature. Having control of the roads meant that the Vodacom network reached places its rival could not. So, when viewers saw the adverts of the huge dog squashed into a tiny kennel or the Sumo wrestler sitting on and crushing a little chair, they would be persuaded to consider the commercials' implied question, 'Is your network too small for you?'

However, it was only when Draftfcb's Francois de Villiers became involved that the Vodacom television campaign really took off. Francois's career in advertising spanned three decades and countless awards, including an honorary award by the South African Academy of Science and Arts and the Pendoring Legend Award, an accolade that had only been awarded once before. Francois had just joined Draftfcb when Vodacom started in 1994. He was a little anxious before his first meeting with Alan because he had heard that he was difficult to please, but before long Francois came to look forward to the campaigns he worked on with Alan.

'Sure, he's difficult,' says Francois, 'but it's just that he expects the best. He is very intolerant of fools, especially those who work for him, and he has a sharp tongue that will rip people to shreds. What I liked about Alan though was that he did not call the shots from his ivory tower. He was accessible, available and hands on with every advert. In fact, he was the marketing department – he owned the brand.'

'The Vodacom brand was my personal baby,' comments Alan. 'I allowed no one to touch it. I worked with some of the greatest brand innovators in the world, but I always had the final say. I was never too busy for my baby, nor did I allow it to be compromised for the sake of money, or anything else for that matter. That's why the custodian of a brand can only ever be the CEO – ultimate power for your ultimate asset.'

Alan had launched the brand the year before with a TV advert that Francois had found disappointing. The commercial featured several shots of sleek-haired, well-dressed professional people driving luxury cars past steel-and-glass buildings while talking on cellphones. In other words, the commercial presented the cellphone as a yuppie tool – exactly what Alan had *not* wanted people to think. It was what people expected from cellular. Francois felt that cellular should be presented as much more than a piece of plastic to make people look cool; the cellular commercials needed soul.

Francois and Alan set about reworking the entire television campaign. For Francois, the fact that Alan did not come from an advertising background created a unique work dynamic.

'I found Alan's way of doing things totally refreshing,' Francois says. 'His lack of formal training was actually a real plus because it meant he saw no limits.'

Alan's imagination tended to override the more practical constraints that usually govern marketing campaigns of all types, namely, time and money.

'Let's use Evita Bezuidenhout or Casper de Vries in our next ad,' Alan would exclaim, clearly delighted at the thought.

'But Casper is in London,' Francois would object. 'We don't have time to arrange it and, anyway, it's too expensive to fly him out.'

Alan didn't see the obstacle. 'But that's not the point! Casper is who we need. What does it matter if we spend a few thousand rand more to get him. Don't be stupid, man, just do it.'

It would be the same with the music used to accompany an advertisement.

'I really like that song. Why can't it be longer?' demanded Alan.

Francois would explain patiently, 'It can't be longer because it will become too expensive to flight the ad. Besides, all the scenes are perfectly synchronised with the music.'

'Change it,' Alan would insist. 'I want an extra five seconds of that song. It's too good to cut it short.'

Alan's demands would at times exasperate Francois, but on the whole he considered the Vodacom boss to be a 'dream client'. 'He saw his company as it should be, and not as it is – not small and unknown, but a huge corporate success,' says Francois.

Alan was looking for a definitive advertising campaign, one that would appeal to both the black and the white markets. It was not going to be easy. Even with apartheid gone, the depressing reality was that, in many ways, the two races remained as far apart as ever. Alan felt that to draw the two audiences together, they needed to laugh about something together, but what was that elusive something? For Francois, the common denominator was storytelling. Each of South Africa's racial groups possess a culture of storytelling. The stories may be written ones – the Herman Charles Bosman books for the English South Africans, the Tolla van der Merwe and Jan Spies campfire tales for the Afrikaners – or verbal ones, such as the ancient myths and legends of the black African groups. The humour in the stories was not in the punchline, but in the way the stories were told; it had to touch people's hearts and minds.

'It's not what the meerkat says that's important,' Francois explains, 'but how he turns his head, how he blinks his eyes, how he moves.'

Francois wanted to tell a story that would make people feel good. The perfect scenario emerged: setting up a pompous wise-guy for a fall so that the underdog would emerge as the hero, a universal theme in the storytelling traditions of all races and cultures. And so the Yebo Gogo script came into being. It features an insolent, self-important young white man being upstaged by a quiet, modest older black man. The yuppie pulls up in his flashy BMW convertible and the first thing the audience sees is his pointy black boots stepping onto the gravel. From his pony-tail and shiny gold chains to the way he shrugs his shoulders into the patchwork leather jacket, the audience is left in no doubt that this crass individual is heading for a fall. With a gaudy blonde girlfriend by his side, the obnoxious man betrays his ignorance by saying 'Yebo Gogo' ('Hello Grandmother') in a slow staccato way to the black grandfather sitting by the roadside selling his windmills, as if he won't quite understand him. The viewers already see him as patronising and insulting.

Sure enough, the insufferable man and the tawdry girlfriend lock themselves out of their car and have to be rescued by the older man, who agrees to call a locksmith, using his cellphone, on condition that Mr Kitsch Cool buys the windmills at an inflated price. The yuppie goes off with all the windmills in his backseat, while the old man chuckles to himself, counting his notes to the sound of James Brown, black as the ace of spades, singing 'I Feel Good'. The ad was clever and funny – audiences loved it. While audiences laughed, they got the message: the cellphone has value regardless of whether you are a yuppie or a nobody.

Francois needed actors who could carry the story so that the varied audience would see the humour in it. Bankole Omotoso, a 52-year-old Nigerian professor of English at the University of the Western Cape was hired to play the part of 'Gogo'. Fluent in four languages, widely travelled, and with 'serious' stage, television and radio work to his name, Bankole acknowledges that it is his Vodacom character that has made him famous. His students love to joke with him and call out Yebo Gogo at the end of a lecture.

'It's sad,' he says with a rueful smile, 'those 30 seconds on TV have made me more famous than 25 years of writing and publishing.'

Michael de Pinna, who plays South Africa's favourite creep in Yebo Gogo, is a serious actor and singer by profession. Since that first advert, Michael has played the part of the hapless yuppie in a number of different ads, appearing as a rugby fan wearing horns, a lip-synching Elvis impersonator in a country town, and a water-skier who loses his leopard skin briefs, to name but three; each time he is rescued by his black cellphone buddy.

Second is Nothing

The political timing of the ads was good. It was a time when both black and white South Africans were prepared to embrace one another. Yebo Gogo meant far more than 'Hello Grandmother'. When Chester Williams dived down for a try in the 1995 Rugby World Cup all the spectators were up on their feet in an instant and cried out in one voice 'Yebo Gogo' – it became a victory cry. It held a universal message that unified the entire country.

'Now that's power in a brand for you,' remarked Francois.

Alan recognised this and he bought the whole concept from the beginning. It was how he perceived Vodacom – a brand for everyone. He didn't want it to be exclusive. It had to embrace every single individual across the race, age and colour spectrum. When Francois presented the concept they budgeted it at a R1 million production that steadily climbed to R3 million. Alan didn't blink.

Alan said to Francois, 'Yebo Gogo was a stroke of genius. I want you to do it again and again, just differently.'

And he did – for twelve years. The Yebo Gogo TV advertising campaign ran from 1994 to 2007, using the same characters in a number of different settings. And every time they sat down to discuss a new ad Alan would ask the same question, 'What's the music?' And the next question would be, 'Can you play it longer?'

As the advertisements gained in notoriety and popularity, the need to push or 'sell' the Vodacom brand on screen diminished. In some commercials the phone never even made an appearance, just the company logo – a sure sign that Vodacom and cellular technology were inextricably linked in people's minds. Alan encouraged Francois to be as creative as possible; there was nothing so outlandish or fantastic that he would not consider.

'Everyone knows that Vodacom is high-tech,' he would remind Francois. 'We don't need to tell anyone that. Do anything you like except high-tech; that's the only rule I have. Instead, make people feel good, touch them where it matters most, and put our logo on it.'

So Francois didn't do high-tech, he did what he calls 'high-touch'. In other words, he wrapped the advertisements in emotion. The commercials had to 'connect' with the viewing public, not merely 'sell' them something. Alan had always stressed the importance of what cellular technology represented – personal empowerment, economic opportunity and social integration – and he insisted that all Vodacom's marketing efforts should reflect this.

'Alan knows what advertising did for his brand,' Francois comments. 'I spend a considerable amount of time trying to get my clients to understand the concepts I'm peddling, but Alan already knew what I was talking about, which is unusual for an engineer! Even the most seasoned advertising directors learned a few tricks from him – he always had a fresh angle.'

The same off-the-wall mentality fuelled the 2000 Vodacom 4U campaign, which introduced per-second billing whereby subscribers would only pay for the actual seconds of airtime used instead of the full minute. The advertisement's byline, 'Make every second count', was linked to extraordinary images of a newborn baby bungee-jumping using its own umbilical cord. Of course, the visuals were largely computer-generated with a real baby's facial expressions digitally blended onto the body of an ultra-realistic 'stunt double' baby doll. The end result: a newborn with a taste for adventure and not a second to waste.

The most surprising aspect of the baby-bungee-jumping ad was the popularity of the music. The soundtrack was initially a song called 'Today', by Smashing Pumpkins, but the band's front man turned down the request to use the song. Draftfcb then roped in a team to write and perform an original score. What the team came up with wasn't even a song – just 40 seconds of words and music meant to sound like a song. Within days after the ad was aired on television, music stores were inundated with calls from people asking for the CD. The musicians were called back to complete the song, which was released under the name BEAM, an acronym of the team members' first names – Brett, Eion, Alistair and Mike. The track was as successful as the original sound bite, climbing to the fifth spot on 5FM's charts within weeks.

The follow-up commercial featuring the same intrepid baby, this time diving into a crowd of youngsters at a nightclub, was just as popular. 'Make every second count' became a huge money-spinner – it was the second-most successful product launched after prepaid. By the end of 2002, Vodacom 4U had signed on 3.5 million subscribers.

In 2005, Draftfcb was asked to come up with a new concept for Vodacom's Vodafone Live! technology, a service that gave subscribers access to almost anything on their cellphones, from songs, images and videos to sports, news and games. The target market was the YAFS – the Young Active Fun South Africans.

The proposed solution came in the form of a meerkat named Mo (short for Maurice). Alan didn't like the original meerkat.

'He's too lifelike and ugly,' Alan told the creative director. 'We need to have a Disney meerkat. Donald Duck doesn't look like a duck, does he? So Mo can't look like a meerkat.'

Mo the Meerkat was redesigned within 24 hours, transformed into an animated creature given to salacious dance sequences and general full-on partying. Mo's first TV appearance featured an impromptu striptease to the tune of Hot Chocolate's 'You Sexy Thing', performed in front of an astonished young woman sitting on her sofa. South African viewers loved the concept so much that they gave the ad a phenomenal 9.24 likeability rating – with 57% of the target audience giving it 10 out of 10. To date, this score has not been bettered by any other Vodacom commercial.

However, there was also a Mo the Meerkat hate club – to them he was nothing more than 'an irritating little shit', as Alan puts it. But since the naysayers were, generally speaking, an older, more conservative bunch (that is, they were most definitely not YAFS), Alan was more amused than alarmed by their venomous dislike of the Vodacom mascot. The important thing was that Mo kept the Vodacom brand fresh and exciting.

The 'Leeuloop' (Lion Walk) advertisement, made for the Afrikaans-speaking community, displayed the same irreverence and risqué humour of the Mo featurettes. Alan had decided that the way to reach the Afrikaans-speaking community was to use one of the popular Afrikaans music hits. But he knew nothing about Afrikaans music, so he turned to his fiancée, Surina, and her son, Chris, for help. They put together a compilation of songs and 'Leeuloop' immediately appealed to him.

Draftfcb was asked to design a 60-second branding ad around the music. It had to amuse people in Vodacom's usual style. Draftfcb approached the original artist, Robbie Wessels, to perform his song with the Blue Bulls cheerleaders as back-up dancers. The 'Leeuloop' – a dance allegedly performed by inebriated, slightly deranged men – gave Vodacom another hit and made Robbie Wessels the top Afrikaans artist in the country. He was booked out for three years after the commercial was aired, but no one wanted to hear anything else except 'Leeuloop'. Shortly afterwards, the

NG Kerk (Dutch Reformed Church) objected to the sexual connotations it contained and Alan agreed to drop the commercial. The fact that the designers had earlier been instructed to edit the rearview shot of the lion's swinging testicles – the lion had a walk-on part in the advert – had, sadly, not been enough. However, Vodacom had already benefited enormously from running the ad. It was played at every rugby match over and over again, while the accompanying ad played on the big screen. It almost became the Blue Bulls' *haka*.

TV wasn't the only medium Alan used to promote Vodacom; he also allocated a significant amount of time and money to billboard advertising. Other than the Cape Town billboard displaying the words 'Welcome to Cape Town, where a cloud covers the mountain and we cover the rest', there was Johannesburg's 'Welcome to Johannesburg. We hope you enjoy your say', which was erected just before the World Summit delegates arrived in the city. This billboard replaced the ruder but much funnier, 'Welcome to Johannesburg. You cover your ass, we'll cover the rest'. Mostly, the billboard drew a lot of laughs, but Alan was forced to take it down as the powers that be felt it was not a positive reflection of the city for prospective tourists.

Motorists were blown away by the billboard in windy Port Elizabeth displaying the words 'Find out if there's wind about' and what appeared to be a construction worker clinging for dear life to a Vodacom billboard. As they drew closer they realised it was a cheeky advertisement by Vodacom to promote its weather service.

The tourist authorities were not amused since they were continually trying to convince the public that Port Elizabeth's nickname, the 'Windy City', was a misnomer. But the students loved it. They kept stealing the mannequin, which irritated the maintenance team. Alan told the maintenance team to let the students take the mannequin and keep replacing it. By this time, it had probably become a tradition or a rite of passage at the university. He wanted them to have it; after all, they were also his customers.

Vodacom's Emergency Service billboard also featured a worker in distress, though this time the mannequin resembled a painter in the same compromised position with his ladder dangling just out of reach. The only text on the billboard reads 'Emergency 112'.

With minimal text, huge lettering, an eye-catching logo and striking humorous three-dimensional visuals, Vodacom's billboard campaigns were immediately noticeable and lived on in the minds of the public long after they had been taken down.

In an August 2007 Markinor survey, Vodacom retained its top spot for Best Advertisements and Best Telecoms Provider in South Africa. It was also voted the company that did the most for community upliftment, and was second only to Coca-Cola as the country's favourite brand. The year before, in a survey of 600 companies in 25 countries undertaken by the International Reputation Institute, Vodacom ranked 52nd worldwide out of 600 companies in 25 countries.

What is the reason that Vodacom's brand has found favour across such a wide audience?

'While the message remains consistent,' says Alan, 'the Vodacom brand is warm, humorous, unpretentious and in touch with all of its 33 million customers.'

Alan's belief in the power of advertising to capture the hearts and minds of the South African public was total. He was irritated if someone complained about or questioned the money he invested in the marketing campaigns, because it appeared to him such an illogical, even pointless objection. Alan's position on advertising is best summed up in the words of Thomas Jefferson, the third president of the USA, who said: 'The man who stops advertising to save money is like the man who stops the clock to save time.'

Alan with his mother, Andronette, in 1952.

Alan with his father, Alan John Alexander, in 1953.

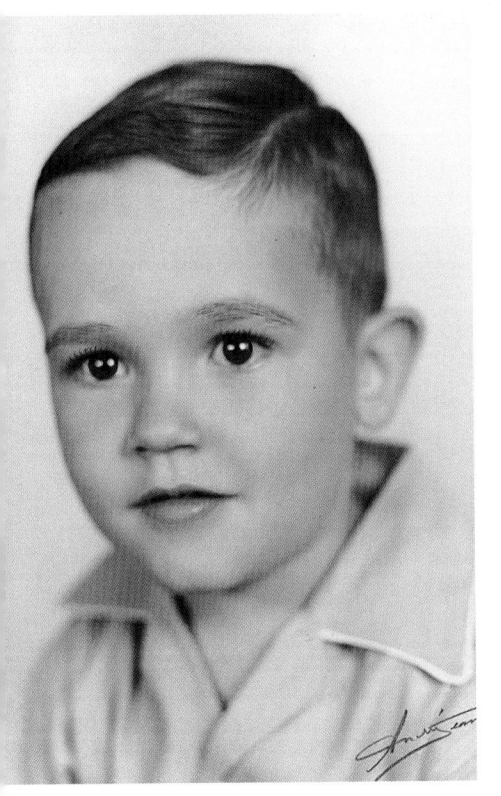

Alan in 1955, age three.

Alan with his brothers Christopher, Anthony and Terence in 1959. The calipers had just been removed from Alan's leg.

Alan joined the Navy for a year in 1970.

Alan's wedding day in 1975. Alan John Alexander and Andronette with their four sons: (left to right) Terence, Anthony, Alan and Christopher.

Alan presents Leon Crouse, Vodacom CFO, with a bronze spotted eagle owl at Leon's farewell function.

From left to right: Alan, Lord Ian MacLaurin (chairman of Tesco, the Vodafone Group and Vodafone Foundation), Phil Williams (Vodafone board), and Andrew Mthembu (Vodacom MD) pay a visit to the well-known Wandie's Place in Soweto.

Sir Christopher Gent, ex Vodafone CEO (second from right), hands over the Vodafone reins to Arun Sarin (first left) in 2004, pictured with (from left to right) Alan, Dr Ivy Matsepe-Casaburri (Minister of Communications), Thabo Mbeki (then President of South Africa) and Phil Williams (Vodafone board).

The opening of the newly refurbished Wynberg Magistrate's Court in 2001. From left to right: Steve Tshwete (Minister of Safety and Security), Joan Joffe (Vodacom's Corporate Relations Executive), Stella Sigcau (Minister of Public Works), Dr Penuell Maduna (Minister of Justice and Constitutional Development) and Alan.

Alan with Michael de Pinna (left) and Bankole Omotoso of Yebo Gogo fame.

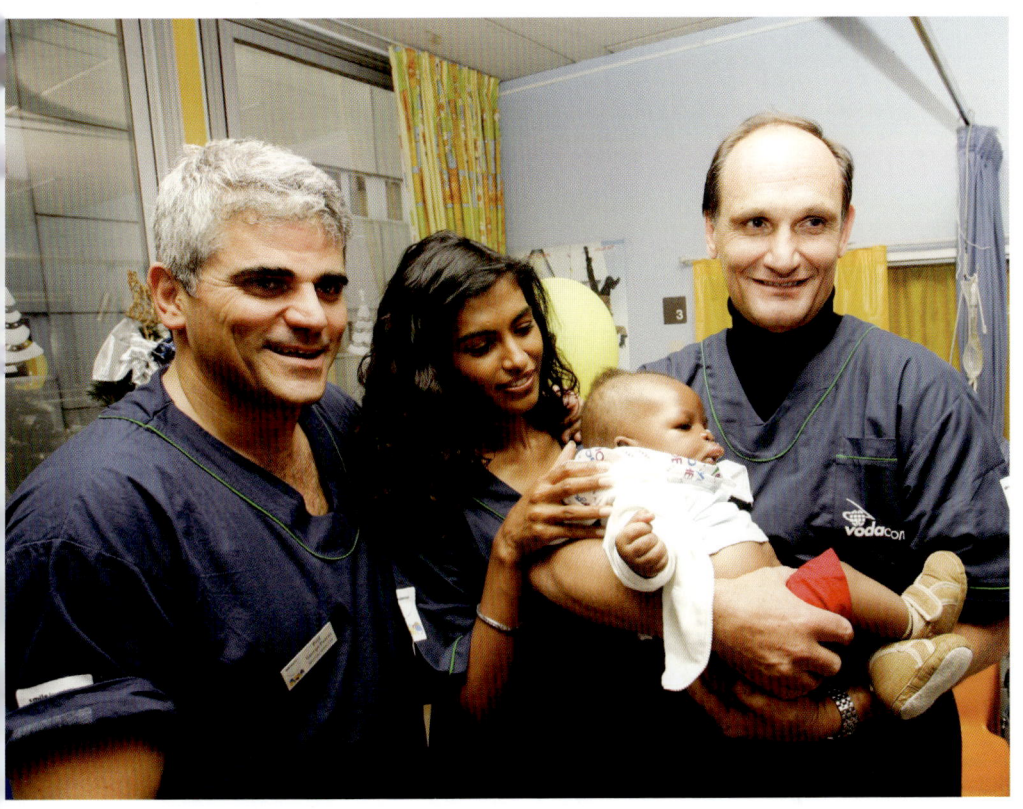

Dr George Psaras, Kerishnie Naicker and Alan pictured with a baby who had just undergone cleft palate surgery.

From left to right: Shameel Joosub, Pieter Uys, Alan and Jacob Zuma.

Wendy Luhabe, the Vodacom board chairperson (2000 to 2005), presents Alan with an Excellence Award on his tenth anniversary at Vodacom.

Nelson Mandela arrives at Vodacom Corporate Park to wish Alan a happy birthday in May 2006.

Alan with his sons – Nicholas (left), Alan Thomas and Matthew (right) – in 2006 after receiving his honorary Doctorate of Business Leadership from the University of South Africa in recognition of 'his remarkable contribution to the world of business'.

Alan and Surina on their wedding day in September 2008, flanked by Irmilee Uys (left) and Americo da Silva (right).

NELSON MANDELA

September 2008

Alan Knott-Craig
Chief Executive
Vodacom

Dear Alan,

It is with sadness that we join the Vodacom family in bidding farewell to you. You have not only built the company and led a team to become "South Africa's number one cellular network" but also distinguished yourself as an outstanding individual with leadership and vision.

Since our early days in the Presidency, we depended on your support and our requests for you to be involved in our projects never fell on deaf ears. We thank you for that support and investing in our country and its future with those efforts. Few business leaders have shown the commitment you demonstrated and even though the contributions always rooted from Vodacom, we know we owe it to your influence and determination to uplift rural communities and eradicate poverty. Your unselfish approach, eagerness and readiness to help have improved millions of lives and we thank you for that.

Although we are bidding farewell to you, we hope that when we meet again, it will be in a different capacity and doubt that you are destined for "retirement" any time soon. However, we join many of your friends and associates in thanking you for the sterling job you did at Vodacom. Indeed, we are proud of you and you should be proud of your achievements.

We hope at least with your new status you will have the time to enjoy with your lovely new wife. We look forward to seeing you and Surina soon.

Best wishes

N R Mandela

Founder: Mr N R Mandela   **Chairperson:** Professor G J Gerwel   **Chief Executive:** Mr Achmat Dangor   **Executive Assistant:** Zelda la Grang

IT Number: 9259/99   PBO Number: 034-681-NPO   Vat Number: 4590213601
PRIVATE BAG X70 000, HOUGHTON, 2041, SOUTH AFRICA
Tel +27 11 728 1000   Fax +27 728 1111
Website: www.nelsonmandela.org

Nelson Mandela's farewell letter to Alan.

Bringing Entertainment to Millions
1995 to 2008

It's easy to make a buck. It's a lot tougher to make a difference.
Tom Brokaw

There were three highlights of the 1995 Rugby World Cup that Alan will never forget as he sat in the crowd at Ellis Park that day. 'The first thing that caught my attention, and that of everyone else in the stands, was the Boeing decked out in South African colours that flew over the stadium. It was as if the hand of God had swept over the spectators. It flew so low every individual felt they could touch it, and that's when the All Blacks lost their first ten points. Then Madiba walked onto the field wearing the No. 6 Springbok jersey. Those 86 000 mostly white spectators would have died for him right there and then. This gesture wrecked the All Blacks' chances of winning from the start. And, of course, there was Joel Stransky's drop kick that happened right in front of me. It was arguably the Best Big Moment in South African rugby for me – and for Joel. The Rugby World Cup of 1995 was one of the greatest sporting events in South African history that decade, and I was there – Vodacom was there.'

Vodacom had signed up as the official cellular supplier to the national rugby squad, providing each Springbok with a three-year airtime contract and a limited edition Motorola Flag cellphone. Under the banner of '*Yebo-Go-Go*', the Vodacom brand had gained a great deal of positive exposure from the Rugby World Cup, but on the day of the Springboks' victory Alan had no thought for Vodacom; he had no thought for anything except for what the game had meant to South Africa.

Vodacom's involvement in sports sponsorship began in 1995 with a dinner invitation from Tokyo Sexwale, who was at the time the premier of Gauteng province. Alan was sure he had been placed next to him at the dinner table for a reason, and he soon found out what it was. Tokyo asked Alan if Vodacom would invest R1.6 million in Soweto's FNB Stadium, which was badly in need of refurbishment if it was to serve as the main venue for the 1996 African Cup of Nations soccer tournament. It was a lot of money for Vodacom in those days, but Alan was delighted to be able to help and agreed to sponsor the security project for the stadium, without consulting his shareholders – again.

Bafana Bafana won the African Cup of Nations the year after Amabokke won the Rugby World Cup, beating Tunisia 2–0 in the final, watched by a capacity crowd of 80 000 people at the fully restored FNB Stadium. Madiba was on the field when the final whistle blew to congratulate captain Nick Tovey and the team, to the rapturous delight of the crowd. That year, Madiba put a spell on the country and the world. South Africans were united in their joy. The country had weathered the initial transition to a democracy and the victories on the sports field lifted their spirits. It made people rise above their differences to embrace a common purpose.

The publicity associated with sporting events had profiled the Vodacom brand to great effect, making it a household name within a short space of time. When the South African Olympic Games team travelled to America for the 1996 Atlanta Games, it did so with a R2.5 million Vodacom sponsorship. Alan had provided the athletes with cellphones and free airtime, a gesture warmly welcomed by the competitors for whom keeping in touch with family and friends back home might otherwise have been an unaffordable luxury. Alan was as delighted as anyone watching when Josia Thugwane won the Men's Marathon – he was the first black South African athlete to win an Olympic gold. At the same games, the peerless Penny Heyns won double gold for the 100-metre and 200-metre breaststroke. In the South African VIP tent, Alan met Penny and signed her up to promote the Vodacom brand, with Sam Ramsamy, the South African Olympic Committee chairman and a dear friend of Alan's, looking on. 'Everything came together,' says Alan. 'Nothing could touch us.'

Alan is perhaps even prouder of Vodacom's more recent sponsorship of the South African Paralympians who participated in the Beijing Paralympics of 2008. The South African team was superb, garnering twelve gold, three silver and six bronze medals, and finishing sixth overall. The sportsmen and -women who participated in the Beijing Paralympics displayed a sporting prowess that few had ever seen before. Natalie du Toit, Ernst van Dyk, Fanie Lombard, Hilton Langenhoven and the rest of the squad exceeded all expectations. Oscar Pistorius, gold medallist in the 400-metre sprint, said: 'The world has to know that we South Africans are winners.'

The country's superb performance on the international sports arena, spurred Alan to look for further opportunities where Vodacom could invest in sport.

Because of his particular passion for cricket, Alan was keen to secure Vodacom's involvement in the game in some way or another. It was also a sport with a huge following in the country, which meant that Vodacom would have access to a captive market. His discussions with South Africa's cricket chief, Ali Bacher, were productive and it was agreed that Vodacom would renovate the Centurion Cricket Park Stadium in Pretoria, provide the national team with cellphone services and invest in training talented up-and-coming youngsters.

The relationship, however, was destined to collapse. Alan discovered that a deal had been signed with MTN, notwithstanding the contract with Vodacom. Disappointed by the cricket administration's behaviour, Alan began legal proceedings, though the parties eventually reached an out-of-court settlement. The experience hurt Alan, for he had acted in good faith and with a genuine desire to help.

But he was not downcast for long. Instead, he set himself the task of making Vodacom the country's biggest and best supporter of South African rugby.

Today, Vodacom sponsors three of South Africa's rugby union teams: the Pretoria-based Blue Bulls, Bloemfontein's Cheetahs, and Cape Town's Western Province Stormers. The company's involvement goes much further than this, however, since it is also the principal sponsor of the Tri-Nations tournament, the Super 14 and the Vodacom Cup, in addition to being the official cellular network supplier to South African Rugby.

Alan was always surprised and appreciative of the fact that the Springbok rugby coaches, Nick Mallett, Jake White and Peter de Villiers, all took it upon themselves to visit him regularly to share their strategy for the Springboks. It was a courtesy that reflected their successes as national coaches.

Vodacom's input at all levels of the game is appreciated everywhere, but perhaps nowhere more warmly than in Pretoria, home of the Blue Bulls. Loftus Versfeld (or simply 'Loftus' for many Bulls fans) is the stadium that hosts the Bulls' home games and it takes its name from Robert Owen Loftus Versfeld, a key figure in Pretoria's sporting history. In more recent times, however, the stadium's name was altered to include the name of the main sponsor. So, from 1998 to 2003 it was called Minolta Loftus, and then, from 2003 to 2005, Securicor Loftus. When Alan secured sponsorship of the stadium, most locals were resigned to the inevitability of a third name change. But Alan did the exact opposite: he recommended reinstatement of the original name, since he appreciated the historical and cultural significance it held for the local community.

By reinstating the name 'Loftus Versfeld', Vodacom went straight to the hearts of the Blue Bulls faithful. As one reporter put it: 'No praise can be too great for Vodacom after [its] earth-shattering announcement. For the first time, a sponsor is thinking further than its nose, and thinking about the culture, the heritage and the history of the sport.'[1] It was hailed a brilliant marketing move and the returns were excellent for Vodacom. Alan, however, does not make any claims to brilliance; his more modest appraisal is: 'I simply did what the community wanted me to do; and they weren't asking for much, were they?'

The establishment of the Vodacom Stadium in Bloemfontein and the sponsorship of the Free State Cheetahs was the result of a meeting between the Free State rugby boss, Harold Verster, and Alan, an introduction arranged by Anthea van Heerden. It did not take long to clinch the deal, which became one of Vodacom's most successful sponsorships, boosting Vodacom's market share to close on 70% in the Free State. The local supporters were loyal to their team and loyal to Vodacom.

Under the guidance of Andrew Mthembu, Vodacom became involved in soccer sponsorship. The sport has a tremendous black following in the country and Alan was not about to neglect this market. For the last fifteen years, Vodacom has sponsored Orlando Pirates, Kaiser Chiefs and Bloemfontein Celtic, three of the country's Premier Soccer League (PSL) teams. Irvin Khoza and Kaiser Motaung, who represented Orlando Pirates and Kaiser Chiefs respectively, maintain that the teams' fans account for 80% of the soccer following in the country.

Alan wanted Vodacom to be involved in sport sponsorship across the country, but for this sponsorship to be effective, it had to be harnessed to sports that had high intensity, high emotion, high loyalty and a huge following. These were sports that were embedded in everyone's hearts and minds, which is the reason that soccer and rugby became so important to Vodacom, and vice versa.

It was interesting for Alan to note that the support for sport varied from one region to another. At the coast, sponsorship of rugby and soccer is less likely to impact on market share than sponsoring the National Sea Rescue Institute (NSRI) and big beach days. In Durban and Cape Town, Vodacom sponsored the typical pursuits of South Africa's coastal communities, such as life-saving, volleyball and surfing programmes. After watching a locally organised beach clean-up at Boggomsbaai one year, Alan decided to introduce a national beach clean-up each December. Hundreds of young students decked out in Vodacom T-shirts would sweep along the beaches twice a day, which was much appreciated by beach lovers.

Alan's association with Ian Weinberger and the NSRI has spanned many years and saved many lives. And although less visible than most of the sponsorships he initiated, Alan is proud of the hi-tech boats of the NSRI with their bold Vodacom branding and brave volunteer crews. Alan has even had the opportunity of experiencing first-hand the exceptional service rendered by the NSRI. At one stage, he would often head down to the coast to test his sailing prowess against the waves in his 41-foot cutter sloop, *Eilean Taigh* ('Island Home' in Gaelic). In the summer of 2003, when Alan was sailing *Eilean Taigh* in Mossel Bay, the gentle 10-knot breeze abruptly whipped up to more than 40 knots. Suddenly, one of the ropes snapped and the spinnaker rope jammed into the genoa. Alan immediately summoned the NSRI volunteers who calmly straightened the sails in the roaring wind. Alan was impressed with their professionalism and bravery, confirming that they more than deserved any form of sponsorship.

There were other sports that Alan simply could not neglect. Golf is a fast-growing leisure activity that attracts the participation of the more affluent, generating a substantial amount of advertising and commercial activity. Alan looked beyond sponsoring the high-profile golf tournaments, and invested in the Caddy Foundation, which provides training in practical and theoretical aspects of the game, and life skills such as literacy and financial planning. A number of caddies who have gone through the programme have gone on to become professional instructors and even club managers.

Round seven of the 1998 Superbike World Championships was held at Kyalami, courtesy of Vodacom sponsorship, which included a round of the World Supersport Series for 600cc motorcyles and the International Sports Racing series. But Alan was after the Formula One Grand Prix to be held in 1999. Bernie Ecclestone, owner of the Grand Prix, one-tickie high and very wealthy, asked Alan if he could arrange for him to meet Mandela. Bernie always gets what Bernie wants, but he couldn't easily get to see Mandela. Alan, through Selwyn Nathan, made a deal with him: Bernie would bring the Grand Prix to South Africa and Alan would arrange for him to have lunch with Mandela. Bernie didn't hesitate; the deal was done. He was ecstatic at being in Madiba's presence and even parted with some money for one of Madiba's many causes. 'There were no free lunches with President Mandela at the Union Buildings,' Alan smiles. 'But in the end, the Grand Prix was too expensive for us to bring to South Africa.'

In 2003, at the urging of Mthobi Tyamzashe, the Director General of Sport, Alan put R27 million into boxing, which was comfortably the biggest investment ever made in the sport. At the announcement of the sponsorship Yebo Gogo celebrity, Michael de Pinna, took to the ring singing, to the delight of the audience. World heavyweight champion, Corrie Sanders, also 'fought' against Louis van Winkel as part of the festivities. The referee was internationally acclaimed Stan Christodoulou.

Alan's wish to bring as many sporting activities to as many people as possible was, in the 1990s, exactly what the new ANC government wanted to hear. The ANC's first Minister for Sport and Recreation, Steve Tshwete, was committed to deracialising sport in the country and welcomed Vodacom's input, which he thought even more laudable considering the company had only been in existence a short while. Alan had many dealings with Steve, and he was a man Alan admired and respected. He came across as a 'rough-and-ready' type of person, but to Alan he was one of the top three gentlemen in politics in the country, someone with no pretences.

Another area in which Alan thought Vodacom could make a contribution was in the arts, and for him, the arts meant music. From the childhood songs his father had played or sang, to the wonderful Cape Town Philharmonic Sunday concerts he had attended while a student at UCT, Alan had always loved music, and he thought it a pity that local music did not have a higher profile. So, when John Roos of the University of South Africa (Unisa) asked Alan if he would be interested in funding its International Music Competitions, he jumped at the chance.

The Unisa International Music Competitions are the only recognised events of their kind on the African continent and have attracted more than 600 first-class musicians from 40 countries. They are rated as five-star events and placed in the same category as Moscow's International Tchaikovsky Competition, the Queen Elisabeth Competition in Belgium and the Van Cliburn International Piano Competition in Texas. To this day, most of the people who write to thank Alan are from the Unisa Music Competitions, which Vodacom has sponsored since 2000.

When Alan opened Vodaworld, he decided to arrange a special concert. With the expert help and support of Hazel Feldman, the young and vibrant violinist Vanessa Mae, arrived with her mother and an entourage of note to play at Vodaworld. Her performances left audiences in raptures, while the purists despaired at her massacre of the violin. Either way, it was a unique and awe-inspiring performance, which Alan had great pleasure in orchestrating.

But the music event that Alan cherishes the most is the Bravo Africa Concert, which, once more with Hazel, brought the Three Tenors – Luciano Pavarotti, José Carreras and Placido Domingo – to South Africa in April 1999. The show, which Vodacom co-sponsored, was a farewell gift to Mandela as his presidency came to an end, and it was held in the majestic grounds of the Union Buildings in Pretoria. The singers were accompanied by a 300-strong choir and the 110-piece South African National Symphony Orchestra. Alan was honoured to meet the three performers. He recalls Carreras as 'clever and funny', Domingo as 'laid-back', and Pavarotti as 'demanding' – an intriguing observation that he steadfastly refuses to elaborate upon.

Alan's investment in sport and the arts not only brought entertainment to millions through live events and television broadcasts; it transformed the company into something more than just a cellular operator: Vodacom became a brand with which people found an affinity.

The Power to do Good
1994 to 2008

*Remember there's no such thing as a small act of kindness. Every act creates
a ripple with no logical end.*
Scott Adams

Alan believes that Vodacom is a company with heart, a company with employees who are inspired to apply energy, skills and resources to help others. Instead of relying only on uncoordinated efforts at social development, Alan's vision was to create a consolidated, meaningful social-development drive. To this end, the Vodacom Foundation came into being as an organisation that would engage in social projects to benefit individuals, groups and communities in need of assistance.

The idea for the Foundation began to take shape during a lengthy lunch-time conversation Alan had with Madiba. It was Alan's second invitation to the Union Buildings but he felt no less nervous than the first. However, his anxiety melted away almost immediately when Madiba extended his hand to Alan, making him feel like an old friend.

The conversation ebbed and flowed naturally for a while. Then Madiba leaned across the table towards Alan and said, 'I would like Vodacom to help us build a school.'

'Where do you want it?' replied Alan instantly.

'Or a clinic,' added Madiba, with a chuckle.

'No problem, we'll do both,' said Alan spontaneously.

Mandela's wish was to improve the lives of the people who lived in the rural area of Bizana, situated in a beautiful valley in the Transkei where he grew up. The Transkei (now the Eastern Cape province) was a *Bantustan* under apartheid – a homeland established by the apartheid government for Xhosa-speaking Africans – which suffered from an almost complete lack of economic and social investment. Although the term 'homeland' had been abolished, the area remained impoverished and its people were in desperate need of schools, hospitals, clinics and basic services.

Alan had agreed to Madiba's proposition without giving a thought to the fact that he would need his shareholders' permission to spend money on the project. But he knew they would not deny a request from Madiba. The president was asking Vodacom to invest in a rural community for the common good. It wasn't a business proposition; it was a straightforward request for help.

And so Alan committed Vodacom to building Cangci Comprehensive Technical High School in Bizana, a poverty-stricken area with a high unemployment rate, severe public health problems and an acute lack of educational facilities. The construction of the school was no easy task; the site chosen had no running water or electricity and the only road was a track winding through the grasslands, leading to the village. The school was built using solar power and a water pump was installed to secure running water. By 1997, the brand new school, along with an associated pre-primary school at Amapisi and a health clinic, were completed. The high school would also serve as a community and adult-education centre. In building the school, the project had made use of and developed skills in the local community, and provided facilities to grow skills further. Alan was satisfied that Vodacom's R12 million investment had been worthwhile.

The old school building – a dilapidated, three-room structure with no equipment and inadequate facilities – was gone; in its place was a ten-classroom school that could accommodate 500 pupils, complete with audio-visual equipment, computers, a science laboratory, a library, a sports field, an administration block and living accommodation for up to eight teachers. In addition to the academic opportunities the new school offered, its computer facilities gave students the chance to interact and engage with the outside world in a way previously unimaginable.

As Alan flew over Bizana on his way to the official opening, he looked down and saw people dotted all along the footpaths that converged at a central point where the ceremony was being held. The occasion was presided over by Chief Daliwonga Mlindazwe (who brought his lounge suite into the tent that had been specially set up for the occasion). Nelson Mandela was the guest of honour. Once more, Alan was struck by Mandela's gracious behaviour, in particular, the manner in which he paid his respects to the Chief as an 'ordinary' citizen, sincerely and seriously. Alan followed suit, hoping that his show of respect would not be thought servile or ingratiating. He didn't disappoint Chief Mlindazwe, who was delighted to see that Alan, like himself, had his arm in a sling (Alan's arm had recently been operated on; the Chief's had been damaged in a car accident). So Alan slipped off his fancy sling and gave it to his host, just as boys exchange toys. One of Alan's favourite memories is that of an old man in the crowd who had spotted Madiba. It was the first time he had seen Madiba in the flesh and his whole face lit up as he gripped Madiba's hand with delight.

It was sad that the school, which was intended to be a beacon of inspiration for the community, initially failed to provide a good education for its children. At the end of the first academic year most students failed their exams, mainly due to the poor quality of the tuition they had received. 'Teaching the teachers' is a common theme in the provision of public education, and Vodacom wasted no time in introducing a development programme for Cangci's teaching staff. Alan was heartened to see the pass rate go up to 90% the following year. Bizana was an important project for Alan, not only because Madiba had personally asked him to take it on, but because the future of so many children depended on the school. It wasn't just a question of throwing money at the project; the school had to produce good results, and it had to be sustainable.

The rejuvenation of Bizana led to many more projects of a similar nature. 'Once Bizana was finished, we knew we couldn't stop there,' says Alan. 'Madiba had set us on our way, but we had no idea how far he wanted us to go. So we kept on looking for new projects. But I knew we had to organise our activities around a more proactive response and that we would need to forge some smart partnerships for greater impact.'

Eventually, after constant urging on the part of Phil Williams, the Vodacom Foundation was set up in 1999 to manage social investment initiatives. Initially, Joan Joffe headed up the Foundation, but she had her hands full with corporate relations, and Alan needed someone who would focus exclusively on the Foundation's projects. Mthobi Tyamzashe ultimately became that person. Alan had dealt with him as the Director General of Sport and had found him to be a personable, dedicated man.

'With Alan I knew I wasn't just getting a boss,' says Mthobi. 'My father died when I was six months old so I adopted Alan as my father. The Vodacom Foundation was more than just a job – it became my family.'

The Foundation's bursary scheme gives above-average scholars and those from disadvantaged backgrounds the financial help they need to study at university. Due to the constant need for Vodacom and South Africa to develop telecommunication-related skills in order to keep pace with the rest of the world, bursaries are awarded to students who are interested in or already engaged in, information technology, computer science, computer engineering, electrical or electronic engineering, law, internal auditing, financial management and accountancy. These students are given the chance to attend a Vodaworld 'open day', where they explore topics with a particular bearing on telecommunications-industry jobs, such as cellular fraud, industry regulations and social investment.

Small gestures by the Foundation are sometimes as important as large financial investments, such as providing children with bicycles so that they don't have to walk long distances to school, which would motivate the learners to improve their end-of-year results. With the help of Afrobike, a non-governmental organisation that promotes cycling as a form of low-cost transport, Vodacom donated over 300 bikes to Maletsana Intermediate School in rural Limpopo. The bikes were sold or rented to the children for a nominal fee to generate funds for maintenance of the bikes and to motivate the children to take care of them. A group of community members also attended a bicycle mechanics workshop and a container was donated to serve as a workshop where children could have their bikes repaired. With all projects, sustainability, skills development and benefits for the wider community are key elements.

As the Foundation grew in size and influence, the number of educational projects it funded also increased. Amongst others, an E-learning and Resource Centre was established, two centres for each of South Africa's nine provinces, where local people learn or develop their computer skills using recycled computers provided by the Foundation.

The Jabavu Public Library and Skills Centre was opened in Soweto in 2008, offering literacy courses, free Internet access, a business corner and an audio-visual section, as well as access to thousands of library books. Its Skills Centre runs baking, sewing and computer literacy courses. Alan had been incredulous that Soweto did not have a library. It was incomprehensible to him that the children in the township did not have access to books, particularly since he had learned to love reading in Oudtshoorn as a child. 'For a child to be denied access to books is to deny a child a life,' he says. The University of Fort Hare Multi-Media Centre in the Eastern Cape provides IT facilities to its 7 000 students, but is of particular relevance and benefit to the lecturers and students of the university's Department of Communication. These projects are but a few of the Vodacom Foundation's ongoing initiatives to contribute to educational development.

The company's Corporate Social Investment (CSI) projects, which the Foundation administers, has a much broader remit than simply education. One morning, out of the blue, Steve Tshwete phoned Alan and asked if they could meet. Alan had worked closely with Steve during Mandela's presidency, when Steve had been Minister of Sport and Recreation. Now, under President Thabo Mbeki's leadership, Steve served as Minister of Safety and Security. Alan genuinely liked Steve whom he believed to be a highly principled man – someone who worked tirelessly to improve the lives of others.

When they met, Steve explained that he needed Alan's help: the Wynberg Magistrate's Court and Police Station in Alexandra, near Sandton, was in urgent need of renovation and Steve believed Vodacom might provide the solution. Alan was eager to do what he could and said that he would go and see for himself how bad things were. Both the courthouse and the police station were in a shocking state of disrepair. Apart from the broken windows, peeling paintwork, shoddy furniture, inadequate lighting and lack of resources (there were no fax machines or computers), it was the air of negativity and apathy that struck Alan most forcibly.

'Everyone looked fed up,' he says. 'I got the feeling that they'd stopped believing things would ever get better so they'd given up. And working in those conditions, who could blame them?'

Some of the staff members told Alan that they felt unsafe at work since there wasn't any proper security and the buildings could be easily broken into. When Alan heard that the magistrate's car was constantly being stolen and that he was often verbally abused and threatened by those he had sentenced, he knew he couldn't walk away.

The two buildings were painted, cleaned and repaired; better lighting and office furniture bought; CCTV and panic buttons installed; an electric fence was erected around the perimeter of the site and security guards were hired to keep watch over the cars. The design of the courtroom was altered so that convicted criminals no longer passed directly in front of the magistrate after they had been convicted. New computers were delivered – and stolen the same night! – so it was agreed that their replacements would be locked in the strong room at night. Alan was especially proud of the new trauma centre where victims of crime could give their statements in private and receive much-needed counselling.

The improvements raised staff morale and efficiency considerably. Local residents no longer regarded the place as threatening and reported incidents of crime willingly. The local community was pleased to see that its law and order officials were being treated with the respect they deserved, which in turn increased the public's confidence in them.

Vodacom handed the buildings over to the state to maintain, but after a year, signs of neglect started showing. Steve called Alan again to a meeting in Cape Town and asked that Vodacom take over the maintenance for the next five years. As a rule, Vodacom did not get involved in maintenance, but Alan decided to intervene.

'This changed our mindset,' he says. 'We couldn't just build a structure and then allow it to go to ruin. In the interests of sustainability, we put a maintenance plan in place for all our projects so that our hard work would not be for nothing.'

On the other side of the prison bars, Vodacom also invested money into improving the lives of convicted criminals by working in conjunction with Readucate, a long-established NGO dedicated to improving literacy levels in disadvantaged communities. By turning prisons into institutions of learning, inmates are empowered to think more positively about themselves and about life outside prison. Vodacom's investment, through the efforts of Readucate, ensured that at least 600 prisoners in Gauteng received literacy training in the hope of making them more employable once released.

'Becoming literate gives a person dignity,' remarks Alan. 'It gives them hope that they can change the course of their lives for something better. By contributing to educating prisoners we feel we can make a contribution to reducing crime in society by giving offenders the skills to become useful citizens outside the prison walls.'

Vodacom became involved in many small projects that made a huge difference to people's lives. Alan was surprised and inspired to learn that there are so many selfless individuals running day-care centres, hospices and shelters for battered women and children on a shoestring budget. It prompted him to mobilise the Foundation to build the first and only Child Abuse Prevention Centre at the time. A sum of R5 million was also donated to prevent women and child abuse, part of which established three *thuthulezas* (places of comfort), which offer counselling to rape victims. Red Nose Day in South Africa is legendary, and Vodacom became one of its sponsors. Established in 1989, the initiative uses the theme of comic relief to raise funds for child and family welfare. Besides taking care of abused children, it provides pre-school care, implements income-generating projects and focuses on poverty eradication.

After his heart attack in 2000 Alan became very aware of health issues. He wanted to make a contribution in the health sector that would make a difference to people's lives. The opportunity came along in the form of Netcare. Ryan Noach, chief operations director of Netcare, went to see Alan that year about an idea he had for an emergency service.

'What struck me about Alan,' remarks Ryan, 'was his ability to get things done. I especially enjoyed his impatience because once he made a decision it had to happen immediately, efficiently and perfectly. Everyone would race to do his bidding because if they didn't perform his temper could reduce them to tears.'

Despite Alan's autocratic style, Ryan was intrigued to note that the people around him almost deified him. He saw Alan as a transformational leader who changed the people and environment around him.

In 2006 when Alan had his second heart attack, he called Ryan, who arranged to have the medical cavalry on standby at the hospital, and so Ryan became his unofficial healthcare provider. 'I still get nervous today when I see his number on my cellphone,' he confesses, 'but I would be pissed off if he didn't call me if he needed help. I was involved in an organisation that looked after 5 million patients a year, but if Alan called and said he had a colleague, friend or shareholder that needed my help, be it here or in Africa, I would drop everything and personally see to it. And it's not an effort. He brings out the best in people, including me.'

In 2000 the Netcare/Vodacom emergency medical service partnership was created, with the establishment of the emergency number 082 911. It handled about 1 million emergency calls per year or 100 000 per month. It was the most-used emergency number in South Africa at one stage. A co-branding deal was also struck, whereby every medical emergency vehicle was branded with Netcare and Vodacom logos. Passion and commitment were the value proposition. Alan offered emergency medical services to every Vodacom subscriber at no additional cost. It was a tangible thing to do for people who were loyal to Vodacom. He promised to contribute to their well-being because they were his customers, a sentiment that was part of Vodacom's ethos.

Netcare also became Vodacom's partner in other health and medical initiatives, such as the Sight for Life Project and The Smile Foundation.

Hundreds of cataract patients who cannot afford the simple yet effective operation to restore their sight have been given hope through a programme sponsored by Vodacom in association with Netcare. Cataracts are the leading cause of blindness in developing countries, and in South Africa there are currently 160 000 people on the waiting list for the operation, with 10 000 added each year. Patients are selected throughout the country during Eye Awareness Week at the Pretoria Eye Institute, during which over 400 operations are performed, as well as other initiatives in Netcare hospitals throughout the year.

'If cataracts cause blindness in a person who supports a family of ten, that leaves ten individuals destitute because their breadwinner cannot provide for them,' says Alan. 'Imagine giving so many people back their livelihood.'

Mthobi remarks, 'It is our contribution to those who have been mothers and fathers to our people. They have shaped our society. Now we have the opportunity to thank them for their contribution by restoring their eyesight.'

Another project of which Alan is justifiably proud is the Smile Foundation, which is run by Marc Lubner. Thousands of children are born with facial abnormalities, such as a cleft lip, a facial injury or Moebius Syndrome, which causes facial paralysis and renders the child unable to smile. The disfigurements are frequently regarded as a form of evil by the community where the child is born and these children are often forced to endure a life of isolation.

'Helping to provide access to life-changing surgery that is usually out of reach for most South Africans is one of the most meaningful causes we have ever supported,' says Alan. 'I watched as the surgeon operated on a young child to repair a cleft palate and I was devastated to think what his future would be if he hadn't had the chance to repair his face. Without surgery this kid would be destroyed before he even had a chance at life. This investment will have a lasting effect.'

'There is no hope for these kids without surgery,' says Mthobi. 'They can't eat, can't talk, and are not accepted. People don't know that there is surgery available that can help them. We have helped to reconstruct hundreds of cleft palates – it has made a huge difference in so many people's lives.'

Alan is impressed with the dedicated and loving commitment of some celebrities to the Foundation's projects. People such as previous Miss South Africa winners Kerishnie Naidoo and Suzette van der Merwe, singing star Danny Kaye, and rugby star Schalk Burger are constant visitors and supporters, carrying balls and teddy bears and, more importantly, hugs and affection, for the children. In a unique sponsorship venture, Vodacom linked its passion for sport with its passion for helping people and launched the Tries for Smiles campaign. For every try scored by Vodacom's sponsored players during the Super 14 tournament, Vodacom undertook to donate R10 000 to the Smile Foundation, up to a limit of R2 million. 'It's such a fantastic idea,' says Schalk. 'I get to make a huge difference to someone's life by just doing my job.'

During a holiday Alan spent in the US, his brother, Chris, broached the subject of building a clinic in Johannesburg, under the leadership of a friend, Dr Rob Kinsley, to operate on children with heart defects. Kinsley, a paediatric thoracic surgeon in the Sunninghill Hospital in Johannesburg, would put together a team of surgeons and medical staff who would make the clinic an unrivalled facility. But a great deal of funding was required before they could bring their project to fruition. Alan took on the project through the Vodacom Foundation and The Walter Sisulu Clinic was established. Children now come from all over Africa to Dr Kinsley's clinic to 'get a new heart'.

'These children are just starting out; their lives have yet to be lived,' remarks Alan. 'All they and their families needed was the money; the care was ready and waiting for them. If Vodacom can do its bit to save these kids' lives, then great – they deserve a second chance.'

Vodacom's involvement in community development projects is not just limited to the Foundation. Within the company, its employees have started an initiative, driven by Suzette van der Merwe, known as Yebo Heroes. This involves people from the company giving their time to fix a building, a garden or computers. They redo the IT network in a police station, brighten up school yards, paint schools and bring in swings. They transform dustbowls into mini green belts. Sometimes they donate part of their salary or work in soup kitchens.

'It is an exceptional initiative,' says Alan, 'that is voluntary and well supported. We have a Yebo Heroes award to recognise the best team at our annual awards, but they do it because they love it.'

It's not only people that benefit from Vodacom's various sponsorship programmes; animals have been the recipients of aid in many forms. Vodacom is a member of the Peace Parks Foundation that aims to link trans-frontier conservation areas, and is a corporate member of the Worldwide Wildlife Fund in South Africa, of which Alan was one of the trustees. Vodacom funds the only full-time gene resource banking centre in Africa, which has developed a technique known as assisted reproduction technology as a conservation tool for the protection of Africa's threatened wildlife species. From the relocation of the Tuli elephants held captive in Brits, to cheetah research and supporting Ann Turner's efforts to save the Southern Ground Hornbill from extinction, Alan is proud of the way Vodacom has created a niche for itself where it can serve nature conservation effectively.

In the Introduction to the book Alan commissioned for the Vodacom Foundation, *The Power to do Good*, he says: 'The Vodacom Group has the ability to be a powerful force for good ... [It] has built a legacy that to my mind is one of our company's most important achievements in our fifteen years of existence. When we report that Vodacom has 35 million customers in five African countries, the truth is that behind that number are 35 million flesh and blood people living in communities where we do business. And if those communities flourish, so will we.'

A Cellular Disneyworld
1996 to 1998

We are creating a new experience. It starts with how you see the building from a distance.
Helmut Jahn

The idea for Vodaworld came to Alan during the 1996 Atlanta Olympics. He and Theo Rutstein took buses or cabs to the city's Centennial Olympic Stadium each day, which gave them time to observe the workings of a typical modern American metropolis. One of Alan's favourite sights was a huge mall where consumers could buy anything electronic under one roof. The mall seemed to draw people in, as if it had some invisible, yet irresistible magnetic power. To Alan, the mall always looked full, and he would watch the throngs of people coming and going with an almost hypnotic fascination.

'Look at that place, Theo!' Alan exclaimed. 'It's got everything electronic anyone could want. The people love it!'

Theo, his eyes also fixed on the mall, nodded. 'Yes, I know,' he agreed, 'but it's not just the shops they like; it's the whole experience of being there that does it.'

'Wouldn't it be great if we could have a cellular mall just like that,' remarked Alan. 'We could call it something like Vodaworld.'

The seed was sown. Alan and Theo began to talk and think about how Vodacom could do something along the same lines. Alan believed Vodacom was a pioneering enterprise – a company that led from the front and didn't back down from challenges. The concept of a 'cellular super mall' was exactly the type of possibility Vodacom should be exploring. Alan's success rate when it came to new ventures was, after all, good – the pre-launch advertising campaign, the distribution network, the highway-coverage programme; all of these 'outrageous' ideas had proved to be effective.

By now, the shareholders were accustomed to Alan's ambitious schemes. However, they were not keen to build what they considered a white elephant, in the middle of nowhere. They weren't convinced that people would drive for miles to buy a cellphone in a mall located in the middle of the bush. Alan insisted that it was time for Vodacom to implement another first. Although they may not always have liked or understood Alan's proposals (presented assuredly by him), they were prepared to let him go ahead with what might be another 'Knott-Craig special'. Alan could start building.

Theo was the only person who was enthusiastic about the idea. When he realised that Alan was serious about it, he recommended a group of architects to design the masterpiece and found the ideal property halfway between Pretoria and Johannesburg, in Midrand. At the time, Midrand was merely a stretch of farmland with no roads, no services and no communications. 'It will grow,' said Theo, so Alan took his advice and started the ball rolling.

Construction began in 1997, and the mall was complete one year later in March and opened to the public. Vodaworld is a one-stop cellular mall where customers sign up for cellular contracts, buy cellphones, have phones repaired, install cellular car kits, get advice on cellular technology, or view the latest technology. A few cafés, restaurants, a cinema, a gym and a nine-hole floodlit golf course are some of Vodaworld's other features.

Alan landscaped every nook and cranny of the Vodaworld garden. He commissioned Ludwig Taschner, Pretoria's foremost rose expert, to create the biggest rose garden in the southern hemisphere in shades of pink and yellow. From his office window in Corporate Park, Alan had a bird's-eye view of his garden, which gave him great pleasure.

The last thing Alan did was to negotiate a deal with the Health and Racquet Club, which entailed relocating their gym from across the highway, to next door to the mall. Alan built bigger and better premises for the gym, with impressive facilities, which the gym used rent-free, on condition that Vodacom employees and customers could have free access to it.

The cost of the project rose monthly as Alan made changes, additions or replaced inferior materials with better ones. He was especially excited about the centre's theatre and conference facilities, which he considered to be the best in the country. And he was similarly proud of the Vodadome – a gigantic circular auditorium with state-of-the-art acoustics that would stage shows, concerts and other events, the like of which had not been seen in the country.

Alan would call Theo at all hours to discuss ideas or to ask for his advice. One night, Theo was woken by his cellphone ringing. He groaned as he picked up the phone. 'It can only be Alan wanting to talk about those blasted building plans.'

'Hello Theo,' said Alan in a bright, cheerful tone. 'Didn't wake you did I? Good. Now listen.'

Theo propped himself up on one elbow and gave Alan a small grunt to let him know he was listening.

'I'm going to put it right in the middle of the mall, Theo; what do think of that?' Alan said triumphantly.

Theo grunted again, but as one who is completely baffled would.

'What is "it" Alan?' he asked in a voice intended to let Alan know how he felt about being woken up at two in the morning.

'It? What do you mean "it"? The conference centre, man!'

Theo let it slide; when Alan was in 'switched-on' mode it was best not to interrupt. He listened while Alan outlined his plan to place the conference centre *within* the main mall, rather than to position it on a site nearby. As he explained, by doing this, every businessman and -woman would have to walk through the mall to get to his or her meeting or seminar in the upstairs venue.

'And getting more people into the mall can only be good for business,' Alan concluded with satisfaction.

'That's great, Alan. Tell me,' Theo asked, 'do you run a property development business or a cellular company?'

'Right now, I'm a property developer,' he responded cheekily. 'Tomorrow I'll go back to selling airtime.'

Theo made his excuses and cut the conversation short – he, for one, needed to sleep.

On another occasion, when Alan became impatient with the building progress, Theo said to him, 'Take it easy Alan; Rome wasn't built in one day.'

'I know,' muttered Alan, 'but if I had been there, it would have happened a lot faster.'

At first, the Vodacom service providers didn't want to set up their cellphone shops in the centre. They had no doubt that Alan would do a good job, but they doubted that the public would take to such an unusual idea. People visited retail centres for many reasons – to buy things, dine, watch movies, and so on – but would they travel all the way to an out-of-town complex selling cellphones?

As Alan said later, 'It was a failure of imagination, I think. They just couldn't get their heads around the idea, so they backed off.'

Without service providers, Vodaworld would disappear, so Alan offered rent-free space as an enticement. This did the trick and the units quickly filled up with suppliers from all areas of cellular technology. Eventually, when the mall took off, Alan had a waiting list of brand names wanting floor space in Vodaworld. With his uncanny knack for business, Shameel Joosub put together clever trade deals, earning Vodacom good rentals and ensuring satisfied dealers.

When Vodaworld was completed, Alan had a R50 million complex in the middle of nowhere and no one paying rent. There would be no rental income for two years due to the deal Alan had made with the suppliers, which meant that the public *had* to like Vodaworld, and they had to like it straight away, or his shareholders would fire him once and for all.

As if there wasn't enough pressure already, the arrival of Vodafone's Sir Julian Horn-Smith and Phil Williams a few days before the opening hardly made things any easier.

However, Phil seemed to admire Alan's new complex. Alan was always grateful for his support, even in the face of the board's disapproval. Phil would always find a way to help Alan out of a predicament or encourage him in his endeavours.

One of the first things Sir Julian said when meeting Alan was, 'I did notice that huge carbuncle on the highway in the middle of nowhere. Who in their right minds would want to traipse out there?'

Then, before he had set foot in the building, Sir Julian came to an abrupt halt, pointing at the cascading fountain towering before him. 'Good lord!

You'll have to get rid of that pond,' he explained dramatically, waving a hand at the landscape architecture that Alan had commissioned specially for Vodaworld.

'I couldn't possibly do that,' replied Alan, determined to let Sir Julian know that he wouldn't be browbeaten. 'That's our reserve water supply in case a fire breaks out in the building.'

Sir Julian guffawed in delight, pleased to see that the Vodacom Number One was as feisty as ever. He patted Alan on the back and walked with him up to the main entrance.

'Sir Julian and I got along very well,' Alan reflects. 'He gave me a hard time about the way I did things, but he believed in Vodacom as much as I did. And what he doesn't know about telecommunications you could write on a pinhead. There isn't much I wouldn't do for him, to tell you the truth.'

Alan arranged board meetings at Vodacom's offices right next door to Vodaworld on days when there were special promotions on offer at the mall, which pulled crowds of people. The Vodafone board members would gaze out the windows of the boardroom, amazed that the cellular mall enjoyed such remarkable success. Alan gleaned satisfaction from their transformation from absolute sceptics to committed believers, even if it was just for a few days.

On the day before the launch, Alan went on a walk-about inspection of the mall with Joan. The steps leading to the majestic mall, the crystal-clear fountains splashing exuberantly, flanked by perfectly aligned palm trees, gave way to an ultra-modern high-tech world inside. Even Alan was impressed. As he walked through the entrance, there were still various signs of the construction process lying around. Alan lost his temper and lashed out at the foreman for sloppy work.

'Alan, don't stress about it,' said Joan, 'people will understand that it's the first day.'

He whipped around to face her. 'You don't understand,' he said vehemently, 'Vodaworld has to be perfect; I won't accept anything less.'

Alan needed a spectacular plan to put Vodaworld on the map. A clever incentive was to offer free return air tickets from Johannesburg to London to the first 1 000 people to sign contracts with Vodacom at Vodaworld. Alan was blown away by the response. On the day *before* the launch just after 5 p.m., people started queuing outside the gates of Vodaworld. The gate-dwellers – hardy souls who had brought tents, bedding and food with them for the long night ahead – were among the thousands of people who had heard or seen the promotional message.

'What the hell are they all doing here so early?' Alan wondered out loud.

'Getting a free plane ticket to London, of course,' said Joan.

When Alan arrived the next day, he saw what he thought to be a crowd of at least 10 000 people waiting to get in. As he stood on the top floor of Vodaworld, he couldn't see the end of the queue that was five abreast in places. Instead of feeling pleased at the huge turnout, Alan felt a rise of panic within him. He had not expected such a tremendous response. Fortunately, the Midrand police force had sent down a troop of men to keep order.

'This could get hectic,' Alan murmured to himself, *'really* hectic.'

In his inimitable style, Alan had set up a carnival on the front steps of the mall: there were thousands of balloons, music, a stand-up comic, and food and drink; there were also Vodacom staff members to hand out bottles of water to those feeling the heat.

Anthea van Heerden, who was the Vodaworld manager, stood next to Alan marvelling at the spectacle. She had been working eighteen-hour days to make sure that every last detail met Alan's exacting standards. She had already marched off a teenager who had hidden in one of the toilets in a bid to get to the front of the queue. In another incident, a young woman had broken through the glass doors and fisted a security guard to force her way in. Anthea was physically slight, but she dragged the woman by the scruff of the neck off the premises. She ran the mall with military precision since Alan expected nothing less.

There was no end to the people – they just kept on coming. The 1 000 free plane tickets were gone in a flash. When it was announced that the tickets had all been given out, not a single person left the queue. And so Alan decided to give away more free tickets. Of course, this meant Alan gained 1 000 extra subscribers, which in turn meant that the merchandising team and contract advisers were selling phones and processing applications well into the night.

'Isn't it good when a plan comes together so beautifully?' Anthea asked rhetorically, as the last of the customers drifted off into the warm October night.

A Cellular Disneyworld

Alan smiled contentedly. 'It feels like the Rugby World Cup all over again.'

Anthea turned to Alan and said, 'Do you know what today reminds me of?'

'No, what?' he asked in return.

'It's just like being at Disneyworld,' she replied. 'It's just perfect.'

Vodaworld put Vodacom on the map. There wasn't another place where people could browse or buy cellular technology 364 days of the year (Vodaworld closed on Christmas Day). The reasoning behind the cellular mall was that the client had access to the latest technology and best expertise in a one-stop shop that was open seven days a week all year round. Customer service didn't come much better than that. The first walk-in Customer Care Centre was set up at Vodaworld. Its operating brief was to ensure that no one walked out of the centre with his or her problem unsolved.

The response from the public was incredible. Many customers said the care centre was the best thing about Vodaworld, and that they really appreciated being able to speak to someone face-to-face if they needed to. This led to care centres being set up in Vodacom franchise outlets across the country. The Vodaworld facility had to be revamped in 2007 to cope with the steadily increasing demand for its services.

Vodacom Corporate Park was built around Vodaworld so that visitors to the complex could see Vodacom in action and so that Vodacom staff could see how their market was working for them – it was a microcosm of Vodacom's national market.

Vodacom's opening of a R125 million Techno-Centre in Cape Town was another landmark event that reinforced the company's commitment to skills development. The six-storey building housed Vodacom's network management centre, billing systems, a 250-workstation customer care centre, a smart card manufacturing plant, mobile switching centre and training facilities. Vodacom's 24-hour support services were also based there. Alan was very pleased with the finished product.

As he applied himself to the job of making Vodacom's customers feel that the company cared about them and not just their spending power, he had not forgotten the needs of an equally important group of people: the Vodacom employees. Alan had seen and worked in enough drab offices to appreciate the importance of good office design. He would grimace with distaste whenever he thought of his early days at Telkom, when he'd been made to sit at a desk behind a door in a gloomy, soulless office as if he was some inferior, second-class citizen who didn't deserve any better.

The Vodacom staff would not be made to feel the same way, Alan resolved; he would see to it personally. And indeed, there is nothing drab or dispirited about the Vodacom offices attached to Vodaworld; quite the opposite, they are bright, airy and comfortable. There are no second-class workstations; each employee's workspace is designed to maximise her or his feeling of well-being.

As Alan explains: 'Getting the work environment right meant a lot to me. It's not just about pay and promotions; people also value the simpler things – a decent desk and chair, good lighting, fresh paint on the walls, those kinds of things.'

In addition to paying close attention to office ergonomics, Alan let his staff know they were appreciated in other ways. Additional facilities included five restaurants, several coffee bars, a crèche, ATMs, a hair stylist and, of course, the gym and the golf course. A wellness programme was introduced, giving staff access to a doctor, psychologist, physiotherapist, chiropractor, dietician and pharmacist. Alan's heart scare had made him something of a health zealot and he would constantly preach to the staff about the need to follow a healthy lifestyle.

Antiretroviral drugs were freely available to HIV-positive staff, which cost the company R3 million each year. HIV testing was not enforced, but if a staff member informed the company privately, Vodacom paid for the medication for the rest of his or her life. If a family member became infected accidentally, the company also paid for that person's treatment. Employees who were HIV positive progressed like anyone else in the company, but Alan insisted they receive treatment and counselling. He had himself tested in front of the staff to encourage transparency about the disease. Vodacom also instituted a bursary scheme for its 4 500 employees.

Alan is adamant he wouldn't have done things any other way. 'I'm really proud that the people of Vodacom have a pleasant working environment,' he maintains. 'I want everyone who works here to love coming to work and I want them to be proud of where they work and be able to show their families that they are valued. After all, they are a big part of Vodacom's success story.'

Stepping into Africa
1995 to 2008

Africa is a cruel country; it takes your heart and grinds it into powdered stone and no one minds.
Elspeth Huxley

The time had come for Alan and Vodacom to move on. If it was to achieve its 20% profit growth target, Vodacom had to find new markets. Alan was reluctant to do it, but it was fast becoming an inescapable truth: Vodacom had to expand into Africa.

His discomfort was natural; Vodacom was still in its infancy and yet the company had developed at a tremendous pace. As Alan says, 'I thought we were already moving fast enough. I was concerned that if we went any faster things would get out of control.'

And yet, deep down, he accepted the need for expansion. Vodacom was an African company as well as a South African one, and its fortunes were tied to those of the continent as a whole. It is rare that a single developing country has all the resources, infrastructure and economic 'know-how' to survive, let alone prosper – which is why mutually beneficial partnerships within a region are vital.

This line of thought prompted the Organisation of African Unity (now the African Union) to give five heads of state, including President Thabo

Mbeki, the mandate to develop a New Partnership for Africa's Development (Nepad), a socio-economic development plan for Africa.

Alan, as one of South Africa's corporate leaders, was someone whose actions would have a direct impact on Nepad. As he remarked: 'If Vodacom prospers it will be good for South Africa, but South Africa cannot continue to grow in isolation. Our neighbouring countries need to share in opportunities for economic development. If Africa improves its economies and corporate governance then foreign investment will follow, leading to prosperity across the continent. Vodacom cannot afford to sit on the sidelines.'

Andrew Mthembu, the then Deputy CEO of Vodacom and MD of Vodacom International says, 'Landing in another African country can be like landing on the moon, a totally different and alien environment. However, you find your feet quickly, probably because you have to. As we saw with the First African in Space project, technology is helping to spur on the African Renaissance. Vodacom is determined for its construction of cellular networks across the continent to play a leading role in Africa's rebirth.'[1]

There was one in-house obstacle that stood in the way of the expansion programme: although the shareholders wanted Vodacom to move into Africa, they imposed limitations. Vodacom was only allowed to operate in sub-Saharan Africa. The rest of the world, north of the equator, was Vodafone's territory. This placed Alan and Vodacom at a disadvantage, since its main rival, MTN, was not subject to the same restriction and had been able to invest in countries as far afield as Syria, Yemen and Afghanistan.

There were other problems that had to be negotiated. First, it usually took a long time to set up a cellular network in a country due to regulatory and licensing issues. There were many conditions that had to be satisfied before an application would even be considered. Interconnection agreements with other network operators had to be negotiated and drawn up, and this took time.

Second, any company thinking of entering a new market will test that market before it makes a commitment. A feasibility study will generate a wealth of useful information – market size, competitor activity, consumer spending profiles, credit levels, and so on – upon which management can base its financial projections. But feasibility studies only work where there are records to show what people earn and where money is spent, amongst other aspects. In countries where a large percentage of economic activity is transacted in cash, which is the case in many African countries, these records simply don't exist. In the Congo, for example, over 70% of the economic activity is generated by the informal sector,[2] which is not accounted for in the published GDP figures. Because of this, it is almost impossible to make accurate financial forecasts, and a decision on whether or not to invest is often based on little more than a gut feeling.

Another important consideration for setting up a new business in Africa is the spending power of the population. In countries where the banking system is open to corruption, fraud and government abuse, people opt for a direct-exchange trading system – cash for goods – rather than use an intermediary such as a bank. However, the cash economy is still subject to external influences, especially if a country's currency is linked to the value of the US dollar. And, because cell-rates are usually dollar-based, a downturn in the US economy can cause a price hike, which means that the person on the street makes fewer calls

A country's relative political stability is a further factor that would-be investors need to take into account. If a country's leaders are perceived as unjust, corrupt or repressive, there is far less chance of investment from external sources. Furthermore, a potential investor may be loathe to put its employees, plant and equipment at risk by placing them in such an unstable environment. Coups, raids and rebel attacks are all part of daily life in some African countries. As Alan confirms, running a company while the country is subjected to violence and political instability is not an easy feat.

But probably the biggest problem in Africa is a lack of infrastructure; in many places it is non-existent. Roads are a good example; a country may only have a few (or indeed no) proper roads, which makes the transportation of people, goods, machinery and equipment extremely difficult. Roads had to be built from scratch in places; security guards were deployed on site to protect equipment; and a dozen creative ways had to be devised to transport heavy equipment down rivers and across forests. Erratic or non-existent power supplies affect the production and delivery of goods and services just as badly. Vodacom would later have to rely heavily on diesel-powered generators to run its base stations in Lesotho and elsewhere because of this problem.

If Alan allowed himself to think about these problems at any great length, the idea of a cellular exploration of Africa appeared unwise, even foolish.

But there was one plus factor that outweighed all these negatives and it was what helped Alan keep his nerve: a cellphone could be used anywhere, a fixed-line phone could not. This was the real beauty of cellular technology as far as Alan saw it. A cellphone went with the user, wherever he or she chose to go, whereas the fixed-line phone was only as portable as the length of its wire. In theory, there was nowhere that cellphone technology could not go. The entire African continent was one gigantic cellular market. Alan made up his mind to go exploring.

The company's first foray into Africa was halfway through 1995, when Vodacom signed an agreement with the Lesotho Telecommunications Company (LTC), the country's fixed-line operator, to set up a cellular network in Lesotho. It is an isolated, mountainous kingdom, with spectacular canyons dotted by thatched huts, completely surrounded by South Africa, where many of the villages can only be reached on horseback, by foot or light aircraft. During the winter months (June to August), snow and ice can make travelling hazardous. While much of the tiny country remains untouched by modernity, developers have laid down roads to reach its mineral and water resources. In more recent years, thousands of people have been forced to seek work in South Africa because of the lack of job opportunities at home. The country is also ravaged by the HIV/AIDS pandemic.

'We went into Lesotho because no one else cared enough to go there,' says Alan. 'It was a small, poor country with about 2 million people, but they also had a right to decent communication like everyone else.'

Vodacom and LTC shared ownership of the new cellular network, which was called Vodacom Lesotho Ltd (VCL), and the remaining 20% was made available to Lesotho's private sector.

The plan was to switch on the network by December 1995 in the Lesotho capital, Maseru, where there was one base station. The network would then be rolled out across the rest of the country. Tariffs would be on a par with those in South Africa and South Africans would be able to use their cellphones in Lesotho.

Three years after Vodacom set up base in Lesotho, hundreds of demonstrators protested for weeks in front of King Letsie's Royal Palace, claiming voting fraud in the May elections that put Prime Minister Pakalitha Mosisili in power. They demanded that the government step down and hold new elections. Troops from South Africa and Botswana entered the country to quell the unrest and to put down an army mutiny. In the chaos that ensued, Alan relocated the billing system to just outside the prime minister's house since it was the safest place to be during the battles that followed. Vodacom didn't leave; it rebuilt its bombed offices and retail stores. It built more base stations, along with a water project and an electricity network. In South Africa the cellular network hires the transmission network; in Lesotho it had to be built from scratch.

Alan also brought some of the Vodacom spirit to the people of Lesotho by injecting a six-digit sponsorship into soccer, an enormously popular sport in the country, and he made further investments in HIV/AIDS health and education initiatives.

Lesotho was a long, hard slog, but eventually the Vodacom network was accessible in all ten districts, key towns and settlements around the country. In 2007 to 2008, Vodacom Lesotho built twelve new base stations and had plans to add a further nine. With a subscriber base of 489 000 at the end of 2008, Vodacom Lesotho holds an 88% market share.

'Vodacom Lesotho's current MD, Godfrey Mbingo, a man with incredible energy, and his experienced predecessor, Merwyn Visagie, have taken cellular in Lesotho to another level altogether,' says Alan.

With Vodacom well established in Lesotho, it was now well placed to extend its operations into other African countries. Alan began thinking that cellular technology could become one of South Africa's major export commodities. Lesotho was only the beginning.

It took six months of planning to enter the Tanzanian cellular market. There were three cellular operators in the country already, with a fourth on the horizon. Vodacom Tanzania opened in August 2000. A year later it had 130 000 customers, as opposed to the anticipated 15 000, and a growth rate of about 1 000 new customers a day. In just eighteen months Vodacom had captured the largest market share in the country. Under the current leadership of MD Dietlof Maré, Vodacom Tanzania has performed exceedingly well despite a difficult and highly competitive operating environment.

Vodacom Tanzania is a joint venture in which the Vodacom Group owns the majority share (about 65%); the remaining portion is owned by Tanzanian shareholders Capsian Construction and Planetel Communications.

When Vodacom entered Tanzania, the competition included Tritel, MIC Tanzania Limited (or tiGo) and one government-owned fixed-line telecommunications operator, Tanzania Telecommunications Company Limited. Shortly after Vodacom's arrival, Celtel paid US$120 million for a 35% stake in the state-owned company, which included a licence to operate a cellular network. By 2008, Vodacom Tanzania had 4.2 million customers, a year-on-year increase of 29.6%, and a market share of 55%.

The figures make good reading, but they only tell half the story. Ivo Lazic of Brolaz (the company that had erected the highway base stations in South Africa in record time a few years earlier) recalls the difficulties of doing the same job in Tanzania: 'The roads were so bad we had to change the shock absorbers on the bakkies every ten days. The drivers had to wear kidney belts to protect them from the pounding they took. Sometimes, six-wheel-drive trucks were the only vehicles tough enough to cope with the terrain. Getting materials was a nightmare, too. We had to build roads and cable cars to haul materials over mountains. I'm not really sure how we managed it, but we did.'

Brolaz even installed a base station at Mount Kilimanjaro in 2001. At 5 895 metres above sea level, the summit was the highest point on the planet at the time covered by a global communication network. So as not to disfigure the view, Vodacom coverage at the summit is provided by a cellular base station at the foot of the mountain at Marangu camp, 3 000 metres away from the summit. The GSM system also covers other high-altitude areas such as La Paz in Bolivia, the highest capital in the world at 4 100 metres, and Syangboche in Nepal, a base camp at Everest at 3 874 metres. Six years later, in May 2007, a Chinese network brought cellphone reception to the top of Mount Everest, making it the highest point in the world to provide cellphone coverage.

Some may argue that it is frivolous to erect a base station to pander the egos of amateur climbers, but being able to summon emergency services via cellphone could mean the difference between life and death for some of the climbers, on what can be a treacherous mountain. Alan stresses that Vodacom did not do this as some sort of publicity stunt – 'Vodacom on top of the world!' – or simply so those at the summit could surprise friends and family by making a mountain-top call. The real boon of having network coverage in this situation is that emergency services can be summoned in the case of a fall or a similar accident.

As Alan says, 'This is why cellphones are so damn good: they're *useful*. If you break a leg 5 000 metres up a mountain, believe me, you'll be glad you packed your phone.'

Although Vodacom entered Tanzania as the fourth cellular operator, it has captured more than half of the market. 'Whenever we invest in a new country,' says Alan, 'we build a bigger network, establish better distribution and create a better brand. It is important for us to be the market leader in the telecommunications business. If you have the largest number of subscribers, you have the economies of scale, and therefore the lowest costs per subscriber. Our investment in Tanzania was worthwhile for Vodacom, and worthwhile for its subscribers.'

On his first visit to the capital of Tanzania, Dar es Salaam, Alan requested a tour of the local shopping mall to determine the retail opportunities available. Jan van Wyk, the first MD of Vodacom Tanzania, took him to a small grocery store.

'This is it?' asked Alan. 'In the whole of Dar es Salaam there's no shopping mall?'

'You can purchase anything you want at any road intersection,' replied Jan, 'from furniture to food, but there's no shopping mall.'

A few years later, Alan was surprised to see world-class hotels and vast shopping malls in the centre of Dar es Salaam. He liked to think that cellular had contributed in some small measure to the progress he encountered in the city.

On a later occasion Alan had the pleasure of being invited to lunch in Dodoma with the prime minister of Tanzania, Edward Lowassa, and his wife. The prime minister told Alan of the plight of Tanzanians who were starving due to a recent drought. Alan agreed to donate R1 million's worth of food to the Tanzanian people, a gesture that endeared Vodacom to Tanzania and further strengthened their relationship.

Africa had not been the best experience for Alan, yet it had not been the worst. Lesotho was a small country where Vodacom had made a small investment. Despite political strife, the cellular network continued to remain stable and rendered an essential service in the country. Vodacom had cut its teeth on Africa in this little kingdom. Tanzania, untouched by tribal rivalries and political upheavals, was perhaps a less complicated venture. It made Alan brave, and he looked forward to taking Vodacom further into Africa.

The Democratic Republic of the Congo (DRC), the continent's third-largest country after Sudan and Algeria, only had 100 000 landlines for its 60 million citizens. The potential for cellular provision in the country was therefore enormous. However, cellular roll-out was not going to be made any easier by an almost complete lack of infrastructure and the dangers of working in a country still at war with itself. Nevertheless, Alan thrived on a challenge, and he was determined to make cellular work in the DRC.

Vodacom's first steps into Africa confirmed Alan's belief in cellular technology as a medium for enriching the lives of ordinary people. Furthermore, he was convinced that advances in cellular technology would take the enrichment process even further. 'Cellphones will have bigger screens with higher resolution, and will make a difference in people's lives in much the same way that television did,' said Alan. 'Television gave people a window to the world. And that's what cellphones will do for Africa. Access to telephony is a great equaliser. In time, cellphones will be the PCs of Africa.'

Vodacom's African experience had just begun. There would be more opportunities, other countries.

16

Infinite Possibilities
2002 to 2008

> *Reality, as usual, beats fiction out of sight.*
> Joseph Conrad

The first thing Alan remembers about his stay in the DRC, is that he was almost killed – twice – both incidents involving crowds out of control. As he watched a stampede of frenzied people approaching, he froze and recalled the words in Michela Wrong's book, *In the Footsteps of Mr. Kurtz*, describing the Congo as 'a vacuum at the heart of the continent... a parody of a functioning state... [in which] normal rules of society were suspended ... an ominous awareness of a world of infinite, sinister possibilities... with a constant sense of chaos and impending violence'.[1] At that moment, a sense of overpowering malignancy chilled him to the bone and he wondered what he was doing in the middle of Joseph Conrad's *Heart of Darkness*.

One has to understand where the DRC has come from to realise the near-impossible situation Vodacom faced when it entered the country. The Democratic Republic of the Congo, as it is known today, has during its turbulent history also been known as the Congo Free State, the Belgian Congo, Congo-Leopoldville, Congo-Kinshasa and Zaire. From 1890 to 1960 the country was a colony of Belgium, which ruthlessly exploited its mineral wealth and treated its citizens abominably; many millions of Congolese died due to exploitation and disease.

There was brief hope for the country when, in 1960, it gained its independence and Patrice Lumumba became Congo's first elected prime minister, but Lumumba was dead within weeks and President Joseph Kasavubu ruled for the next five years. From 1965 to 1997 Congo was given the name 'Zaire' after the accession to power of the flamboyant, cunning and exploitative Mobutu Sese Seko. Under Sese Seko's rule, the country was afflicted by civil war, ethnic strife, sham elections, a non-existent infrastructure, crippling corruption and a struggling economy. When the war in neighbouring Rwanda spilled over into Zaire in 1997, the chaos that ensued gave the anti-Mobutu rebels a chance to capture the capital, Kinshasa, and install Laurent Kabila as president. After his assassination in 2001, his quiet-spoken, publicity-shy son, Joseph Kabila became the Congo's president, the world's youngest head of state, who promised to rule by consensus. Despite a peace deal and the formation of a transitional government in 2003, the conflict continues to the present day.

The Congo Civil War, as it is often referred to, has to date claimed over 3 million lives, and is possibly the worst tragedy to unfold in Africa in recent decades. Fighting is fuelled by the country's vast mineral wealth, with all sides taking advantage of the anarchy to plunder the natural resources. In recent years, one particular mineral, coltan (short for Columbite-tantalite), has been at the centre of the conflict. It is a key element in the manufacture of cellphones, computer chips, nuclear reactors, and PlayStations. The market for the mineral has greatly increased in recent years, exacerbating conflict in the DRC.

Despite the instability in the country and Alan's misgivings, Vodacom forged a partnership with the Congolese Wireless Network in May 2002, inheriting 12 000 subscribers in the process. Initially, the network only covered three parts of Africa's third-largest country: Kinshasa and the mining towns of Mbuji-Mayi and Lubumbashi. 'We chose these three cities because there was peace in those areas,' commented Andrew Mthembu. 'Vodacom would wait for cues from the government as to where peace would be opening up in other areas before venturing any further.'

When Vodacom took over the Congolese Wireless Network, it had to do a SIM swap; in other words, the new network was taking over the old one. Because Vodacom had a better quality system, the existing 12 000 subscribers needed upgraded SIM cards as did the new customers, which amounted to a total of 40 000 subscribers.

Alan flew to the Congo with his bodyguard, Gawie, in tow; Andrew Mthembu, who spearheaded all the African initiatives through Vodacom International Holdings; Joan Joffe, who headed up marketing; Dot Field, whose primary job was public relations and to take care of Alan; and Anthea van Heerden, who was looking after marketing and logistics in the DRC.

When Alan reflects on his time in the DRC, he speaks affectionately of the people but with concern about the place. He found the Congolese, apart from the odd exception, to be unfailingly friendly, polite and engaging. Similar to hundreds of millions of Africans across the continent, the local people go about their daily lives as best they can, refusing to let chronic poverty, poor governance, disease and war destroy their spirits. At the markets, wooden tomato boxes under a dilapidated umbrella display a pitiful array of goods – a few tomatoes, a bunch of bananas or a bottle of petrol. Petrol is sold and consumed by the bottle, with vehicles travelling only as far as the bottle will take them. Some of the tomato boxes also function as informal 'banks'. Although Congo's official currency is the Congolese franc (CDF), it is such an unstable currency that US dollars are widely used in its place. The 'banks' on the side of the road exchange the locals' francs for dollars to enable them to purchase what they need.

Alan was captivated by the natural sophistication of the Congolese women. Despite the heat and mud, they sauntered down the potholed streets in their gorgeous hats and designer shoes as if they were ambling down the boulevards of Paris, scurrying for cover from the intermittent downpours. In spite of the poverty, a cult of fashionistas, who have appointed as their source of inspiration Congolese music legend Papa Wemba, manage to buy expensive clothing from designers such as Dior and Versace at great personal sacrifice. They even hire porters to carry them across Kinshasa's notoriously muddy roads.

Getting around the Congo, Alan discovered, is no easy matter. The road system is primitive and often in poor condition – with 'potholes so big you could lose a car in them', according to Alan. Private cars are a rarity and they mostly belong to the government, Kinshasa-based United Nations staff, aid agency workers and executives of the larger mining companies. The Volkswagen kombi taxis are unsafe, unreliable and uncomfortable, but can still be seen packed with people sitting, standing and even lying on top of one another. Sometimes all the seats are ripped out of the taxis and wooden benches are installed so that more people can be squeezed into a vehicle. Much the same can be said about the irregular train service. Alan soon found out that for the vast majority of Congolese the only options were to walk or cycle, or to use a handmade canoe to traverse the vast waterway system that criss-crosses the country.

When it comes to making long journeys across the countryside, trucks laden with goods and passengers set off at dawn, when the air is cool and there is less chance of the trucks' engines overheating. The vehicles are always accompanied by truck boys known as *mutshungas*. Dressed in greasy torn overalls, the truck boys carry wedges to slip under the tyres when the truck gets stuck. Shouting cries of encouragement to the driver, the passengers join in, making the vehicle's journey a team effort. The truck boys' duties also include changing wheels, repairing and maintaining the vehicle and ensuring that nothing is stolen.

While in Kinshasa, Alan and the others stayed at the five-star Meimling Hotel, a majestic building clinging to its fading colonial splendour, with a huge wrought-iron gate adorning its entrance. Alan was booked into the palatial presidential suite. Though stunning in every other respect, he was annoyed that his room's air-conditioning was not working. And, for those lucky enough to afford hotel accommodation in the Congo, the availability of air-conditioning is the whole point of making a booking in the first place. It was so hot Alan was sure that he could have fried an egg on the window sill if he had so chosen. Dot went off to complain to the hotel management and demanded that the air-conditioner be repaired before the end of the day or the bill would not be paid.

In the evening, the group enjoyed fine French cuisine at a nearby Belgian restaurant situated in the most disreputable backstreets of the capital. Beggars, some crippled, roamed the streets searching for food and begging for dollars. Though Alan saw none, he knew that Kinshasa housed gangs that also took to the streets at night, in search of something more than a few dollars. Muggings, kidnappings and robberies were commonplace. The never-ending warfare had left many buildings damaged, while modern high-rise buildings remained unoccupied and already showed signs of decay. And yet here was a luxurious restaurant set amid the squalor, complete with plush velvet furnishings, ornate chandeliers, fine crystal and fabulous food.

'It was very odd,' Alan recalls, 'almost unreal. What went on inside that restaurant had no bearing on what went on outside. When we left, we were accompanied by bodyguards carrying AK-47s. To us it seemed crazy, but to the Congolese it was just the way things were; it was no big deal.'

The party of five then proceeded to a candlelit market in Kinshasa, unprepared for the allure of a thousand flickering candles lighting up the shabby stalls. Even the most extravagant Christmas lights would not have matched the ambience radiating from the run-down marketplace. Their car split a pathway through the steady throng of people. Out of nowhere, two lunatics ran up to the car, banging on the windows and rocking the vehicle. We are going to be crushed to death, thought Alan, glancing at the panic-stricken faces of his companions. But the driver kept his cool and averted a possible tragedy, mumbling something about a drug-induced high.

Back at the hotel, and still feeling slightly unnerved, Alan went to bed. The air-conditioning had not been fixed, but he was too tired to do anything about it. He longed to open a window to let a little air into the room, but didn't, since he knew that doing so would also let in the mosquitoes. Exhausted, hot and disoriented, Alan fell into a fitful sleep.

At five minutes to midnight, he woke with a start to the sound of someone banging urgently on the bedroom door. He sat bolt upright in bed and listened intently. But there was no further knocking; instead, he heard two or three low voices muttering something incomprehensible, followed by a scratching noise and the jangle of keys. Alan's heart was racing and his throat was as dry as sandpaper. This is it, he thought, the Congolese army has been sent to take me out or kidnap me for ransom.

A key turned in the lock and the door swung open. Three men stepped noiselessly into the room but stopped when they saw Alan sitting up in bed, staring at them. Then one of the men took a pace forward and raised his arm in Alan's direction, holding what looked like a gun with a silencer attached to it. Alan closed his eyes.

The ceiling light came on and Alan slowly opened his eyes to see a man with a hand drill pointing at the air-conditioning unit above his head.

'Sorry, sir,' the man said, still pointing at the faulty unit with his drill, 'but we need to fix the air-con.'

Alan couldn't believe what he was hearing. Here he was lying helplessly in bed waiting to be 'taken out' and in walk the air-con technicians making a night call.

When he regained his composure, Alan was ready to explode. 'Just leave it,' he fumed.

'We can't,' said the spokesman, 'we have to fix it by midnight or we will be in big trouble. The manager said you won't pay for the room if the air-con is not fixed today, and it's still today,' he said, looking at his watch.

'Just fuckin' leave, okay,' Alan cursed. 'I'll pay for the bloody room. I just don't want you here right now.'

When Alan related the story at breakfast the next morning, the reaction was not as he had expected it to be: the team found it by far the funniest thing they had heard in months and begged him to tell it again. This didn't improve Alan's mood; everything about the incident was so preposterous that he didn't think getting angry would achieve anything.

'It could only happen here; only in the crazy Congo,' he muttered as he headed outside.

If Alan's fear in his room that night had been unfounded, the events associated with the distribution of SIM cards were genuinely unnerving. The SIM exchange would take place at the Grand Hotel. It had been agreed with the hotel management that Alan could use one of the conference rooms for swapping out the SIM cards. Desks had been set up with a chair on either side – one for the Vodacom staff member and one for the client. The Vodacom adviser was given twenty minutes per person, in which he or she would explain the purpose and function of the SIM card, how to fit it, how to buy and add airtime, and to try and match it with the same cellphone number as the previous SIM card – mission impossible.

The morning was an utter disaster from start to finish. A mass of people had gathered outside, packed tightly against the hotel's main doors. When Alan arrived mid-morning, he could hear the clamour of voices demanding access to the building and the shudder of the doors into the conference centre as the heaving crowd pressed forward. The guards had to use their rifles as batons to stop the people at the front from breaking past them into the hotel.

Anthea, Andrew and Alan looked at each other. No one was panicking yet, but they could see the anxiety in each other's eyes.

'How shall we handle this?' asked Anthea, for whom 'handling things' usually came easily.

'This is a bloody catastrophe,' Alan bellowed.

The room quickly filled with people pushing and shoving. It was obvious that there was no hope of allocating the cards properly – the twenty-minute-per-person idea was a non-starter. Alan went from desk to desk telling each SIM card adviser to pass out the cards as fast as possible, and not to worry about matching each person to his or her unique number.

'Quick as you can,' he urged. 'Let's get this room cleared before anyone gets hurt.'

Alan had seen several people with nasty looking head wounds, either the result of a rifle-butt blow or simply from the inevitable accidental collisions that occur in this sort of situation. The sooner they could empty the room, the fewer casualties there would be.

Seeing the chaos, Anthea had jumped onto a table to address the crowd, but no one could hear her properly. Even if they could, most would not have understood what she was saying since she was shouting in English. Her repeated message of 'Please stand back, there are enough SIM cards for all of you', went unheeded. Many of the people who had come to collect their SIM cards had travelled miles to get there, which had taken some of them four days to cover. No one was about to leave without a card in hand.

Not all the people could be helped on the first day, so the conference centre was booked for the next day. However, Alan was told that the hotel was not prepared to risk further damage to its premises and reputation, and that he must do his work outside the hotel. Chairs were set out in the vast dusty backyard of the hotel for the people to sit on, while a raised platform held the desks and chairs used by Vodacom staff. The Congolese, it was hoped, would take a seat in the 'waiting room', wait their turn to be called up onto the platform to receive their SIM cards in small groups of three or four people, and exit through the back gates.

Alan stepped outside with much trepidation the following morning. He glanced at the new arrivals pressed up against the three-metre high solid steel gates, shuddering and buckling under their weight. As the gates swung open, the people hesitantly made their way toward the chairs. Then they broke out into a run, faster and faster, until they became a human torrent crushing everything in their path. Alan watched shoes flying in the air, handbags dragged across the sand and people ploughing to the ground as the mass dashed toward him. The crowd rushed past him as if possessed by demons, heaving and sweating as they made a beeline for the desks. Chairs were sent flying in a shower of white confetti, people were knocked to the ground in the rush to get up on the stage, and then, when they tried to leave, they found that the back gates had been inadvertently locked by hotel staff.

More panic ensued. People were irate, tempers were flaring; any minute and there would be full-scale violence unleashed and people would get hurt. The crowd started ramming against the gate, shouting and chanting. Then Alan saw Anthea run straight into the crowd and scale a six-foot wall in black stilettos, a beautiful blonde in white. Standing on top of that wall, she raised her hands in fists above her head and started chanting '*Vodacom, Vodacom, Vodacom!*' breaking out into song and making up the lyrics as she went along extolling the virtues of Vodacom. The people stopped and gaped at her, and burst into spontaneous laughter. Soon the whole crowd was singing with her.

This diversion bought Alan some time. He stormed off to the hotel manager and almost grabbed him by the collar. With his teeth gritted to control himself he said, 'If you don't fuckin' open that gate right now, I'm going to break it down.' It was something of an extreme empty threat, but it worked.

Alan's first three days in Kinshasa had been nothing short of a nightmare. But he came away thinking that the Congolese were the warmest, kindest people he had ever met – just not in crowds. They possess nothing, he thought, but they have heart.

With the SIM card distribution complete and the Vodacom team still miraculously intact, Alan was able to concentrate on other matters. He opened a Vodacom shop for the new Congolese subscribers, which immediately became a centre of attraction. The fact that the building was beautiful and air-conditioned was part of its appeal, but it was mainly the kudos afforded those seen in the shop that explained its popularity. The cellphone users would come and sit in the shop for a long time, not because the service was slow, but because they wanted as many of their friends, work colleagues and family members as possible to see them inside the store.

As always, coverage had to be first class. Alan asked Ivo (of Brolaz) to put up the base stations. By now, Ivo had become accustomed to working in less-than-perfect environments, but the Congo operation was more taxing than anything they had encountered before. Without road or rail links, Ivo was obliged to use the Congo River to transport the equipment and materials. The freight was put on barges and then ferried up-river to various drop-off points. But this proved hopeless – the barges were 50 years old, very slow and prone to breakdowns. Theft was a problem; so too was sabotage, despite there being guards on the vessels. In the end, planes were contracted to do the work, which saved time and money.

Getting the material from the airport to the base-station sites was also fraught with difficulties. Apart from the poor condition of the roads, Ivo and his team had to contend with the roadblocks that appeared at regular intervals. The roadblock personnel were always armed and were very interested in what Ivo had in his trucks. A bribe was often the only answer, since refusing to 'cooperate' in this way usually led to a night or two in jail. Ivo and his 'co-offenders' would then have to be bailed out (where bail monies ended up was anyone's guess). It was only when Ivo got a letter from the president to authorise their presence in Kinshasa that the guards at the roadblocks let them through – for a fee.

Alan reckoned the potential market in the Congo would be 6 million people out of a population of 60 million at the time, and he aimed to reach half of these people within ten years. In nine months of operations, Vodacom reached 200 000 subscribers, and in 2008 it had a subscriber base of 3.3 million. Its estimated market share was about 41%, while its main competitor Celtel had 37%. The remaining market was shared between tiGo (9%) and Congo Chine Telecom (13%).

'The Democratic Republic of the Congo is not our greatest investment by far, and probably never will be, but it has done more for the Congolese people in terms of economic development and peace (such as it is) than any other single event in the past 50 years,' says Alan.

Despite the obvious benefits of cellular for the country, running a cellular service in the Congo is fraught with difficulties on a daily basis. There were three coup attempts in the Congo while Dietlof Maré was running Vodacom Congo. When civil war breaks out it comes to the streets. Dietlof had put disaster recovery plans in place and with every rebel take-over attempt he kept the Vodacom network running. Despite a tank shell deliberately aimed and fired at the Vodacom offices, he evacuated all the people from the building, all the while keeping the network going. The first thing the rebels do when they arrive is cut the power. Vodacom's network is key to communications in the country and if it goes down, the government goes down too. During the first coup, amidst shelling and hails of bullets, Dietlof watched the power go down, while Alan's voice on his cellphone screamed at him to get out. But he felt responsible to keep Vodacom in operation. He couldn't just leave. Eventually Dietlof bribed one of the guards to run across the road through the cross-fire to switch on the generator and Vodacom continued to provide a service to its subscribers in spite of the war raging in the streets. It was all in a day's work in the Congo.

Alan struggles to understand the ways of the Congo. 'It is a country of contradictions,' he says. 'With all its hopes and aspirations and beautiful people, it lives in the grip of constant civil war. It is a vast country of bloodshed and corruption; yet its ordinary people, 60 million of them, carry on regardless – they are Congo's greatest asset.'

The One that Got Away
2001 to 2006

People go to Africa and confirm what they already have in their heads and so they fail to see what is there in front of them. That is what people have come to expect. It's not viewed as a serious continent. It's a place of strange, bizarre and illogical things, where people don't do what common sense demands.
Chinua Achebe

As the plane descended to land in Lagos in March 2004, Alan peered through the window at the gently curving bay that hugged the coastline of Nigeria, a country where he was about to invest US$250 million of his shareholders' money into a cellular network. Andrew Mthembu, his tall frame cramped into the seat next to Alan, was to manage that investment as part of his African portfolio.

It hadn't been easy to convince Vodafone or Telkom to invest in Nigeria, but Alan's third shareholder, Rembrandt, was always supportive of his decisions. Although it was a country with vast potential, they regarded it as a risky venture, not least because, in their view, Nigeria was synonymous with corrupt business practices. It had been pointed out to Alan that Transparency International, the global corruption watchdog, believed Nigeria to be one of the world's most corrupt nations. The fact that Nigeria is not the only place where corruption exists does not in any way minimise the harm that it has brought to Nigerians. Above all, corruption has tarnished the image of the country, created by its inability to deal with unethical conduct.

The giving and receiving of bribes is commonplace and occurs at all levels and in all sectors of society – from the need to pay a spurious 'immigration fee' to airport customs officials when arriving in the country, to having to bribe checkpoint guards to ensure smooth passage, to having your car stopped by a police officer keen to supplement his meagre salary via roadside extortion. Corruption had become so blatant and widespread that it appeared to have been legalised in Nigeria.[1]

Driving into Lagos, Alan and Andrew passed miles of shacks teeming with people and informal markets. Nigeria swelled to a population of over 132 million across 36 states in 2004, making it the eighth-most populous country in the world. The country grew so quickly, fuelled by Nigeria's booming oil industry in the 1970s, that its infrastructure, not to mention its institutional framework, was left behind. Although Nigeria is the eighth-largest oil exporter, corruption and mismanagement in 2004 swallowed about 40% of Nigeria's US$20 billion annual oil income. Despite its oil riches, 70% of the country's population lives below the poverty line.[2]

En route to the hotel, Alan was fascinated to discover a 'computer city' in the open air. There was nothing they couldn't buy at the computer bazaar – gadgets, screens, laptops, gizmos – all at half price. Telecomms Road in Lagos was another revelation, an electronic bazaar on wheels that came close to the concept of Vodaworld with a unique twist. As Alan looked out of the taxi window, a row of battered cars lined each side of the street with their boots open, displaying a chaotic array of cellphones and cellphone accessories.

'What a great system,' remarked Alan. 'At the end of the day you close the boot, drive home with your shop stowed in the back of the car, and return to the same spot in the morning to continue trading.'

'Now that's what I call innovation with an African flavour,' smiled Andrew. 'We're going to make a name for Vodacom on this road.'

At the beginning of the decade, Nigeria had the third-lowest density of telephones in the world, averaging fewer than four telephone lines for every 1 000 inhabitants. The lamentable state of the country's infrastructure and electricity supply, however, made the roll-out of cellular coverage exceptionally difficult. Network operators struggled to protect margins while maintaining quality of service. Despite the obstacles, customer demand continued to outpace capacity, forcing networks to limit the

The One that Got Away

supply of new SIM packs to the market. In short, Nigeria was not an easy operating environment, but its huge untapped consumer market offered great potential.

The first time Alan explored the possibility of breaking into the Nigerian cellular market had been in 2001 when the Nigerian government invited bids for cellular licences. The timing was good but the circumstances were not ideal. Although there was a provision in the shareholders' agreement stipulating that Vodacom could not pursue business opportunities north of the equator, Vodafone relented when an opportunity to invest in a cellular network in Nigeria presented itself. Alan and Andrew discussed the possibility of a joint venture with Nigerian billionaire and CEO of Globalcom, Mike Adenuga. However, days before the bidding for the cellular licence closed, Vodafone withdrew its approval for Vodacom to go ahead.

Alan was disappointed that Vodacom had missed out on entering the Nigerian cellular market since he felt it was the last big opportunity in Africa, but he agreed that it was a risky venture. Despite a controversial business history, today Globalcom is the second-largest network operator in Nigeria, with 14 million subscribers, not far behind MTN with 18 million.

Instead of dwelling on lost opportunities, Alan outbid three rivals in 2002 to win a licence for Vodacom to operate its network in Mozambique. As the country's second GSM operator, Vodacom formed a partnership with Emotel, a consortium of local businesspeople, public figures and a war veteran association. One of Vodacom's challenges would be to battle out the customer turf with the competition, mCel, owned by the state and German company Detecon, and entrenched in the country with 100 000 subscribers.

About 20 million people live in Mozambique where years of civil war have destroyed the country's infrastructure and social fabric. Although considered to be Africa's fastest-growing economy, poverty is rife. Vodacom forecast a total market of some 2 million customers after ten years of operations and expected to win a market share of at least 50%.

Cellular operations went up fast. The core network was built in three months and a six-figure customer base was reached in six months. With MD José dos Santos at the helm, Vodacom Mozambique reached a customer base of 1.3 million in 2008. Mozambique wasn't one of Vodacom's most lucrative investments, but with its current expansion to the north of the country it has become a promising investment.

Two years later, faced with competition at home from a third cellular operator, Cell C, and MTN's exceptional success in Nigeria, Alan began to reconsider Nigeria. In 2004 there were four network operators in Nigeria: MTN; Econet Wireless Nigeria (EWN, now Vmobile); Globalcom and NITEL, the state-owned utility managed by an external party. The single biggest challenge facing the cellular operators was keeping pace with demand as capacity expansion proved to be a struggle.

As Alan said to the press, 'The cellular cake is so big in Nigeria that if both MTN and Vodacom were to establish a cellular service there, there are so many Nigerians wanting telephones that we would certainly be hard pressed to service everybody. There are definitely enough potential subscribers to satisfy four operators, never mind two.'[3]

By March 2004, after months of extensive due diligence, Vodacom's negotiations with Nigeria's second-largest mobile firm, EWN were concluded to everyone's satisfaction with a view to concluding a joint venture.

The agreement with EWN was of special concern to Telkom's US-based shareholder, SBC Communications, which had a stake in Telkom through the Thinthana Consortium with Malaysia Telecoms, and through Telkom, served on the Vodacom board. The US Foreign Corrupt Practices Act (FCPA), enforced by the US Department of Justice (DOJ), prohibits US companies from either directly or indirectly giving anything of value to a foreign official for a corrupt purpose. The Americans in Telkom were hesitant to invest in Nigeria because if the DOJ found any US corporation guilty of contravening the Act, or buying into a company that had previously done so, a stiff fine and a possible jail sentence would be imposed. Shawn McKenzie, the SBC-appointed COO of Telkom at the time, said the American holding company would never approve the deal unless Alan took the proposal directly to the SBC CEO himself, Ed Sullivan. Alan met with Ed over a game of golf at Fancourt and assured him that Vodacom would operate in Nigeria with 'honesty, trust, good faith and professionalism', and that he would withdraw at the slightest suggestion of any damage to the reputation of its shareholders.

On 1 April 2004, the agreement between Vodacom and EWN became effective. The deal involved a five-year management contract of EWN, with the option to purchase, to ensure there would be no difficulties with the FCPA. Vodacom had the right to withdraw immediately if the Act's rules were not adhered to. Alan had spent well over R1 million on forensic teams to ensure that the agreement and EWN's company practices were sound.

But Vodacom's foray into Nigeria was challenged by EWN's minority shareholder, Econet Wireless Limited (EWL), headed by Strive Masiyiwa, who was a controversial figure in telecommunications circles. Masiyiwa maintained that he had first rights to the 33% in EWN that Vodacom had agreed to buy. He instituted legal action against Vodacom, accusing the company of inducing a breach of contract between himself and EWN, and claiming US$1.5 billion in damages.

However, Masiyiwa's own position was less than secure. He had been unable to secure finance for the proposed EWN deal (a fact he later acknowledged), and he faced accusations of mismanagement and cronyism from the EWN directors. Matters were further complicated by the fact that Masiyiwa was a founding partner of EWN, in which he held a 5% equity stake and a management contract to run the Nigerian operation. The EWN directors had voted to revoke all three – partnership, shareholding and management contracts.

Masiyiwa became a thorn in Alan's side. Since the court case wasn't proceeding as quickly as he wanted it to, Masiyiwa resorted to other measures to manipulate the situation to his advantage. If Alan sent a private letter to the EWN chairman, it was published in the press the following day; the US DOJ received a constant stream of information; and, in the end, Masiyiwa was there to ensure that he put a spoke in the wheel of the final deal.

The press reported: 'Masiyiwa became like a priest following Vodacom around Nigeria, looking for even the slightest sin. That Vodacom's overseas shareholders were already jittery was common knowledge, and it didn't take much to push them overboard. That came in the form of someone forwarding corruption allegations to the US authorities.'[4]

Despite this volatile background, negotiations between EWN and Vodacom continued. At one stage, Alan wondered if Nigeria was so important to Vodacom that it was worth the relentless hammering to which it was being subjected. Yet it was that important; it couldn't be ignored.

Alan stayed on in Nigeria until the deal had been concluded to his satisfaction and then flew to Phuket in early April 2004 for a much-needed holiday, leaving Andrew and his team behind to finalise the remaining details.

Within three weeks the deal went sour. By the time Alan landed in Johannesburg on 19 April 2004 his cellphone was ringing. It was Phil Williams telling him there was a serious problem in Nigeria and he was to 'fix' it immediately. The issue at stake was the payment of brokerage fees, which are legal and normal practice in Nigeria. Alan found that although the agreement between Vodacom and EWN stipulated that the brokerage fees were not to be paid until after the completion of the due diligence and the signing of the management agreement, they had been paid by the Nigerian operator days before the management agreement was signed. There was no corruption in respect of the brokerage fees, but it was regarded as a slip in corporate governance since Vodacom had to authorise payment personally. From the moment the management contract was signed, Vodacom was formally responsible for the company – past and present.

Alan was told that Masiyiwa had been the original party authorising all the payments on behalf of EWN, but when Masiyiwa was questioned by the press he referred to the issue as 'this matter of bribery' and that he had 'an obligation to cooperate with law enforcement agencies'.[5] EWN, suggesting that he was motivated by revenge, accused Masiyiwa of trying to spoil its deal with Vodacom.

On Alan's return, Andrew Mthembu, who headed up the Nigerian negotiations, had insisted that the commissions be reversed or Vodacom would pull out of the deal. All the monies had been reversed by 23 April. Alan and some of his colleagues departed for Lagos. They spent weeks checking and rechecking every transaction, and instituting even more stringent controls, even though they had no formal control of the company. But it wasn't good enough for the US authorities.

Alan wrote an email to his board with a proposal as to how he envisaged solving the Nigerian dilemma:

> *To some extent we are in a stalemate position with regards to our envisaged transaction in Nigeria. Whilst the commercial promise remains appealing, concerns relating to the US Department of Justice are stifling the appetite of at least SBC and to a lesser extent Vodafone. We are never going to escape the continuous barrage of real and imagined allegations of Strive and his cohorts to the DOJ, and the DOJ is never going to be able to totally dismiss them.*

The fact is that you, our shareholders, have been more than vigilant and cautious, our management team in Nigeria has been more than vigilant and cautious, and my colleagues and I have been ensuring to the absolute best of our ability that we have enough controls in place in Nigeria and enough resources to exercise these controls. That is far more than most companies are doing in Nigeria, and we should not be afraid to say so. We are committed to running a clean business, always have been, and always have done so.

As a display of good faith and commitment to a process which would ensure a trouble-free business in Nigeria, I would like to suggest that I visit the DOJ and explain not only our current situation, but also what we have done to remedy any failing we might have experienced. There has been no FCPA violation; there has been no dishonesty on our part. We cannot undo our mistakes, but we can react rapidly and repair whatever damage has been done, introduce measures to prevent any more mistakes, and move on.

If the DOJ did not give its blessing, then Alan suggested that Vodacom would have no choice but to move out of Nigeria with as much grace and as little damage as possible. It made him sick to the stomach to admit defeat because he knew that so many people had worked so hard to get the cellular deal up and running.

Alan flew to Washington DC on 22 May 2004 in a last-ditch attempt to save the agreement, but the Washington lawyers were clear: there was no way the deal could go ahead without courting more trouble.

On 27 May 2004, a special Vodacom Group board meeting was called in Midrand at which Alan, mindful of his promise to Ed Sullivan, recommended that Vodacom withdraw from Nigeria. The board agreed and, three days later, after meeting with the Nigerian shareholders at the Dorchester hotel in London, the agreement with the Nigerian company was terminated by mutual consent.

The market was shocked at Vodacom's hasty retreat from Nigeria, which was exacerbated by the negative publicity relating to the speculation around bribery and corruption. It was only after returning from his meeting with the Nigerians in London that Alan could face the media. He asserted that Vodacom's ethics and good governance had been compromised in Nigeria and that the company had had no alternative but to exit.

Added to the incredible disappointment of the broken deal, Andrew Mthembu resigned. Alan had spent ten years working with Andrew and was saddened that he had lost one of his best people. In fact, Andrew was being groomed to take over Alan's position as Chief Executive of Vodacom. Not only was Andrew an asset to Vodacom, he was also a valued friend to Alan. When Andrew left, Alan felt as if he had lost a member of his family.

By September 2004, the Vodacom board finally declared Nigeria to be 'over'. Nigeria was a year of Alan's life that he would have dearly loved to rewind and start over, but instead he focused on the next bend around the corner. Vodacom had escaped Nigeria scarred and battle-weary, but with its capital secure. Alan more or less kept his connections intact and a group of about 30 ex-Vodacom people under the leadership of Willem Swart remained behind to help EWN run the company.

Although Alan was disillusioned by the Nigerian experience, he made sure not to burn any bridges. 'The fact that we have withdrawn from this venture does not mean Nigeria is off limits,' he said to the media. Though he said he had 'lost his appetite for the moment', Nigeria was too important a market to ignore. However, he was emphatic that he would not go in and knowingly expose the company and its shareholders to inappropriate risk.

A year later, Vodacom was once again engaged in fresh talks with Vmobile (formerly EWN). The press dubbed Vodacom 'the comeback kid' of Nigeria's telecoms industry. Many saw Vodacom's re-entry into the Nigerian market as an attempt to surpass the performance of its rival MTN, which had experienced massive growth and phenomenal performance through its investment in Nigeria. In fact, the MTN Group had overtaken Vodacom by becoming the largest mobile network in Africa in terms of subscriber base and revenue. And this had been simply due to MTN's investment in Nigeria. Despite the speculation about Vodacom's motivation for returning to Nigeria, the fact of the matter was that due to the exit of SBC from Telkom and the improvement of governance within the Nigerian cellular company, Vodacom was once again able to consider a possible investment in Vmobile. At this point, the major challenge was no longer American anticorruption legislation, but the shareholder litigation in Vmobile, which needed to be resolved before Alan could make any investment.

Vodacom entered into a consortium with The Virgin Group in a joint bid for a controlling stake in Vmobile, but the agreement lapsed as the process dragged its feet. Late in 2005, the Vodacom board gave Alan approval to pursue the Nigerian deal on its own for the third time around. There was still huge potential, the price was right and Vodacom had been there before – the company knew the ropes. MTC, a Middle Eastern company, was the opposing bidder. This time, Alan played his cards carefully.

Vmobile made an offer to both EWL and Vodacom simultaneously, which the latter accepted and the former rejected. Alan was confident that this time Vodacom would at last own a little piece of Nigeria's cellular market.

Then, in early 2006, Vodafone suddenly pulled out. Alan was stunned. There was no coherent reason for the turnaround. He angrily fought Vodafone's decision, pointing out that Vodacom would never again get this chance to double the value of the company. Vodafone stood its ground and then, in a startling move, Telkom sided with Vodafone. Alan could not believe that he had spent so much time and energy on a perfect deal, only to be forced to retreat for no good reason with his reputation in shreds. MTC and Vmobile were left to negotiate the deal.

MTC bought a 65% controlling interest in Vmobile and re-named the company (using one of its brand names) Celtel. In two years, Celtel doubled its subscriber base. By October 2008, Nigeria's cellular market totalled 61 million subscribers, with 1.77 million new clients coming on-stream each month.

Another opportunity to invest in Nigeria came around shortly afterwards, but it was fraught with difficulties and far too expensive, and Alan was not in the right frame of mind to entertain any notion of buying into the Nigerian telecoms industry.

Once Nigeria was well and truly lost, the board decided to expand its African operations in Ghana. Although he was reluctant, Alan dutifully went off to Ghana at the shareholders' insistence with a business proposition, and was well received. Alan didn't even blink when his shareholders pulled out of this deal too. Vodafone returned to Ghana in its own capacity and set up a Vodafone cellular network in the country, maintaining that northern Africa was still its territory, as stipulated in the original contract. Tens of millions of rands poured down the tubes in Nigeria and Ghana – empty promises – all of it, thought Alan.

Alan is ambivalent about Nigeria. He had learnt much about Africa and its people. It didn't endear him to the politics of Africa, but he found the people vibrant and brave in the face of a vicious circle of adversity and poverty. He had also learned a great deal about Washington and the American justice system, and he had been disappointed in both. Alan had spent night after night turning the events in Nigeria over in his head, replaying different scenarios, but at the end of the day, the fact remained that Vodacom had missed out on its next big opportunity.

Nigeria was without a doubt the biggest disappointment of Alan's life.

New Millennium: New World – New Life
2000 to 2008

What appears to be the end may really be a new beginning.
Anonymous

The year 2000 was the Chinese Year of the Dragon, Alan's Chinese zodiac year of birth – 1952. The dragon is a symbol of good fortune and immense power, a respected and honoured master of authority; confident and fearless in the face of challenges. This is my year, thought Alan, this is going to be my best year ever. He couldn't have been more wrong.

Internationally, the good news was that the Y2K millennium bug never materialised. But three months later, in March, the dotcom bubble burst, wiping out scores of high-tech companies that had invested and speculated millions on the Internet in the mistaken belief that this was a 'recession-proof' market. Closer to home, Nelson Mandela stepped down as president of South Africa to make way for Thabo Mbeki. Alan had nothing against Mbeki, but with the country in Madiba's hands he had felt the future to be more secure. Overnight, South Africa seemed to be on shaky ground.

Alan berated himself for being such a wimp. In the interests of progress, it was important to release the familiar and embrace the new. Alan's career was at its pinnacle. Vodacom had become a formidable business with a market capitalisation of R70 billion, which would make it one of the country's five biggest companies if it went public. With a turnover close to R10 billion, Vodacom had proven over and over that it had a winning formula.

In September 2000, Vodacom shareholder Rembrandt restructured into two listed companies, namely, Remgro Limited and VenFin Limited. Remgro represented Rembrandt's established interests in tobacco, financial services, mining and industry, while the telecommunication and technology interests were accommodated in VenFin Limited, which included shareholding in Vodacom. Alan was pleased that Dillie Malherbe was retained on the Vodacom board as VenFin's representative since he made a sound contribution to their discussions.

Five years later, in November 2005, Vodafone bought VenFin's 13.5% stake in Vodacom for R16 billion, making the company a 50% shareholder in Vodacom with Telkom. It was the second-largest direct foreign investment in post-apartheid South Africa. Alan hoped that the deal would spur Vodafone on to give Vodacom free rein to pursue new markets and earn fresh revenue. On a personal level, however, he would miss Dillie's involvement on the board; his non-interventionist approach to Alan's management style and his valuable contributions over the years that had made a visible difference to every meeting.

However, it was on a personal level that Alan was to undergo a transformation that would change his life.

In April 2000, Alan was in London for the annual Vodafone Spring Ball. While exercising in the gym of his hotel, he was gripped by terrible chest pains and collapsed to the floor. At the age of 48, he was exceptionally fit and had the stamina of a man half his age, and yet he had had a heart attack. The supplements he had been taking were partly to blame for inducing the blood clots in his heart, but he knew that the hours he kept and the demands of running a multi-billion rand company had taken their toll on his health too.

Following his recuperation, Alan returned to work with the intention of taking things much easier than before. However, he was soon immersed in the demented pace that drove Vodacom forward; except now, Alan no longer found it stimulating.

When Vodacom had started out, there was no blueprint showing Alan how to start up a new industry; he had had to rely on his wits, which made his job unpredictable, challenging and fun. He could be as creative and imaginative as he wished, taking his ideas to new heights that no one had dreamed possible, further adding to the thrill he felt working for Vodacom. Alan loved his work. When a journalist asked him how many hours a days he spent running Vodacom, Alan replied that he didn't understand the question. He lived and breathed Vodacom. It *was* his life.

But now that the company was firmly established as the top cellular operator, the emphasis had switched from innovation to consolidation. Although this made commercial sense, Alan missed the days when inventive thought counted for at least as much as financial expediency. Nowadays he seemed to do a lot more delegating and supervising and a lot less doing and controlling.

Another source of tension at the time was Alan's changed relationship with Telkom. In 1997, the US-based SBC Communications had partnered with Telkom Malaysia to buy 30% of Telkom for R5.5 billion, and the Americans were sent to run the South African organisation.

'SBC is a solid company,' says Alan, 'but for the six years that Telkom was under American management they pretty much made a hash of it and made my life hell, and I know the feeling was mutual. With the exception of the last American COO of Telkom, Shawn McKenzie, I'm sure they would have hung me out to dry at the first opportunity. They certainly tried, opportunity or not. But they forgot one thing, they were guests in our country, and I was not. And I would not allow them to intimidate me.'

Alan suspected that the Americans did not like his hands-on, somewhat autocratic management style, or his refusal to play a subservient role to them.

'They seemed to regard Vodacom as a Telkom subsidiary and me as their lackey when, in fact, they only played a shareholder role in the company,' he says. 'Anyway, I refused to be deferential to them.'

Alan even received an affidavit from someone in senior management at Telkom, which is still in his possession, confirming that 'there exists a conspiracy by the American senior management of Telkom to undermine Alan Knott-Craig and they desire to see him removed from his position as CEO of the Vodacom Group'. At one board meeting, an American non-executive director of Vodacom got up and said, 'I absolutely insist that Alan be fired right now', in reaction to something controversial that Alan had said or purportedly not done. It wasn't the first time that he had been threatened with being fired, and he was certain it wouldn't be the last.

Vodafone, VenFin and the Vodacom chairperson at the time, Wendy Luhabe, were incensed by the outburst, but Phil Williams calmed everyone down. These personal attacks, more than anything else, strengthened Alan's relationship with Wendy. Most of the Americans who headed up Telkom refused to see Alan; it was only when Shawn McKenzie of SBC became the Telkom COO under Sizwe Nxsana, the Telkom CEO, that Alan was able to forge a productive working relationship. But, as Alan says ruefully, 'The damage had already been done. Besides, I'd pissed too many people off by that stage. I continued to treat them with the same contempt they held for me.' Phil had his hands full trying to keep the peace.

By way of contrast, Alan's relationship with Vodacom's chairs was far more positive. The personal rapport he developed with Alwyn Martin, Dr Hasmukh Gajjar, Wendy Luhabe and Advocate Oyama Mabandla (the successive Vodacom chairs Alan worked under) meant that Alan rarely had cause to complain. He had a suspicion that Telkom's American management had initially briefed some of them to oust him, but they became his staunchest supporters.

Despite the board's support of Alan in the face of Telkom's hostility toward him, it created a great deal of unnecessary tension. 'Eventually, it became unbearable,' remarks Alan, 'and I suppose the situation was a contributing factor to my heart attack in 2000.'

Alan voiced his concerns to Phil Williams, urging him to ask the board to release him from his position.

'Phil,' Alan started carefully, 'if I had to choose a time to leave Vodacom it would be now.'

Phil was visibly startled. 'What's brought this on, Alan? You need to put your heart attack behind you now.'

'That's part of the reason I need to leave,' Alan admitted. 'But it's more than that. I've changed. Vodacom has changed. Now, it's all about making more money, and that on its own is boring as hell. When I started at Vodacom no one believed in cellular. Now everyone is hooked. The gold rush is over.'

'The board won't let you go easily, you know that,' remarked Phil.

The board, as Phil had predicted, refused to countenance the idea.

They needed Alan to stay where he was for the good of the company and the shareholders. To sweeten the bad news – bad news as far as Alan was concerned – they gave him a generous raise. How ironic, thought Alan. When I was killing myself working eighteen hours a day, I earned a pitiful salary. Now that I want to leave, they offer me a serious package.

But Alan wasn't interested in more money; money wouldn't alleviate the general feeling of dissatisfaction and restlessness that possessed him. The heart attack had changed him, he knew that, but quite *how* it had changed him he could not say. He just felt *different*. And because he felt unfulfilled and unsure about what life he should be leading, he became increasingly irritable. At home, he became argumentative, intolerant and distant. His relationship with Janet began to suffer, but he refused to accept the fact that his marriage was failing. Things between the couple got so bad that in December 2001 they agreed to separate. Two months later, having accepted that their marriage could not be saved, Alan and Janet divorced on amicable terms.

When Alan reflects on his marriage to Janet, he realises that from the time he started at Vodacom, he had slipped into another world, leaving Janet behind. He had become careless of his relationship with her. Vodacom was like Hollywood – a place full of egos searching for the spotlight, of wild ideas and people for whom the word 'normal' was anathema, of non-stop action performed at breakneck speed without a safety net. If you couldn't keep up, you were dropped without a thought. And if someone got lost along the way, no one even noticed.

And for a long time Alan had been able to keep up. In fact, he had been out at the front of the pack setting the pace. He had felt invincible; he could go on forever, firing on all eight cylinders at once. The heart attack reminded him that he was neither invincible nor unstoppable; it also made him think more seriously about relationships that he had taken for granted for too long.

Because Vodacom had been his all-consuming passion, Alan had spent little time with his three boys when they were growing up as teenagers. Janet had taken charge of their upbringing; the only time he became involved was when they needed discipline, in which case he would be as tough on them as his own father had been on him. One month of every year was always spent at the beach house in Boggomsbaai. They had a wonderful time, but that hardly made up for the separate lives they lived the remainder of the year. But the heart attack mellowed him, making him more approachable, and he began to enjoy a relaxed relationship with his adult sons. He knew that the boys had taken strain during the months following the divorce, but he took comfort in the fact that they were all adults who would eventually be able to accept that although their parents were no longer together, they were loved beyond measure.

For months after the divorce, Alan was withdrawn and dispirited. He stayed with his lifelong friend Les Cohen in Sandton, while his assistant Rae found a house for him to buy in Waterkloof, Pretoria. He had no furniture to his name and was glad of the curtains the previous owner had left behind. But he had a view and a rose garden, which lifted his spirits. His youngest son, Matthew, moved in with him. For a while, Alan wasn't sure who was looking after whom, but he was glad of the company. Janet had been his companion for more than 25 years, and the thought of living alone had chilled him to the core. With hindsight, he knew that Janet had been a good wife who had never complained about his long hours and the constant trips into Africa and abroad. She was a nurturer whose priority had been her family.

As Alan tried to pick up the pieces of his life, he returned his attention to Vodacom, vowing to himself that he would do things differently this time. But before he could make his next move, he had to wait for what seemed like an eternity for the entry of the third cellular operator and a decision on access to the 1 800 spectrum. MTN and Vodacom had been limited to using the overcrowded GSM 900 network spectrum, which was becoming problematic. 'You can only knit so many jerseys from one ball of wool,' said Alan, 'and spectrum is just like that.'

Alan welcomed another mobile network operator into the market and waited eagerly for Cell C's appearance. Competition made everyone think smarter and that, so he maintained, could only be a good thing.

Cell C was formed by a consortium of Lebanese businessmen, led by Talaat Laham, and South African BEE companies and trusts. The third licence, eventually awarded to Cell C, took three-and-a-half years to process. Bidding started in late 1998, the licence was awarded in mid-2001, and the service was launched in November 2001. The first network licence had taken just six months to finalise.

'Those three years screwed Cell C,' says Alan. 'The process was all about bad losers not being able to accept defeat. They started the race, and when the losers became unhappy with their lot, they asked for the race to be re-run – which would, of course, give them another chance. I have seen it happen again and again in other industries. It becomes a farce.'

Amidst the discussions around granting the third cellular network licence, the availability of frequencies or spectrum became a long, drawn-out saga. The spectrum is the most important resource for cellular network operators; they cannot function without it. Despite threats of a court case and various negotiations between Vodacom, MTN and the Independent Communications Authority of South Africa (Icasa), the regulator allocated Cell C sole use of the 1 800 Meg bandwidth for three years, placing all three networks at a disadvantage. MTN and Vodacom would have to continue sharing the now-overcrowded 900 Meg bandwidth, which impacted on network quality in congested areas. What might at first sight have seemed like a good proposition to Cell C was, in fact, anything but. The lower-frequency bandwidth (the 900 Meg) gave better penetration since low frequencies can travel through physical barriers more easily than high frequencies – the 1 800 Meg bandwidth.

Ideally, Vodacom and MTN needed to give Cell C some 900 spectrum and Cell C needed to give away some 1 800 spectrum in return. But Cell C didn't want to do it. Alan couldn't understand why they didn't see the value of operating in both spectrums.

'Icasa's decision was a big mistake,' remarks Alan. 'If it had stopped to think, the regulator would have brought down the costs of cellular and Cell C would have been in a stronger position. I had gone to great lengths to point out the benefits of using both spectrums and it had been ignored. But perhaps it was just part of a political game of which I was unaware.'

Cell C soon ran into difficulties, as Alan explains: 'It didn't take Cell C long to figure out that it couldn't build an efficient network with the 1 800 spectrum alone, so it asked us for some of ours.'

Despite the frequency saga, Alan had a good relationship with Talaat, having travelled to Lebanon together to take in the sights and flavours of a country that Alan considered to be one of the most beautiful in the world. They agreed that Cell C could 'roam' on Vodacom's network, for which it would have to pay a negotiated fee.

'It was a great deal for both of us,' says Alan. 'Whatever market share Cell C gained, it always came back to us; and whatever market share we lost it still came back to us.'

Cell C shared some of the towers and distribution channels that Vodacom had set up and there was a genuinely productive and healthy relationship between the two network operators. As Alan says, 'We shared more easily with Cell C than we had ever done with MTN.'

Cell C's cardinal mistake, according to Alan, was its decision to build its own network, an incredibly expensive procedure that the shared-facilities agreement should have rendered unnecessary. As well as the cost of establishing its own network, Cell C was still obligated to pay Vodacom for using its network – even if it no longer intended using it.

'It's like having a car in the garage and not driving it. I think that Cell C might have used its money better,' is Alan's terse assessment.

With a third player in the cellular market, Alan was not about to rest on his laurels. Vodacom could not for a minute take its market lead for granted. It was important to stay ahead of the pack, and the way to do that was to continue to out-innovate the competition. On Vodacom's seventh anniversary in 2001, the company launched a new product that billed customers by the second instead of by the minute. Vodacom 4U was a prepaid spin-off targeted at teenagers. The trick was to introduce Vodacom 4U to the youth market without smothering Vodago, which was aimed at adults over the age of 25. Alan recognised the enormous spending power of the youth and specifically commissioned the design of a product that would grab the attention of this fickle market. 'If anyone over 30 likes the product, I'll scrap it,' he told his engineers.

The concept had to appeal to the teenage lifestyle. The idea was not only to provide a new service, but to offer a holistic cellular experience. Vodacom 4U included ultra-cheap SMS rates, a prepaid or contract option, an application for an international student identity card, and an SMS dictionary. In its first year Vodacom 4U attracted 760 000 customers, almost as many people as were connected to Vodacom in the first four years of the company's existence. The image of the bungee-jumping baby and the catchy tune, 'Seize the moment, seize the day', had the sort of off-beat charm and humour that Alan was looking for. But, more importantly, it was precisely what the target market was looking for – something subtle yet distinctive without a deliberately 'cool' image.

Building on the cellular experience, Vodacom launched its My Life service in 2002 and Look4me two years later. My Life offered subscribers Internet access and a combined photo-and-text message capability by blending together General Packet Radio Service (GPRS) and Multi-media Messaging Service (MMS). Alan found it interesting that his first 'real' job at Telkom in the 1980s had been to build an X.25 packet network, and here he was again launching packet communication with wireless access. My Life was a cellular effort to bridge the digital divide since it gave the majority of people in the country access to the Internet through their cellphones, where previously it would have been out of reach due to the exorbitant cost of purchasing a computer.

Look4me enabled subscribers to track any other Vodacom cellphone user as long as that person had given his or her consent. The idea behind the concept was to offer people peace of mind knowing they could check the location of family members, especially that of their children. The new feature was welcomed by the police because it could help 'trap' a criminal using a Look4me-enabled cellphone at the scene of a crime. The man convicted of killing former first lady, Marike de Klerk, made a call to his girlfriend from De Klerk's cellphone. The call was picked up by a mast 50 metres from the complex where the murder took place.

When the idea of bringing third generation (3G) technology to South Africa was first suggested, Alan had been reluctant. The high licence costs involved had proved disastrous in Europe, where 3G had failed dismally. Alan did not want the same to happen in South Africa. In essence, 3G combined a mobile phone, a laptop, PC and television in one package, which provided a whole new way of communicating, gaining information, conducting business, learning and accessing entertainment.

After a conversation with Lothar Pauly, a man Alan admired for his technical expertise, Alan decided to lead from the front with the launch of 3G. His decision was also prompted by the regulator's ruling not to charge a licence fee, probably in the light of the failure of that approach in Europe. With everything he had done, being first had given him the edge. Being there first had made Vodacom the biggest provider of cellular in the country.

Vodacom spent R400 million rolling out the initial 3G sites in the major metropolitan areas and then rolled out a further 1 000 3G sites for an additional R835 million. Mobile broadband, upon which 3G was based, was already revolutionising the way in which people did business; it meant, for example, that an employee could work out of the office without compromising his or her productivity. The advantages of this technology included simplicity, convenience, value-for-money, wide-ranging coverage, easy activation and mobility. 3G customers could stay connected for as long as they liked because they only paid for the amount of data they sent and received – and not for the length of time they were connected.

Telkom had been the sole provider of broadband, and then Vodacom started to fly, providing some stiff competition; speeds became faster and the price of 3G was cut by 99%. Alan focused on volume to get the technology into as many hands as possible, and much to his surprise, the company started making money from it. In retrospect, he believes that the introduction of 3G was Vodacom's most significant contribution to the cellular market in the first decade of the new millennium. 'It wasn't new. We just took advantage of an opportunity that nobody else wanted,' is how he puts it.

With cellphone penetration in South Africa at 80%, Vodacom was constantly looking for opportunities to expand its growth horizontally in the market. In 2006 the company prepared to compete with Multichoice's DStv in the pay-TV market, since cellphones could now double up as satellite decoders. Alan could see a time in the not-too-distant future when people would go to one company to buy their TV package, telephone, Internet and data transmission as a bundle. And, by setting up a Bluetooth connection between the cellphone and the television, satellite channels could also be viewed at home on a bigger screen.

'Think about a world without expensive satellite dishes and decoders,' says Alan. 'Imagine sitting in a rural area watching Bafana Bafana win the World Cup! The cellphone could make the perfect decoder. The possibilities are endless.'

It wasn't only new technology that was transforming cellular businesses, the regulatory environment also brought about change that would have a profound impact on network operators.

The Electronic Communications Act of 2007 allowed operators to build their own fixed-line networks rather than being forced to lease lines from Telkom, and Alan intended to do just that. Vodacom started laying fibre optic lines in metropolitan areas that year in order to gain additional data capacity and to end its reliance upon Telkom. The fact that true broadband demanded fixed lines was, of course, a major factor.

Telkom, confronted by the newly empowered cellphone providers, also faced competition in the form of Neotel, the new national telecommunications operator that had just been awarded a R100 million contract to supply services to the government in preference to Telkom. Pressured from all sides, Telkom started making noises to the effect that it would have to establish its own mobile phone business if it was to remain a force in the telecommunications industry.

As Telkom and Vodacom sped toward a collision course, each encroaching on the other's traditional territory, Telkom admitted that 'if presented with a bona fide offer from Vodafone, the board would be obliged to consider it'. The scene was set for Vodafone to step in and take advantage of Telkom's invitation for it to acquire a greater share of South Africa's largest cellular company. Soon after, in 2008, Vodafone offered Telkom R22.5 billion for 15% of its equity in Vodacom, placing a value of R150 billion on Vodacom. It was a source of great pride to Alan that the little company he had started fifteen years previously had grown from nothing to R150 billion in just over a decade. The offer was made on condition that Telkom unbundled the rest of its stake to its shareholders. Some was to be sold to BEE partners, some was allocated to the Vodacom staff and the rest listed on the Johannesburg Stock Exchange (JSE). The sale gave Vodafone management control of Vodacom.

Vodacom was listed on the JSE in May 2009, eight months after Alan retired. Fortunately, Alan was spared the controversy surrounding the move. After spending R200 million preparing for the listing, Icasa and trade union federation, Cosatu, launched an urgent interdict the day before the event to block the listing, after having approved the deal months before. The rand plunged by 3%; government was accused of meddling; and foreign investors saw the move as confirmation that South Africa was an unstable business investment. The listing went ahead as planned and Icasa issued an apology a week later saying they had 'fallen off their horse'.[1] Once again, Alan was not impressed with Icasa's performance, and he sympathised with Pieter Uys having to deal with this challenge in his first months as Vodacom CEO.

From fledgling start-up to listed company, Vodacom had come a long way since launching a revolutionary technology upon a disbelieving market. In the first eight years of its existence until 2000, Vodacom's customer base had topped 3 million. From 2000 to 2008, the following eight years, Vodacom's customer base grew to 33 million. The company's growth had been nothing short of spectacular and the numbers had rocketed beyond comparison. But for Alan, the first couple of years had been the most intense. He felt as if he had been part of a team inventing the wheel, and he had given everything he had within him to make it work, to the exclusion of all else in his life. It saddens him to think that if he hadn't had another heart attack in 2006, his life wouldn't have been any different. He would still be chasing that wheel.

Alan knew that he had not only built a solid company, but that he had empowered people by opening up the lines of communication previously out of reach to the majority of the population. A simple little handset had given millions of South Africans the chance to participate more fully in the economic, social and cultural life of the country, which Alan considered immensely enriching – for them and for him. It was no small feat, and he was grateful that he had been given the unique opportunity of being a pivotal part of the cellphone revolution in the country. But the satisfaction Alan gained from his professional achievements was not replicated in his personal life. He saw his heart attacks as a brief intervention, intense and painful, to set him on a different course. He had been given another chance and he had to make it count, every second of it. The question still stood, 'What happens next?'

The Legacy
2008

One day your life will flash before your eyes, make sure it's worth watching.
Anonymous

The entire audience rose to its feet – journalists, investment analysts, government officials and shareholders – to give Alan a standing ovation that left him momentarily speechless. It was an unprecedented, spontaneous tribute to a man they regarded as the father of cellular in Africa – the architect of a multi-billion rand industry that has added real value to the lives of millions. Alan was deeply moved by this unexpected gesture, one which he would always regard as one of the highlights of his career at Vodacom.

In June 2008, for the fourteenth year running, Alan presented Vodacom's financials to an audience of critics and admirers alike. The figures reflected double-digit growth, an operating profit of R12.5 billion, an income of some R50 billion, and 33 million customers in five African countries – an exceptional achievement under the leadership of a man whose priority was not to build a financial empire, but to empower people through the gift of communication. Through an innocuous handset, the face of communication on the continent had been revolutionised and an indelible imprint had been left on the social fabric of its people.

The success of the cellular industry in South Africa and the growth of Vodacom is a case study in visionary leadership, constant commitment to excellence, the will to succeed at all costs, and an ability to inspire people to visualise and realise a dream. In an interview a few years ago, Alan said to the contrary: 'I am no visionary, nor a great intellectual, nor do I have the patience to read the fine print. But I have the ability to learn quickly, to make people excited about what they are doing, and to get the job done.'[1]

On the announcement of his retirement in June 2008 Alan received a number of letters from people who clearly thought that he had more than just the ability to learn and to get the job done. The late Dr Ivy Matsepe-Casaburri, Minister of Communications from 1999 until her death in April 2009, said in a personal letter to him: 'Your tenacity, business acumen, inspiration and the talent to build a world-class network have immensely contributed to a better life for millions of South Africans.' Perhaps that is what Jack Clarke spotted in Alan Knott-Craig the day he chose someone to head up Vodacom – the power to lead a team to change people's lives for the better.

Above all, Alan's drive to be first, to be the best, was behind every success that carried Vodacom to the top. At the core of Alan's philosophy is the notion that if he is not going to win, then it isn't worth doing. His father's words, 'First is first and second is nothing' will always be his mantra.

Alan attributes his success with Vodacom to five critical factors, one of which is distribution. A company's ability to get its product out the door and into the hands of its customers will determine its likely success or failure. Aware of the impact Vodacom's distribution system could have, Alan started to negotiate with cellular dealers for exclusive distribution of Vodacom products months before the licence was granted. In fact, it seemed all he did in 1993 was to negotiate distribution deals. Once the large corporations such as Pick 'n Pay and Game had bought into his concept, the rest seemed to fall into place. He lined up dealerships across the country and gave them a product that would walk off the shelves. But Alan didn't just sit back and watch the distribution channel work for him. He created personal relationships with his dealers, so much so that many of them became lifelong friends. He showed an interest in solving their problems and set them up to be successful. In return, they gave him their loyalty and ensured his success.

After establishing a first-rate distribution network, Alan turned his attention to another critical success factor. Coverage is a cellular network's product, maintains Alan, not cellphones. He knew that if he provided more coverage than the competition he would also gain more customers. Coverage is the number one priority for cellphone users; it is the thing they care about most. As a result, Alan invested heavily in it. By December 1994, Vodacom covered all the major highways and gained a foothold in the local market that it has never lost. 'It was a question of the haves and the have-nots,' says Alan. 'You either had coverage or you didn't. And if you did, you were set for success; the customers followed you willingly.'

Alan then set about creating brand awareness, which was (and still is) a vital component of Vodacom's success. The first Vodacom advertisements ran on television seven months before the product was available. He spent R10 million on advertising at this early stage because he believed that if he was the first to establish his brand, then Vodacom would become the leader in the cellular industry right from the beginning. The move paid off – literally, since Vodacom's financial position has gone from strength to strength thanks to effective brand awareness campaigns. Focusing on a consistent message and constant visibility, the brand exuded humour and warmth, which touched the hearts of the nation. The Yebo Gogo brand became part of the vocabulary and culture of an entire generation, providing Vodacom with more mileage than any other company in the country.

While there never has been a price war in South Africa between the cellular providers since 1994, price and product are fundamentally important to Vodacom's financial health. Where products were concerned, prepaid airtime was the magic formula that found a market like no other cellular product before it. It was the golden key to unlock the door of economic opportunity, especially for the millions of black South Africans for whom the door had remained resolutely shut during apartheid. Prepaid airtime was a first for Vodacom and for the world. Today prepaid is not only a huge part of Vodacom's business in South Africa, but also of its operations elsewhere on the continent. Two other products that have contributed to Vodacom's success are SMS and Vodacom 4U. For the first five years almost no one used SMS. Alan then took a strategic stand and offered SMS free of charge, much to the dismay of his competitors. Usage shot up and kept growing, even after Vodacom started charging for the service again.

Vodacom 4U cornered the youth market for the company, making it the 'coolest' brand in the country. Billing airtime per second seemed like an insane concept, but the youth market bought into it with such enthusiasm that it spent more than the standard prepaid customers.

Regardless of the cost, Alan invested in a full range of technology because he believed that people want to communicate on the most advanced level possible. 'So what if it takes a while to get your money back,' says Alan. 'You don't price in this industry based on cost. If you did, the first people who joined the network would have paid a fortune and business would have stopped right there and then. You have to take a good financial hiding in the first few years. It took us seven years to become cash-flow positive on voice, and data communication won't be an overnight success either. It takes time.'

Vodacom couldn't remain exclusively in South Africa. Since 1995 the company has extended its field of operation to include other African nations. Alan believes that a company's commercial well-being cannot be measured in isolation; it needs to be considered in the context of regional economic performance. If South Africa's neighbours can improve their economies and corporate governance, the southern African region will become a much more attractive proposition to foreign investors.

In Africa, cellular communication is, in effect, the only communication, since fixed-line infrastructure is at best poor, at worst non-existent. This means that there is no limit to the level of penetration achievable on the continent. The cellular company that can effectively market its brand in other African countries can then start to think about the international market. This transition will only be possible via alliances forged with large international groupings, since the sums involved in establishing cellular overseas will be substantial. And the key to success in any expansion exercise is consistency of product and service. Customers want to know that if they use a Vodacom cellphone in New York, New Delhi or Sydney, the experience they have will be equally good. Providing consistency of service at the highest standard possible is the surest way of keeping existing customers and attracting new ones. This explains why Alan was prepared to commit the same level of expertise and resources to each and every Vodacom roll-out programme – in South Africa, Lesotho, Tanzania, Mozambique and the DRC – to ensure the same high level of brand consistency wherever Vodacom products and services were available.

The Legacy

The possibility of total cellular penetration is not as far-fetched as it may seem. It is certainly an idea that Alan has given a great deal of thought to.

'I don't see why cellular penetration can't be 100%,' he says. 'Who says you need money to have a cellphone? You can get second-hand phones for next to nothing. You can receive calls and it doesn't cost you a bean. You need never make a call, but you can call your voicemail and emergency number free of charge, and you can send free "Please Call Me" requests. To me, that sounds very appealing.'

Alan's outstanding leadership and unique business acumen are qualities that have also been acknowledged and appreciated within the academic community. In May 2006, as Vodacom reached its 20 million customer mark and posted a revenue of R31 billion, Alan was awarded an honorary Doctorate of Business Leadership by Unisa in recognition of 'his remarkable contribution to the world of business'. Alan, more comfortable with praising others than receiving praise himself, simply told the press he was 'quite chuffed' with the award. Although he is, of course, immensely and justifiably proud of the honour bestowed on him, he did not feel the need to broadcast this through the media. Two years later, he was awarded a second honorary doctorate from the Nelson Mandela Metropolitan University in Port Elizabeth.

Alan had introduced the Vodacom CEO Awards to create a culture of excellence and to establish role models for Vodacom staff and everyone associated with the company. On the eve of his retirement, Alan was presented with his own personal CEO Award by the new CEO, Pieter Uys. The award, said Pieter, was an 'official recognition of the enormous personal contribution you have made over the last decade and a half of your life, often at huge cost to yourself. We hereby recognise not only your vision, but the commitment and dedication that you so uniquely brought to realise that vision. We want to thank you for leading us so fearlessly and so clearly. We want to thank you for inspiring us, teaching us to think big and to always go toward the future with courage.'

Doctorates bestowed in recognition of exceptional achievements; an unexpected standing ovation; a tribute to his leadership – these must be amongst Alan's most treasured memories. Yet he cites meeting Nelson Mandela and being in a position to make a contribution to some of his projects as an especially rewarding experience.

'People worship Madiba and anything he touches, yet there is a rare humility about him,' says Alan. 'And this is where his power lies. We've lost that since he left the presidency. It was Madiba who taught me the secret of life: always let people know how important they are and they will do anything for you. It takes little effort and it comes back to you in more ways than you can imagine.'

On his birthday in May 2006, Alan was chatting to a journalist in his office when he was interrupted by a telephone call from Dot Field, Group Executive: Corporate Communications for Vodacom.

'Alan, there's someone downstairs who wants to wish you happy birthday,' she said.

'Dot, I'm in the middle of an interview,' Alan answered impatiently.

Dot insisted, 'Believe me, Alan, you want to come downstairs. Just do it.'

Alan hurried downstairs, where Dot directed him out onto the pavement in front of the Vodacom offices. A cavalcade of black cars stood end-to-end right outside the building. One of the back doors of the first car opened and out stepped Madiba in full view of the entire Vodacom staff contingent with their noses pressed up against the windows. 'I must be dreaming,' thought Alan. Madiba smiled broadly and stepped forward to shake his hand.

'I was in the area and I thought I would stop by and wish you happy birthday,' Mandela said.

Alan, visibly overwhelmed, somehow found the words to thank him.

Not long after, Alan invited Madiba to lunch at Vodacom Corporate Park to meet his staff, shareholders and business partners. Madiba, gracious as always, accepted. As he entered the Vodacom building, staff members hung over the balconies, cheering and clapping; pictures were taken; hand after hand was shaken; smiles were given all around; and the Vodacom choir sang like it had never sung before.

If Alan had been 'quite chuffed' when Unisa gave him his degree, he would probably concede that he was 'very chuffed' the day Nelson Mandela visited Vodacom and touched the lives of everyone present that day.

The first school and clinic Vodacom built were at Madiba's request, which led to the establishment of the Vodacom Foundation.

'In my fifteen years as CEO of Vodacom, this must be one of our most important achievements. There can be nothing more meaningful than to mend a child's heart; give someone back his sight; or provide access to life-changing surgery so that a young girl can smile. The people who make the Foundation their life's work – caregivers, doctors, my staff members, ordinary people – have inspired me and confirmed my belief in the power within each one of us to be a force for good. The work of the Foundation has made me proud to be associated with Vodacom.'

So how does Vodacom continue to remain a sound company with its CEO of fifteen years making his exit?

'Simple,' says Alan. 'Don't tamper with the current successful management of the company.'

Pieter Uys, formerly Vodacom's COO, emerged as the logical successor to Alan. Over the last few years he had taken over the reins of the company on many occasions and has in-depth knowledge of what needs to be done to ensure that the company remains successful.

Although Leon Crouse, Vodacom's former financial manager and Alan's right-hand man, also left Vodacom, the core team that remains is exceptionally talented and committed. The technical expertise of the company's senior engineers is unparalleled, since they have been with Vodacom since its inception. So, when Alan left, he did so happy in the knowledge that Vodacom was in safe hands and that its future was filled with promise.

Every End is a New Beginning
2009

Don't ask yourself what the world needs; ask yourself what makes you come alive. And then go and do that. Because what the world needs is people who have come alive.
Harold Whitman

In the end, I chose a new life. Sometimes when you think you are done, another beginning presents itself; tentative and nebulous at first, it becomes a flickering glimmer of light. For a long time I felt my life had come full circle. The hours I spent staring at that heart monitor lulled me into a state of introspection, where I reassessed my life in the minutest detail. In retrospect, I don't consider my heart attacks to be a misfortune; they were a refuge that made me stop and change direction. I was so high on success that no one could touch me, but I had reached a point where I needed to stop and see what I was worth to myself. I had poured my heart and soul into Vodacom to the exclusion of everything else, which I now knew I could no longer do – even if it had taken two physical breakdowns to make me see this. There is nothing more compelling than standing at the edge of your life – peering into the void – and wondering what the hell you are doing.

Vodacom was a living, breathing dream come true. It was an inspiring, absorbing part of my life. In fact, it *was* my life. At times it was tempestuous and frenzied, like a torrid love affair, which inevitably must run its course, but it was exhilarating all the same. As one success followed another, I believed I was invincible. But eventually it consumed me. I don't believe in half measures – it's either all or nothing – and I gave Vodacom my all. And, if I could turn back the clock, I wouldn't change a single thing. Regardless of the light and dark shades that coloured my experiences, I know that my life became richer for all that Vodacom gave me. It is a life few would have the chance to experience. It made me brave. But in the end, it left me cold.

The first five years were challenging, thrilling, exacting – I was stretched to my limits. But as soon as Vodacom became a successful corporation, bureaucracy slipped in and took over. The company became a lumbering creature that I couldn't tame. Once established, Vodacom seemed to lose some of its innovative spirit, and so did I. Don't get me wrong, the company was always flying, but it was dragging too many people, too many procedures in its slipstream. Everyone wanted a piece of the action and it became impossible to act with any real, meaningful independence. I couldn't make a decision without going through the all-important *processes*. I began to lose my enthusiasm for what had been the most wonderful job in the world; I became a bore. And when that happened, I knew I had to get out.

If I was asked to nominate the single most challenging aspect of my life at Vodacom, I would have to say it was managing the board's expectations. But I could handle it and I enjoyed it in a perverse way. At best, my relationship with the board was like a game of chess: two wary opponents probing for weaknesses, using strategy and guile to outmanoeuvre the other. At worst, it resembled a boxing match: two pugnacious fighters engaged in all-out attack in round after round of a bloody, bruising contest.

Perhaps strife and discord are inevitable in such situations. After all, Vodacom was both a free-spirited enterprise *and* a corporate behemoth. Where I would continually press for swift, decisive action, the board would invariably call for a slower, more considered response. I argued that things needed to be done today (or better yet, yesterday) because I knew that it was only by leading from the front – acting and not reacting – that Vodacom would gain irresistible momentum. And with momentum comes growth, which is what we both wanted.

Of course, my relationship with the board was not all doom and gloom; by and large we got done what we needed to, and I think we did a pretty good job together. Some board members I worked particularly well with, most notably Phil Williams of Vodafone, who, right from the beginning, did all he could to help me. A consummate professional and long-time friend, Phil is also blessed with the ability to see and bring out the best in people, including me. His understanding of human nature is uncanny; I have lost count of the times he has left me marvelling at some nuance of behaviour or action that he has picked up in someone. Phil saw the person behind every success, failure, joy and disappointment. He had a singular approach that often made the biggest difference. When Phil left Vodafone, things were not the same. I had lost a valued colleague as well as a close friend, which made his departure all the harder to bear.

Although I became skilled at getting what I wanted from the board, there were times it kept my hands tied, specifically when it came to expansion. Our forays into Africa had left me demoralised. We tackled a difficult market in the Congo amidst crumbling infrastructure and continuous civil war; in Mozambique we continued to butt heads with a ten-year incumbent; in Tanzania we fought continuous price wars; but in each case we were successful beyond expectations. Yet, no matter how hard we tried, Nigeria always remained out of reach. Amidst allegations of bribery and corruption, media leaks and litigation, I worked harder than ever before to make sure that Vodacom would become part of Nigeria's cellular realm, but it slipped through my fingers. If I had made a mistake I would have been prepared to let it go, but the deal was good.

The Nigeria episode taught me that there are limits to what a person can accomplish in a single lifetime; that to fail at something is not a crime, nor something to be ashamed of, provided you have given it your best shot. I can honestly say that I gave Nigeria my best shot. With disappointment comes wisdom, the wisdom to choose between hitting your head against a brick wall or opening the door and walking out. I walked away.

Before I left the company, there was one more thing I wanted to do. The last decision I made at Vodacom was to put together a R7.5 million BEE deal for the benefit of our staff and ordinary black South African citizens, and not simply a few prominent individuals. Royal Bafokeng Holdings and Thebe Investment Corporation were our preferred investment partners. I was pleased that the entire staff complement received equity in the company, including myself. But there was a catch. In order to cash in on those shares employees had to have worked for the company for five years from the time they were issued, and I was leaving Vodacom before the year was up. It was a sensible arrangement, and I was simply unlucky to have been leaving the company at the 'wrong' time. But it still felt odd to be saying goodbye as a salaried employee, not a shareholder, especially since I had, as much as anyone, actually shared – physically, mentally and emotionally – in all the experiences, good and bad, that Vodacom had undergone.

My settlement – the one stipulated in my contract – was what I was entitled to, no more, no less, which is how things were meant to be. On my retirement as CEO of Vodacom, the company was worth R150 billion and paying R6 billion in dividends per annum. I was happy with the legacy I was leaving behind.

The compromise I reached with the board in 2006 was that I would work for another three years – the last six months as a consultant, an arrangement that was extended until 2011. I wasn't prepared to stay on any longer because my peace of mind was at stake. I had been sent two messages loud and clear to get out while I was still in one piece. I had to start listening.

Looking back at what Vodacom has become, it is incredible to think that in the beginning no one believed in the potential of cellphones. Telkom didn't want to invest in a technology that had no track record. Jack Clarke made Telkom do it. Then he persuaded me to run the new cellphone company – a job nobody else was keen to take. I'm glad I did. Jack's unflagging enthusiasm and his formidable intellect helped me to grow and develop in ways that I would never have imagined possible. Once I'd met Jack and benefited from his wisdom, I was so eager to join him that I told him I'd work for free as long as he gave me the chance to run with Vodacom. His reply was, 'You make this company work, and we'll make it up to you.' We didn't disappoint one another.

But Telkom fired Jack to make way for someone else to become chairman. He went home and passed away a few years later. I saw him a few days before he died. We talked business, as we always did, and he thanked me for remembering him, as he always did when we spoke, which was at least once a year. It saddened me that a man of such vision had been sidelined in what could only have been a politically expedient move.

The corporate world is not the place that will teach you how to become an entrepreneur. It will smother your ideas and drive you to drink. It is not the ultimate pinnacle of success; it is a place where sheep go to graze. If you want to be an entrepreneur, go out on a limb and do things differently. But it won't happen overnight and it won't come easy. The best way I can put it is to be impatiently patient. Don't wait for success to come to you; go out and find it. Get busy making plans, but don't plan all your life. Believe it before you can achieve it and then set clear goals. Setting goals is the only way to make a dream come true. Then make it happen.

Once you have a clear vision of what you want to achieve, surround yourself with effective people. Successful companies know that the best person for the job does not necessarily have the most impressive CV or the most experience; it's principally about finding people with the right attitude. Attitude is more important than talent, money, experience or education. Great attitude coupled with a desire to achieve is the hallmark of the most successful individuals.

The only way to inspire people to achieve is through decisive leadership. Leadership is not a one-day thing; it is a constant commitment to excellence that has to be practised every day. Your actions have to motivate them to do more, to become more. You have to make your team believe that they can achieve your vision. But it needs to be about the dream. Forget about making money – focus on the passion. The money will follow.

Besides, the true measure of wealth is what you're worth if you lost all your money. So set about building something of true lasting value. If you become successful, be kind and generous. It makes the winning even more worthwhile. At the moment of greatest accomplishment, don't lose your sense of balance and humility. Don't lose yourself along the way. Take time to think and read; play a little and be good to others.

One of the most common misconceptions is that success is due to some stroke of genius, some elusive quality that only a unique set of individuals possesses. You don't have to be wealthy, super-intelligent or influential to succeed. Status, intellect and money have very little to do with it; becoming successful is purely a state of mind. You just have to want to be the best, and to want this with every fibre of your being. When I crouched on the starting line with adrenalin coursing through my veins and every nerve in my body taut with suspense, I still had my doubts. But I was more afraid of mediocrity. I had to finish what I started, and I had to finish well. I like to think I did just that.

With that, I turned my attention to creating a new life for myself. After my divorce I decided that I would not attempt marriage again. I had experienced the best and the worst of it, and I wasn't sure that I would be able to sustain a commitment of that nature again. I don't easily trust people and it takes a long time before someone really gets to know me. But as often happens in life, the unexpected comes along and sweeps you off your feet without any warning. Surina had come into my life along the way and before long we were talking about making a long-term commitment. I have found that in marriage, the first time round, you take a lot for granted. It's like flowing down a river: you just let it take you. The second time you pay more attention to the scenery while also watching out for the rapids. You become more aware of the world's beauties, and its dangers, which is exactly what makes life worth living.

We held a small, intimate ceremony at Fancourt in September 2008, with a few close friends in attendance. Dot Field tirelessly organised the wedding down to the last flawless detail, ensuring that we had a perfect day. My old friend Americo da Silva was my best man; Wendy Luhabe read a verse from the Bible; and Pieter Uys's daughter, Irmilee, was Surina's bridesmaid. It was a happy event. Through the sunshine I saw the faces of my parents, my sons, my brothers, my friends, and the new joy in my life – my three-month-old granddaughter, Juliet. It gave me great pleasure to know that they were all there to celebrate the start of a new chapter in my life. As I walked down the aisle into the spring freshness, I glanced at my wife, the beautiful Surina, and I couldn't wait to go home.

Notes

Chapter 4
1. 'Faster Calls, Faster Cash'. *Cape Argus*, 8 July 1993.
2. 'Faster Calls, Faster Cash'.
3. Z.B. Molefe, 'A Real Revolution'. *City Press*, 22 August 1993.

Chapter 5
1. D. McLeod, 'Licence to Disagree'. *Financial Mail*, 27 July 2007.
2. Molefe, 'A Real Revolution'.
3. D. Biggs. 'Tavern of the Seas Column'. *Cape Argus*, 30 September 1993.
4. J. van der Walt, *Yebo Gogo. It's a Deal: How Vodacom became a Partner in the New South Africa* (Vodacom, 2003).

Chapter 6
1. Van der Walt, *Yebo Gogo*.
2. Van der Walt, *Yebo Gogo*.
3. Van der Walt, *Yebo Gogo*.

Chapter 7
1. T. Betty, 'Cellular Phones' Prices Cut'. *Sunday Times*, 13 February 1994.
2. F. Greyling, 'Vodacom has 100 000 Subscribers'. *Beeld*, 28 October 1994.

Chapter 9
1. 'Road Link "Vital for Many Users"'. *The Star*, 24 May 1994.
2. V. Pienaar, 'Strategy for Strong Retailer Base Paid Off'. *Business Day*, 30 March 1995.

Chapter 10
1. 'Spotlight on Social Issues'. *Cape Times*, 3 February 1993.
2. 'Faster Calls, Faster Cash'.

3. F. Botha, 'Pre-paid Cellular Calls the Shots'. *Business Report*, 2 December 1996.
4. G. Gordon, 'Vodacom's Message gets Cheap'. *Sunday Times*, 14 June 1998.
5. Gordon, 'Vodacom's Message gets Cheap'.
6. 'New Products Spur Growth of the Cellphone Industry in SA'. *Sowetan*, 12 December 1997.

Chapter 12
1. M. Smit, 'Yebo Gogo! Loftus Versfeld has Returned to Sport'. *Business Day*, 2 September 2005.

Chapter 15
1. 'Vodacom Rolls out DR Congo Network'. BBC News Online, 27 May 2002, www.news.bbc.co.uk/2/low/business/2010584.stm (accessed 29 May 2009).
2. 'Rich Rewards from Moving into Africa'. *Business Day*, 17 October 2002.

Chapter 16
1. M. Wrong, *In the Footsteps of Mr. Kurtz: Living on the Brink of Disaster in Mobutu's Congo* (Harper Perennial, 2002), pp. 4, 10–11.

Chapter 17
1. D. Ihenacho, 'Nigeria's Anti-corruption Shenanigan'. Nigeria World Online, 21 June 2004, www.nigeriaworld.com/columnist/ihenacho/062104.html (accessed 29 May 2009).
2. 'Corruption Costs Nigeria 40% of Oil Wealth, Official Says'. The Boston Globe Online, 17 December 2004, www.boston.com/.../2004/.../17/ (accessed 29 May 2009).
3. N. Moodley, 'Vodacom Sees Nigeria Market Big Enough for Four'. *Engineering News*, 16 January 2004.
4. M. Gebhardt, 'MTN's Gold Mine has Become Vodacom's Heart of Darkness'. *Business Report*, 3 June 2004.
5. M. Bidoli, 'Twins on a Quest'. *Financial Mail*, 11 June 2004.

Chapter 18
1. B. Naidu, '"We Got it Wrong"– Icasa'. *Business Times*, 21 June 2009.

Chapter 19
1. A. Knott-Craig in 'We Pay Tribute to an African Cellular Pioneer'. *Vodaworld*, Spring 2008.

References

Knott-Craig, A. 2002. *Knott-Craig History: Family Lines*. Cape Town: Interactive Africa.

Marinovich, G., ed. 2008. *Prospects of Babel: New Imagery from the Congo*. Johannesburg: Vodacom/Silver Halide Publishing.

Naidoo, R. 2007. *The Life and Times of Vodacom as Covered by the Media from 1993 to 2007*. Cape Town: Interactive Africa.

Van der Walt, J. 2003. *Yebo Gogo. It's a Deal: How Vodacom Became a Partner in the New South Africa*. Midrand: Vodacom.

Vodacom. *Annual Reports*. Midrand: Vodacom.

Vodacom Foundation. 2008. *The Power to do Good*. Cape Town: Interactive Africa.

Vodaworld. 2008. 'We Pay Tribute to an African Cellular Pioneer'. Spring 2008.

Wrong, M. 2002. *In the Footsteps of Mr. Kurtz: Living on the Brink of Disaster in Mobutu's Congo*. New York: Harper Perennial.

Index

Ackerman, Raymond 77
Adenuga, Mike 161
Advance Mobile Phone System (AMPS) 36
affirmative action 26
Africa
  business conditions 142–43
  cellphone industry 142, 144–48, 184
African Cup of Nations 116
African National Congress (ANC) 36
  and cellular telephony 58–61
  and privatisation 46–47
Afrobike 126
Amabokke 116
Amapisi Pre-Primary School 124
analogue systems 26, 36, 37, 39
Anglovaal 50
anti-apartheid demonstrations 25
apartheid 24, 25
Armscor 89
Armstrong, Neil 72
Atlanta 133
Attieh, Mark 81

Bacher, Ali 117
Bafana Bafana 116, 178
Barlow Rand 50, 53
Barret, Dan 82
base stations 65, 71, 86–91, 143, 146, 156–57

beach clean-ups 119
Beale, Lena 29
BEAM 111
Beck, John 85
Beets, Allan 65
Bell, *Doctor* 15
Beltel videotext 30–32
Bets, Ben 42, 50–51
billboards 83, 113–14
birds and tree towers 90–91
Bizana 124, 125
Black Economic Empowerment (BEE) 60–62, 190–91
Bloemfontein Celtic (football team) 119
Blue Bulls (rugby team) 117–18
Blue Label 81
Boggomsbaai 10, 63, 119, 173
Bold, Anthony 50
Boschendal 18
Bosman, Herman Charles 108
Botha, *Doctor* 15
boxing 120
Boyce, Dr Charles 28, 29, 30
boycott of South Africa 40
Bravo Africa Concert 121
broadband *see* third generation (3G) technology
Brolaz 86, 87, 90, 146, 156–57
Burger, Schalk 131

C450 standard   35, 36
Caddy Foundation   120
Cangci Comprehensive Technical High
    School   124, 125
Cape Town   15, 19, 24, 83, 113
Capsian Construction   145
car phones   35, 36
Carrim, Yusuf (Doc)   82
cataract patients   130
Celli, Dr Gabrielle   36
Cell C   162, 174–76
cellphone industry   37–39, 46–47, 56,
    58–61, 63, 64–65, 69–71, 105
  in Africa   142, 144–48, 184
  and African National
    Congress   58–61
  and Black Economic Empowerment
    60–62
  in Democratic Republic of
    Congo   149, 150–51, 154–58
  early attitudes to   54, 68
  economic impact   92–93, 103, 180
  and fraud   80
  in Ghana   167
  in Lesotho   144–45
  licensing   55, 174–75
  malls   133–39
  in Mozambique   161
  in Nigeria   160–61, 162–67
  regulator   65, 69, 175, 177
  spectrum   174, 175
  in Tanzania   145–47
  technology   88
  tender process   48–49
  townships   77–78
  trial phase   69–70
  World Trade Centre negotiations,
    1993   60
  see also Cell C; MTN; Vodacom
Cellstar Cellular Network   53
CellWatch   94
Celtel   146, 157, 167
Centurion Cricket Park Stadium
    (Pretoria)   117

Chaphe, Bob   96, 99, 100, 101–02
Chatz Cellular   81
Chatz, Selwyn   81
Cheetahs (rugby team)   117, 118
Chelsea Hospital   8
child abuse prevention centre   129
Child Welfare   10
children with heart defects   131–32
Christodoulou, Stan   120
Clarke, Brian   96
Clarke, Jack   34–35, 37–38, 41, 49,
    55–56, 59, 62, 66, 84, 182, 191
Coetzee, Ibeth   70
Cohen, Les   174
Cointel   81
coltan (Columbite-tantalite)   150
community service telephones   49–50,
    53, 54, 77–78
Congo Chine Telecom   157
Congolese Wireless Network (CWN)
    150
Congress of South African Trade
    Unions (Cosatu)   60, 179
Conrad, Joseph   149
Convention for a Democratic South
    Africa (Codesa)   48
Coopers and Lybrand   41
Craig, John Ziervogel (paternal great-
    grandfather)   14–15
cricket   117
crime prevention   94
Crouse, Leon   42, 57, 80, 95, 187

Da Silva, Americo Alberto Seixal
    Ferreira   27, 31, 36, 193
Dar es Salaam   147
De Klerk, F.W.   59
De Klerk, Marike   177
De Pinna, Michael   109, 120
De Romão, Jesus   27
De Villiers, Dawie   41
De Villiers, Francois   106–11
De Villiers, Jacques   18

Index

De Villiers, Peter   118
De Vries, Casper   107–08
Democratic Republic of Congo (DRC)   143, 147–48, 149–58
Detecon   161
Dodoma   147
Dos Santos, José   161
dotcom bubble   169
Draftfcb (Lindsay Smithers)   106, 111–12
Drakensberg   90
Du Preez, Robert   82
Du Toit, Danie   41, 45, 51, 56
Du Toit, Natalie   117
Dutch Reformed Church   113

Ecclestone, Bernie   120
Econet Wireless Limited (EWL)   163, 167
Econet Wireless Nigeria (EWN)   162, 166
   see also Vmobile
Eilean Taigh   119
E-learning and Resource Centre   126
Electronic Communications Act   178–79
Ellis Park   115
Elsie (housekeeper)   13
Emotel   161
Engelbrecht, Johan   45, 50
Evaton   77–78
Eye Awareness Week   130

facial disfigurement in children   130–31
Feldman, Hazel   121
Field, Dot   151, 152, 186, 193
Finlayson, Paul and Gill   82
FNB Stadium (Soweto)   116
Foreign Corrupt Practices Act (USA)   162, 165
Fourie, Piet   82

Gajjar, Hasmukh   172
Game   76, 82, 105, 182
Geissler, Phil   95
general election, *1994*   69, 70–71
General Packet Radio Service (GPRS)   177
Global System for Mobile Communications (GSM)   37, 38, 39, 40, 45, 88
   see also GSM Association
Globalcom   161, 162
golf   120
Graaff-Reinet   25
Graaff-Reinet Advertiser (newspaper)   15
Grand Hotel (Kinshasa)   154, 155–56
Granny Rae   see Knott-Craig, Rae
Greeff, Rhynie   8
Grid, The   95
GSM Association   97

Hall, Gawie   2–3, 151
Hani, Chris   48
Health and Racquet Club   134–35
health clinics   124
heart attacks   1, 2–6, 8–10
Henning, David   55
Henry, Peter   27
Herman, Alan   82
Hertzog, Albert   73
Het Suid-Western (newspaper)   14
Het Zuid-Westen (newspaper)   14
Heyns, Penny   116–17
Hibbard, Shane   50
Higson, Ben   50
HIV/AIDS   140, 145
Horn-Smith, Sir Julian   42, 55, 61, 136–37
Hyatt Regency Hotel (London)   8

Independent Communications Authority of South Africa (Icasa)   175, 179

Interactive Africa 106
International Telecommunications Union 40
Internet 97, 177

Jabavu Public Library and Skills Centre (Soweto) 127
Jacobs, *Doctor* 5
Joffe, Joan 100–01, 126, 137, 138, 151
Joffe, Sean 82
Johannesburg 113
Johannesburg Stock Exchange (JSE) 179
Jones, Isabel 99
Joosub, Shameel 80, 136

Kabila, Joseph 150
Kabila, Laurent 150
Kaiser Chiefs (football team) 119
Karoo 12, 13
Kasavubu, Joseph 150
Kaye, Danny 131
Kennedy, Dennis 74
Keyes, Derek 41
Khoza, Irvin 119
Khoza, Reuel 56
King, Dr Jeff 3, 7
Kinshasa 150, 151, 152–53, 157
Kinsley, Dr Rob 131
Knott, Elizabeth Jane (paternal great-grandmother) 14–15
Knott-Craig, Alan
  boyhood 12–14, 15–19, 20, 21–22
    birth 13
    bullied at school 15–16
    challenges bicycle gang 16–17
    domestic chores 17
    garage experiments 21–22
    holidays 19
    homes in Oudtshoorn 14
    military service 19–20, 22
    movies 18–19
    reading 18
    relationship with parents 17, 18
    schools 19
    scouting 17
    sport 17, 19
    Sundays in Oudtshoorn 12–13, 18
  family history 14–15, 17–18
  health 2, 140
    erratic heartbeat 6–7
    at the gym 1, 2, 8
    heart attacks 1, 2–6, 8–10, 129, 170, 180, 188
    near-death experiences 4–5, 7
    panic attacks 6
    Perthes 13, 15
  home life
    children 29–30, 173–74
    divorce 173, 174, 193
    financial situation 29, 30, 50
    at Louis Botha Children's Home 29
    marriage to Janet 27, 173
    marriage to Surina 193
    retreat at Boggomsbaai 10, 63, 173
    sailing 119
    at Wingate Park (Pretoria) 30
  personality
    attitudes to leadership and success 192
    as a businessman 31, 81–82, 85, 87, 89, 107, 190, 192
    and corporate world 191–92
    energy and enthusiasm 44, 129, 182, 189
    management style 103, 107, 129, 171, 182, 192
    musical tastes 14, 121
    as a student 25
    temper 17, 107, 129, 137
    unconventional thinker 67, 134
  at Post Office and Telkom 22–25, 27–32, 34

advocacy of cellphone technology 36–41, 43, 47
attitude to institutional culture 51
Beltel videotext 30–32
building pinball machines 27
commercialisation 34
computerising cable records 27–28
digging trenches 23–24
investigation into cellphone technology 35–36, 37–38, 74
manual writing for Wits Technikon 29
neighbourliness of farmers 23
opinion of cellphone tendering 49–50
organisation of annual conference 44–45
packet switching network 30
at Pinelands 27–28
in Pretoria 28–29, 30–32
resignation 50
studying for MBL degree 32
as technician 22–25
workshop 24
at University of Cape Town 19, 22, 23, 25–27
bursary from Post Office 22, 23
relationship with father 22, 24, 25
at Smuts Hall 25
thesis 26–27
at Vodacom 1–2, 10–11, 50–71, 74–187
and Africa 141, 142, 143–44, 147, 148, 168, 184, 190
and Americans 168, 171–72
awards 97, 185
contracts 78–79
customer care 70
dealers 80–82, 182
in Democratic Republic of Congo 148, 149–58
disillusionment 171, 173
employees 139–40
financial management 57, 184
general election, *1994* 70–71
in Ghana 167
honorary doctorates 185, 186
in Lebanon 175
in Lesotho 144–45
lessons from World Trade Centre negotiations, *1993* 60
marketing 76–77, 104–08, 110–14, 183
in Mozambique 161
MTN jamming incident 99–102
network coverage 83–91, 103, 183
in Nigeria 159, 160, 161, 162–68
packet switching 177
prepaid airtime 95–97, 183
relationship with board 61–62, 66–68, 79, 84, 123, 134, 136, 137, 164–65, 171, 172–73, 189–90, 191
and Rembrandt 67–68
retirement from 179, 182, 188, 190–91
and social development 123–32, 186–87
sponsorship of sport and arts 115–22
takeaway phones 75–76
in Tanzania 146–47
third generation (3G) technology 177–78
township phone shops 77–78
and Vodafone 56–57, 61–62, 66–67, 79, 84, 96, 137
and Vodaworld 133–39
voicemail 97–98
Knott-Craig, Alan John Alexander (father) 13, 15, 17, 22, 24, 25

Knott-Craig, Alan Thomas (son) 29
Knott-Craig, Andronette
  (mother) 13, 15, 17–18
Knott-Craig, Angus (uncle) 15
Knott-Craig, Arthur (uncle) 15
Knott-Craig, Christopher (brother) 9, 16, 17, 131
Knott-Craig, Derek (uncle) 15, 18
Knott-Craig, Elizabeth (aunt) 15
Knott-Craig, Janet (wife, née Schorn) 10, 27, 28, 173–74
Knott-Craig, Juliet (granddaughter) 193
Knott-Craig, Matthew (son) 30, 174
Knott-Craig, Nicholas (son) 10, 29
Knott-Craig, Rae (paternal grandmother) 15
Knott-Craig, Ronald Charles (paternal grandfather) 15, 24
Knott-Craig, Surina (wife, née Larsson) 3, 5, 6, 55, 112
Knott-Craig, Terry (brother) 17
Knott-Craig, Tony (brother) 17
Knott-Craig newspapers 14–15
Komga 13, 19, 25
KPMG 99, 100
Kruger Park 90
Kyalami 120

Lagos 159, 160, 164
Laham, Talaat 174, 175
Langenhoven, C.J. 14
Langenhoven, Hilton 117
Lazic, Ivo 86–87, 88, 89, 90, 146, 156–57
leadership 192
Lebanon 175
Leeuloop (dance) 112–13
Lesotho 144–45
Lesotho Telecommunications Company (LTC) 144
Letsie, *King* (Lesotho) 144
liberalism 26
life-saving 119
literacy training in prisons 128–29
Loftus Versfeld Stadium (Pretoria) 118
Lombard, Fanie 117
Louis Botha Children's Home (Pretoria) 29
Lowassa, Edward 147
Lubner, Marc 130
Luhabe, Wendy 92, 172, 193
Lumumba, Patrice 150

Mabandla, Oyama 172
Mae, Vanessa 121
Malan, Dawie 30
Maletsana Intermediate School (Limpopo) 126
Malherbe, Dillie 42, 55, 59, 61, 62, 170
Mallett, Nick 118
Mandela, Nelson (Madiba) 10, 33, 59, 101–03, 115, 116, 120, 121, 123–24, 125, 169, 185–86
Maré, Dietlof 145, 157, 158
Martin, Alwyn 172
Martinnen, Kari 40–41
Masiyiwa, Strive 163, 164
Matsepe-Casaburri, Dr Ivy 182
Maxwell, Ian 65
Mbeki, Thabo 141, 169
Mbingo, Godfrey 145
mCel 161
McKenzie, Shawn 162, 171, 172
McKinnon, Athol 19
Meimling Hotel (Kinshasa) 152, 153–54
Meyer, Abe 21–22
Meyer, Roelf 60
MIC Tanzania Limited 146
  see also tiGo
Midrand 134
military service 19–20, 22
Mlindazwe, Daliwonga 125

Index

Mo the Meerkat 112
mobile telephony 36–38
Moebius Syndrome 130
Moholi, Pinky 59
Morija Mission Station (Lesotho) 14
Morokweng (Limpopo) 78
Morris, Guy 82
Moseneke, Dikgang 84
Mosisili, Pakalitha 144
Mostert, Karin 82
Motaung, Kaiser 119
Motlana, Dr Ntatho 59, 60
motorcycle racing 120
Motorola 93
Mount Everest 146
Mount Kilimanjaro 146
mountaineers 146
Mozambique 161
MTC 167
Mthembu, Andrew 8, 118, 142, 150, 151, 154, 159, 161, 163, 164, 166
MTN 50, 53, 54, 60, 62, 65, 68, 69, 77, 85, 94, 96, 98–102, 103, 106, 117, 142, 161, 162, 166, 174, 175
Multi-media Messaging Service (MMS) 177
MXit 95
Mykonos 90

Naidoo, Kerishnie 131
Naidoo, Ravi 106
Nathan, Selwyn 120
National Party 25–26, 72
National Sea Rescue Institute (NSRI) 119
National Union of Mineworkers (NUM) 62
Naudé, Lionel 50
Navy 20
near-death experiences 4–5, 7
Neotel 179
Netcare 129–30
New Partnership for Africa's Development (Nepad) 142

Ngcaba, Andile 46–47, 59, 61
Nigeria 159–61
Nightall, Chris 61, 79
NITEL 162
Noach, Ryan 3, 129–30
Nugter, Adrian 97
Nxsana, Sizwe 172

Olivetti South Africa 30–31
Olympic Games, Atlanta, *1996* 116, 133
Omotoso, Bankole 109
Oosthuizen, Ters 49, 53, 55
Organisation of African Unity 141
Orlando Pirates (football team) 119
Oudtshoorn 12, 14, 19, 20, 21, 24, 25
Ouma Agnes (maternal grandmother) 13, 18, 19
Oupa Tony (maternal grandfather) 13, 19
Outeniqua mountains 12, 17

packet switching 30, 177
Paralympic Games team, *2008* 117
Pasley, Rob 50
Pauly, Lothar 177
Peace Parks Foundation 132
Peet, Sir John 55, 57
Perthes 13, 15
Peters family 19
Pick 'n Pay 77, 105, 182
Pistorius, Oscar 117
places of comfort see *thuthulezas*
Planetel Communications 145
Please Call Me 95
Pollock, Graeme 19
Port Elizabeth 113
Post Office 21, 22–25, 27–29, 30–32
Posts and Telecommunications Workers Association (POTWA) 60, 62
Postmaster General 60
Prefcor 76

prepaid airtime   95–97, 183
Procter, Mike   19

Queensberrybay (Wild Coast)   13

Ramaphosa, Cyril   60, 61
Ramsamy, Sam   117
Rand Show (Pretoria)   75
rape victims   129
Readucate   128
Red Nose Day   129
Rembrandt   42, 51, 52, 53, 55, 61, 62, 67–68, 104, 159, 170
Remgro Limited   170
Rhodes, Cecil John   14, 18
Richmark   81
Riha, Peter   10
Roos, John   121
Royal Bafokeng Holdings   190
Royal Brompton Hospital (London)   8–9
rugby   115–16, 117–18, 119
  World Cup, *1995*   115–16
Rupert, Johann   42, 51, 68
Rutstein, Theo   72–76, 77, 79, 133–34, 135–36

Sanders, Corrie   120
SAS Pretorius   20
SBC Communications   162, 164, 166, 171, 172
Schmidt, Kevin   8–9
schools   124
Scott, Alvin   44–45
Scott, Stuart   36
Seko, Mobutu Sese   150
Sellschop, Jacques   98, 100–01
September, Reuben   44
Sexwale, Tokyo   116
Shell House   58, 59
Shirk, Leon   65, 93, 97, 103
Shope-Mafole, Lyndall   59
Short Message Service (SMS)   94, 183

Siemens   45, 80, 86, 96
Sight for Life Project   130
Singleton, Amanda   40
Smile Foundation   130–31
soccer   118–19, 145
Sommerville, Blaise   82
South African Clothing and Textile Workers Union (SACTWU)   62
South African government policy on communications   40, 41, 42, 47, 48–49
South African National Symphony Orchestra   121
St George's Cathedral (Cape Town)   25
storytelling and advertising   108
Subscriber Identity Module (SIM) cards   65, 93–94, 154–56
Sullivan, Ed   162, 165
Sunninghill Hospital (Johannesburg)   7, 131
Suntel   50, 56
Supercall   81
surfing   119
Surtee, Yusuf   101
Swart, Willem   50, 166
Swartberg mountains   12, 17
Sybil, Hymie   76

Tanzania   145–47
Tanzania Telecommunications Company Limited   146
Taschner, Ludwig   134
teachers   125
television   72–73, 178
Teljoy   73, 74, 75, 76, 79–80
Telkom   34–36, 37, 40, 41–42, 45, 46, 47–48, 50–51, 86–87, 103, 172, 191
  relationship with Vodacom   55, 66, 68, 159, 162, 171, 179
Telkom93 conference   44–47
Thomas (boyhood friend)   13

Index

Theart, Francois (Naki)   70
Thebe Investment Corporation   190
third generation (3G) technology   177–78
Three Tenors   121
Thugwane, Josia   116
thuthulezas (places of comfort)   129
tiGo   157
Total Access Communication System (TACS)   36, 39
Tovey, Neil   116
township phone shops   77–78
Transkei   124
tree towers   89–91
Tries for Smiles   131
Tritel   146
trust   31
Tshwete, Steve   120–21, 127, 128
Turner, Ann   132
Tyamzashe, Mthobi   120, 126, 130, 131

Union Buildings (Pretoria)   101, 121, 123
Unisa International Music Competitions   121
Unitas Hospital   3–5
university bursaries   126
University of Cape Town (UCT)   19, 25–27
University of Fort Hare Multi-Media Centre   127
Uys, Irmilee   193
Uys, Pieter   31, 50, 87, 179, 185, 187

Van Aardt, Loodt   50
Van der Merwe, Suzette   131, 132
Van Dyk, Ernst   117
Van Heerden, Anthea   118, 138–39, 151, 154, 155, 156
Van Rensburg, Eugene   48
Van Winkel, Louis   120
Van Wyk, Jan   147

Van Zyl, Rae   3, 174
Varejes, Gavin   81
VenFin Limited   170, 172
Verster, Harold   118
Verwoerd, H.F.   25
Vian, Frankie   36
Victor, Graham   8
Virgin Group   167
Visagie, Merwyn   145
Visser, Thys   42
Vlok, Barry   50
Vmobile   166, 167
  see also Econet Wireless Nigeria
Vodacom   42, 50, 64–71, 74–142, 144–51, 154–87
  advertising   66, 69, 75, 83, 106–14, 183
  in Africa   141, 142, 143, 144–48, 184
  awards   97, 103
  base stations   65, 71, 86–91, 143, 146, 156–57
  billboards   83, 113–14
  billing system   65, 111, 176, 184
  and Black Economic Empowerment   61–62, 190–91
  board   55, 61–62, 66–68, 79, 84, 97, 123, 134, 136, 137, 164–65, 171, 172–73, 189–90, 191
  branding of   104–05, 107, 122, 183
  choir   186
  competition with MTN   98–102
  contracts   76, 79
  and crime prevention   94
  culture   173
  customer care   70, 139
  dealers   80–82, 182
  distribution   76–77, 80–81, 182
  employees   139–40
  and environmental lobby   89
  ethics   163–66
  fibre optic lines   178–79
  financial performance   53–54, 57, 80, 141, 169–70, 181, 184

and Ghana   167
handsets   78–79, 80
Internet service   97, 177
listing on Johannesburg Stock Exchange   179
Look4me   177
marketing   74–76, 104–06, 183
name and logo   51–52
Netcare/Vodacom emergency medical service   130
network coverage   83–91, 103, 183
and Nigeria   159, 161, 162–67
and pay-television   178
prepaid airtime   95–97, 183
recruitment   51
relationship with Cell C   175–76
relationship with Telkom   55, 66, 68, 159, 162, 171, 179
service providers   80, 136
SIM cards   65, 93–94, 154–56
and social development   *see* Vodacom Foundation
sponsorship of sport and arts   115–22
subscribers   71, 79–80, 85, 95, 96, 103, 112, 130, 145, 146, 157, 161, 176, 180
survey results   114
takeaway phones   75–76
tariffs   68–69
tendering bid   52–55
third generation (3G) technology   177–78
tree towers   89–91
voice mail   97–98
work environment   140
Vodacom 4U   81, 111, 176, 183, 184
Vodacom Congo   149, 150–51, 154–58
Vodacom Connector Pack   94
Vodacom Corporate Park   139
Vodacom Foundation   123, 125–32, 186–87
Vodacom Lesotho   144–45
Vodacom Mozambique   161

Vodacom Stadium (Bloemfontein)   118
Vodacom Tanzania   145–47
Vodacom Techno-Centre (Cape Town)   139
Vodafone   42, 53, 55, 56–57, 61–62, 65, 66–67, 79, 84, 96, 137, 142, 159, 161, 164, 167, 170, 172, 179
Vodago   96, 97, 176
Vodamail   98
Vodaworld (magazine)   106
Vodaworld (Midrand)   10, 105–06, 121, 126, 133–39
volleyball   119

Walter Sisulu Clinic   131
Washington DC   165
Weinberger, Ian   119
Welgemoed, Dr Piet   42, 47, 59
Wemba, Papa   151
Wessels, Robbie   112
Western Province Stormers (rugby team)   117
Whent, Sir Gerald   42, 56, 67
White, Jake   118
Wilderness   13
Williams, Chester   110
Williams, Phil   2, 56, 67, 125, 136, 164, 172, 190
Wireless Application Service Provider (WASP)   81–82
Wolmarans, Barry   82
Wood, Eric   30
Worcester Advertiser (newspaper)   15
World Trade Centre (Kempton Park)   60, 61
Worldwide Wildlife Fund   132
Wrong, Michela   149
Wynberg Magistrate's Court and Police Station (Alexandra)   127–28

Y2K   169
Yebo Gogo   108–10, 183
Yebo Heroes   132

Zaina, Virgilio   30–31